I NEVER KNEW THERE WAS A WORD FOR IT

Adam Jacot de Boinod, hunter of perfect and obscure bon mots, is a true linguistic **bowerbird** (a person who collects an astonishing array of – sometimes useless – objects). He trawled the languages of the world for exotic specimens in his bestselling books *The Wonder of Whiffling*, *The Meaning of Tingo* and hit follow-up *Toujours Tingo*.

In memory of my father

I Never Knew There Was a Word For It

ADAM JACOT DE BOINOD

With illustrations by Sandra Howgate

PENGUIN BOOKS

Peng...

Peng...

Pe...

Penguin ...

Penguin B...

Penguin Books Ltd, Registered Offices: 80 Strand, London WC2R 0RL, England

www.penguin.com

The Meaning of Tingo first published in Penguin Books 2005
Toujours Tingo first published in Penguin Books 2007
The Wonder of Whiffling first published in Particular Books 2009
Published under this title with a new Introduction in Penguin Books 2010

1

Printed in Great Britain by Clays Ltd, St Ives plc

A CIP catalogue record for this book is available from the British Library

978–0–141–02839–2

www.greenpenguin.co.uk

Contents

Toujours Tingo

The Wonder of Whiffling

Introduction

My name is Adam Jacot de Boinod and I'm hopelessly addicted to strange words. I've spent the last six years compulsively hunting down unusual vocabulary and now have written three books collecting my very best and most unusual discoveries.

All three are included in this volume, which I've called *I Never Knew There Was a Word For It*, because I didn't. My vocabulary is now ten times richer than it was six years ago, as I hope yours will soon be too . . . Let me tell you a little about each book:

The Meaning of Tingo

My interest in unusual words was triggered when one day, working as a researcher for the BBC programme *QI*, I picked up a weighty Albanian dictionary to discover that they have no less than twenty-seven words for eyebrow and the same number for different types of moustache, ranging from a **mustaqe madh**, or bushy, to a **mustaqe posht**, one which droops down at both ends.

My curiosity rapidly became a passion. I was soon unable to go near a bookshop or library without sniffing out the often dusty shelf where the foreign language dictionaries were kept. I started to collect my favourites: **nakhur**, for example, a Persian word meaning 'a camel that gives no milk until her nostrils are tickled'; Many described strange or unbelievable things. How, when and where, for example, would a man be described as a **marilopotes**, the Ancient Greek for 'a gulper of coaldust'? And could the Japanese samurai really have used the verb **tsuji-giri**, meaning 'to try out a new sword on a passer-by'? Others expressed concepts that seemed all too familiar. We have all met a **Zechpreller**, 'someone who leaves without paying the bill'; worked with a **neko-neko**, the Indonesian for 'one who has a creative idea which only makes things worse'; or spent too much time with an **ataoso**, the Central American Spanish for 'one who sees problems with everything'. It was fascinating to find thoughts that lie on the tip of an English tongue, crystallized into vocabulary. From the Zambian **sekaseka**, 'to laugh without reason', through the Czech **nedovtipa**, 'one who finds it difficult to take a hint', to the Japanese **bakku-shan**, 'a woman who only appears pretty when seen from behind'.

In the end my passion became an obsession. I combed over two million words in countless dictionaries. I trawled the internet, phoned embassies, and tracked down foreign language speakers who could confirm my findings. I discovered that in Afrikaans, frogs go **kwaak-kwaak**, in Korea owls go **buung-buung**, while in Denmark Rice Crispies go **Knisper! Knasper! Knupser!** And that in Easter Island **tingo** means to borrow things from a friend's house one by one until there's nothing left.

Luckily for my sanity, Penguin then signed me up to write the book that was to become *The Meaning of Tingo,* which meant I had an editor to help me decide which of the thousands of great words should make it into the final book but, goodness, it was hard to leave some out. The book came out in 2005 and was an instant hit. It has since been published in eleven different languages and Tingo-mania spread all round the globe.

Toujours Tingo

I was delighted when the book's fans demanded a sequel as I felt like I was only just getting started. This time I found such delights as **okuri–okami**, the Japanese word for 'a man who feigns thoughtfulness by offering to see a girl home only to molest her once he gets in the door' (literally, 'a see-you-home wolf'); **kaelling**, the Danish for 'a woman who stands on the steps of her house yelling obscenities at her kids'; and **belochnik**, the Russian for 'a thief specializing in stealing linen off clothes lines' (an activity that was supposedly very lucrative in the early 1980s). And how could I have missed the German **Kiebitz**, 'an onlooker at a card game who interferes with unwanted advice' or the Portuguese **pesamenteiro**, 'one who habitually joins groups of mourners at the home of a deceased person, ostensibly to offer condolences but in reality to partake of the refreshments which he expects will be served'?

In this book I ventured into over two hundred new languages. The Ndebele of Southern Africa have the word **dii–koyna**, meaning 'to destroy one's own property in anger', an impulse surely felt by most of us at some time or another, if not acted upon. From the Bakweri language of Cameroon we have **wo–mba**, a charming word to describe 'the smiling in sleep by children'; and from the Buli language of Ghana the verb **pelinti**, 'to move very hot food around inside one's mouth in order to avoid too close a contact'. And doubtless there are many among us who have found ourselves disturbed by a **butika roka** (Gilbertese, Oceania) 'a brother-in-law coming round too often'.

Once again, of course, many of the more unusual words relate closely to the local specifics of their cultures. Most of us are unlikely to need the verb **sendula**, (from the Mambwe of Zambia) meaning 'to find accidentally a dead animal in the forest', which carries with it the secondary meaning 'and be excited at the thought that a lion or leopard might still be around'. But even if we never have the call to use these expressions, it's surely enriching to know that in Finnish, **poronkusema** is 'the distance equal to how far a reindeer can travel without urinating'; while **manantsona**, from the Malagasy of Madagascar, is 'to smell or sniff before entering a house, as a dog does'. We may not share the same climate, but we can all too easily imagine the use of words like **hanyauku**, (Rukwangali, Namibia) 'to walk on tiptoe on warm sand', **barbarian-on** (Ik, Nilo-Saharan), 'to sit in a group of people warming up in the morning sun', or **dynke** (Norwegian), 'the act of dunking somebody's face in snow'.

Half as long again as *The Meaning of Tingo*, this second bite into the substantial cherry of world languages allowed me to venture in depth into all sorts of new areas. There are more examples of 'false friends', from the Czech word **host**, which confusingly means 'guest', to the Estonian **sober**, a perhaps unlikely word for 'a male friend'. There are the intriguing meanings of the names of cities and countries, Palindromes and even national anthems, as well as a series of worldwide idioms, which join the words in confirming that the challenges, joys and disappointments of human existence are all too similar around the world. English's admonitory 'Don't count your chickens', for example, is echoed in most languages, becoming, in Danish: **man skal ikke sælge skindet, før bjørnen er skudt** 'one should not sell the fur before the bear has been shot'; in Turkish, **dereyi görmeden paçaları sıvama**, 'don't roll up your trouser-legs before you see the stream' and in the Ndonga language of Namibia **ino manga**

ondjupa ongombe inaayi vala, 'don't hang the churning calabash before the cow has calved'.

The Wonder Of Whiffling

While I was working on the previous two books, scouring libraries and second-hand bookshops, riffling through reference books from around the world to find words with unusual and delightful meanings, I kept coming across splendid English dictionaries too. Not just the mighty twenty-volume *Oxford English Dictionary*, but collections covering dialect, slang and subsidiary areas, such as Jamaican or Newfoundland English. Sneaking the occasional glance away from my main task I realized there was a wealth of little-known or forgotten words in our language, from its origins in Anglo-Saxon, through Old and Middle English and Tudor–Stuart, then on to the rural dialects collected so lovingly by Victorian lexicographers, the argot of nineteenth-century criminals, slang from the two world wars, right up to our contemporary world and the jargon that has grown up around such activities as darts, birding and working in an office. Offered the chance, it seemed only right to gather the best examples together and complete my trilogy: bringing, as it were, the original idea home.

Some of our English words mean much the same as they've always meant. Others have changed beyond recognition, such as **racket**, which originally meant the palm of the hand; **grape**, a hook for gathering fruit; or **muddle**, to wallow in mud. Then there are those words that have fallen out of use, but would undoubtedly make handy additions to any vocabulary today. Don't most of us know a **blatteroon** (1645), a person who will not stop talking, not to mention a shot-clog (1599), a drinking companion only tolerated because he pays for the drinks. And if one day we feel **mumpish** (1721), sullenly angry, shouldn't we seek the company of a **grinagog** (1565), one who is always grinning?

The dialects of Britain provide a wealth of coinages. In the Midlands, for example, we find a jaisy, a polite and effeminate man, and in Yorkshire a **stridewallops**, a tall and awkward woman. If you tuck too much into the clotted cream in Cornwall you might end up **ploffy**, plump; in Shropshire, hold back on the beer or you might develop **joblocks**, fleshy, hanging cheeks; and down in Wiltshire hands that have been left too long in the washtub are **quobbled**. The Geordies have the evocative word **dottle** for the tobacco left in the pipe after smoking, and in Lincolnshire **charmings** are paper and rag chewed into small pieces by mice. In Suffolk to **nuddle** is to walk alone with the head held low; and in Hampshire to **vuddle** is to spoil a child by injudicious petting. And don't we all know someone who's **crambazzled** (Yorkshire), prematurely aged through drink and a dissolute life?

Like English itself, my research hasn't stopped at the shores of the Channel. How about a **call-dog** (Jamaican English), a fish too small for human consumption or a **twack** (Newfoundland English) a shopper who looks at goods, inquires about prices but buys nothing. Slang from elsewhere offers us everything from a **waterboy** (US police), a boxer who can be bribed or coerced into losing, to a **shubie** (Australian), someone who buys surfing gear and clothing but doesn't actually surf. In Canada, a **cougar** describes an older woman on the prowl for a younger man, while in the US a **quirkyalone** is someone who doesn't fall in love easily, but waits for the right person to come along.

Returning to the mainstream, it's good to know that there are such sound English words as **rumblegumption**, meaning common sense, or **ugsomeness**, loathing. **Snirtle** is to laugh in a quiet, suppressed or restrained manner, while to **snoach** is to speak through the nose. If you are **clipsome**, you are eminently embraceable; when **clumpst**, your hands are stiff with cold. To **boondoggle** is to carry out valueless work in order to convey the impression that one is busy, while to **limbeck** is to rack the brain in an effort to have a new idea.

As for **whiffling**, well, that turned out to be a word with a host of meanings. In eighteenth-century Oxford and Cambridge, a whiffler was one who examined candidates for degrees, while elsewhere a whiffler was an officer who cleared the way for a procession, as well as being the name for the man with the whip in Morris dancing. The word also means to blow or scatter with gusts of air, to move or think erratically, as well as applying to geese descending rapidly from a height once the decision to land has been made. In the underworld slang of Victorian times, a whiffler was one who cried out in pain, while in the cosier world of P.G. Wodehouse, whiffled was what you were when you'd had one too many of Jeeves's special cocktails.

As a self-confessed **bowerbird** (one who collects an astonishing array of sometimes useless objects), I've greatly enjoyed putting together all three collections. I sincerely hope that you enjoy reading them, and that they save you both from **mulligrubs**, depression of spirits, and **onomatomania**, vexation in having difficulty finding the right word.

In compiling all three books I've done my level best to check the accuracy of all the words included, but any comments or even favourite examples of words of your own are welcomed at the book's two websites: for foreign languages **www.themeaningoftingo.com** – and for English **www.thewonderofwhiffling.com** (There were some very helpful responses to my previous books, for which I remain grateful.)

Adam Jacot de Boinod

Acknowledgements

I am deeply grateful to the following people for their advice and help on all three books: Giles Andreae, Martin Bowden, Joss Buckley, Candida Clark, Anna Coverdale, Nick Emley, Natasha Fairweather, William Hartston, Beatrix Jacot de Boinod, Nigel Kempner, Nick and Galia Kullmann, Kate Lawson, Alf Lawrie, John Lloyd, Sarah McDougall, Yaron Meshoulam, Tony Morris, David Prest and David Shariatmadari.

In particular I must thank my agent, Peter Straus, my illustrator Sandra Howgate, my editor at Penguin, Georgina Laycock; and Mark McCrum for his invaluable work on the text.

The Meaning of Tingo

Meeting and Greeting

ai jiao de maque bu zhang rou
(Chinese)
*sparrows that love to chirp won't put on
weight*

¡Hola!

The first and most essential word in all languages is surely 'hello', the word that enables one human being to converse with another:

aa (Diola, Senegal)
beeta (Soninke, Mali, Senegal and Ivory Coast)
bok (Croatian)
boozhoo (Ojibwe, USA and Canada)
daw-daw (Jutlandish, Denmark)
ella (Awabakal, Australia)
i ay (Huaorani, Ecuador)
khaumykhyghyz (Bashkir, Russia)
nark (Phorhépecha, Mexico)
rozhbash (Kurdi, Iraq and Iran)
samba (Lega, Congo)
wali-wali (Limbe, Sierra Leone)
xawaxan (Toltichi Yokuts, California, USA)
yoga (Ateso, Uganda)
yoyo (Kwakiutl, Canada)

But it may not even be a word. In the Gilbert Islands of the Pacific, **arou pairi** describes the process of rubbing noses in greeting. For the Japanese, bowing is an important part of the process and a sign

of respect: **ojigi** is the act of bowing; **eshaku** describes a slight bow (of about 15 degrees); **keirei**, a full bow (of about 45 degrees); while **saikeirei** is a very low, worshipful type of bow that involves the nose nearly touching the hands. When one meets someone extremely important, one might even consider **pekopeko**, bowing one's head repeatedly in a fawning or grovelling manner.

Just say the word

Sometimes a single word works hard. In Sri Lanka, for example, the Sinhala word **ayubowan** means not only 'good morning', but also 'good afternoon', 'good evening', 'good night' and 'goodbye'.

Expectant

The frustration of waiting for someone to turn up is beautifully encapsulated in the Inuit word **iktsuarpok**, meaning 'to go outside often to see if someone is coming'. As for the frustration of the caller, there's always the Russian **dozvonit'sya** which doesn't simply mean to ring a doorbell, but to ring it until one gets an answer (it's also used for getting through on the telephone).

Hey you!

Once the first encounter is out of the way the correct form of address is important. Most of us know the difference between the intimate French **tu** and the more impersonal (and polite) **vous**. A similar distinction exists in Arabic between **anta** ('you' singular) and **antum** ('you' plural) – addressing an important person with **anta** (**anti** is the feminine version) rather than **antum** would be considered impolite.

In Vietnam there are no fewer than eighteen words for 'you', the use of which depends on whom you are addressing, whether a child or a senior citizen, whether formally or informally. And in the Western Australian Aboriginal language of Jiwali there are four words for 'we': **ngali** means 'we two including you'; **ngaliju** means 'we two excluding you'; **nganthurru** means 'we all including you'; and **nganthurraju** means 'we all excluding you'.

Cripes!

Exclamations are generally used to express a sudden reaction: to something frightening, incredible, spectacular, shocking or wonderful. Best not attempted by the visitor, they are better heard from the mouth of the native speaker than read off the page:

aaberdi (Algerian) a cry used when learning fearful news
aawwaah (Dardja, Algeria) a shout of doubt or hesitation
aãx (Karuk, North America) how disgusting!
aduh (Malay) ouch or wow!
aduhai (Indonesian) an expression of admiration
alaih (Ulwa, Nicaragua) gosh! goodness! help!
alalau (Quechuan, Peru) brrr! (of cold)
amit-amit (Indonesian) forgive me!

ammazza (Italian) it's a killer! wow!

asshe (Hausa, Nigeria) a cry of grief at distressing news

bambule (Italian) cheers! (preceding the lighting of a joint)

cq (Albanian) a negative exclamation of mild disappointment

hoppla (German) whoops!

naa (Japanese) that's great!

nabocklish (Irish Gaelic) don't meddle with it!

oho (Hausa, Nigeria) I don't care

oop (Ancient Greek) a cry to make rowers stop pulling

sa (Afrikaans) catch him!

savul (Turkish) get out of the way!

schwupp (German) quick as a flash

shahbash (Anglo-Indian) well done! (or well bowled!, as said in cricket by a wicket-keeper to the bowler)

tao (Chinese) that's the way it goes

taetae tiria (Cook Islands Maori) throw it away, it's dirty!

uf (Danish) ugh! yuk!

usch då (Swedish) oh, you poor thing!

y-eazziik (Dardja, Algeria) an expression used exclusively by women to criticize another person's action

zut (French) dash it!

Chinwag

The niceties of what in English is baldly known as 'conversation' are well caught in other languages:

ho'oponopono (Hawaiian) solving a problem by talking it out

samir (Persian) one who converses at night by moonlight

begadang (Indonesian) to stay up all night talking

glossalgos (Ancient Greek) talking till one's tongue aches

Breakdown in communication

Whether the person you are talking to suffers from **latah** (Indonesian), the uncontrollable habit of saying embarrassing things, or from **chenyin** (Chinese), hesitating and muttering to oneself, conversation may not always be quite as we'd like it:

catra patra (Turkish) the speaking of a language incorrectly
and brokenly

nyelonong (Indonesian) to interrupt without apology

akkisuitok (Inuit) never to answer

dui niu tanqin (Chinese) to talk over someone's head or
address the wrong audience (literally, to play the lute to a
cow)

'a'ama (Hawaiian) someone who speaks rapidly, hiding their
meaning from one person whilst communicating it to
another

dakat' (Russian) to keep saying yes

dialogue de sourds (French) a discussion in which neither
party listens to the other (literally, dialogue of the deaf)

mokita (Kiriwana, Papua New Guinea) the truth that all know
but no one talks about

Tittle-tattle

Gossip – perhaps more accurately encapsulated in the Cook Island Maori word **'o'onitua**, 'to speak evil of someone in their absence' – is a pretty universal curse. But it's not always unjustified. In Rapa Nui (Easter Island) **anga-anga** denotes the thought, perhaps groundless, that one is being gossiped about, but it also carries the sense that this may have arisen from one's own feeling of guilt. A more gentle form of gossip is to be found in Jamaica, where the patois word **labrish** means not only gossip and jokes, but also songs and nostalgic memories of school.

False friends

Those who learn languages other than their own will sometimes come across words which look or sound the same as English, but mean very different things. Though a possible source of confusion, these false friends (as linguists call them) are much more likely to provide humour – as any Englishwoman who says 'bless' to her new Icelandic boyfriend will soon discover:

hubbi (Arabic) friendly
kill (Arabic) good friend
bless (Icelandic) goodbye
no (Andean Sabela) correct
aye (Amharic, Ethiopia) no
fart (Turkish) talking nonsense
machete (Aukan, Suriname) how

The unspeakable ...

Cursing and swearing are practised worldwide, and they generally involve using the local version of a small set of words describing an even smaller set of taboos that surround God, the family, sex and the more unpleasant bodily functions. Occasionally, apparently inoffensive words acquire a darker overtone, such as the Chinese **wang bah dahn**, which literally means a turtle egg but is used as an insult for politicians. And offensive phrases can often be beguilingly inventive:

> **zolst farliren aleh tseyner achitz eynm, un dos zol dir vey ton** (Yiddish) may you lose all your teeth but one and may that one ache
> **así te tragues un pavo y todas las plumas se conviertan en cuchillas de afeitar** (Spanish) may all your turkey's feathers turn into razor blades

... the unmentionable

Taboo subjects, relating to local threats or fears, are often quirky in the extreme. Albanians, for example, never use the word for 'wolf'. They say instead **mbyllizogojen**, a contraction of a sentence meaning 'may God close his mouth'. Another Albanian taboo-contraction is the word for fairy, **shtozovalle**, which means may 'God increase their round-dances'. Similarly, in the Sami language of Northern Scandinavia and the Yakuts language of Russia, the original name for bear is replaced by a word meaning 'our lord' or 'good father'. In Russian itself, for similar reasons, a bear is called a **medved'** or 'honey-eater'.

... and the unutterable

In Masai the name of a dead child, woman or warrior is not spoken again and, if their name is also a word used every day, then it is no longer used by the bereaved family. The Sakalavas of Madagascar do not tell their own name or that of their village to strangers to prevent any mischievous use. The Todas of Southern India dislike uttering their own name and, if asked, will get someone else to say it.

Shocking soundalikes

The French invented the word **ordinateur**, supposedly in order to avoid using the first two syllables of the word computer (**con** is slang for vagina and **pute** for whore). Creek Indians in America avoid their native words for earth (**fakki**) and meat (**apiswa**) because of their resemblance to rude English words.

In Japan, four (**shi**) and nine (**ku**) are unlucky numbers, because the words sound the same as those for 'death' and 'pain or worry' respectively. As a result, some hospitals don't have the numbers 4, 9, 14, 19, or 42 for any of their rooms. Forty-two (**shi-ni**) means to die, 420 (**shi-ni-rei**) means a dead spirit and 24 (**ni-shi**) is double death. Nor do some hospitals use the number 43 (**shi-zan**), especially in the maternity ward, as it means stillbirth.

Fare well

Many expressions for goodbye offer the hope that the other person will travel or fare well. But it is not always said. **Yerdengh-nga** is a Wagiman word from Australia, meaning 'to clear off without telling anyone where you are going'. Similarly, in Indonesia, **minggat** means 'to leave home for good without saying goodbye'.

Snobs and chauffeurs

Words don't necessarily keep the same meaning. Simple descriptive words such as 'rain' or 'water' are clear and necessary enough to be unlikely to change. Other more complex words have often come on quite a journey since they were first coined:

al-kuhul (Arabic) originally, powder to darken the eyelids; then taken up by alchemists to refer to any fine powder; then applied in chemistry to any refined liquid obtained by distillation or purification, especially to alcohol of wine, which then was shortened to alcohol

chauffer (French) to heat; then meant the driver of an early steam-powered car; subsequently growing to chauffeur

An Arabian goodbye

In Syrian Arabic, goodbye is generally a three-part sequence: a) **bxa-trak**, by your leave; b) **ma'assalama**, with peace; c) **'allaysallmak**, God keep you. If a) is said first, then b) is the reply and then c) may be used. If b) is said first, then c) is obligatory.

---

hashhashin (Arabic) one who smokes or chews hashish; came to mean assassin

manu operare (Latin) to work by hand; then narrowed to the act of cultivating; then to the dressing that was added to the soil, manure

prestige (French) conjuror's trick; the sense of illusion gave way to that of glamour which was then interpreted more narrowly as social standing or wealth

sine nobilitate (Latin) without nobility; originally referred to any member of the lower classes; then to somebody who despised their own class and aspired to membership of a higher one; thus snob

theriake (Greek) an antidote against a poisonous bite; came to mean the practice of giving medicine in sugar syrup to disguise its taste; thus treacle

From Top to Toe

chi non ha cervello abbia
gambe *(Italian)*
*he who has not got a good brain
ought to have good legs*

Use your onion . . .

English-speakers are not the only ones to use food metaphors – bean, loaf, noodle, etc. – to describe the head. The Spanish **cebolla** means both 'head' and 'onion', while the Portuguese expression

cabeça d'alho xoxo literally means 'he has a head of rotten garlic' (in other words, 'he is crazy'). Moving from vegetables to fruit, the French for 'to rack your brains' is **se presser le citron** – 'to squeeze the lemon'.

. . . or use your nut

In Hawaii, a different item of food takes centre stage. The word **puniu** means 'the skull of a man which resembles a coconut'. Hawaiian has also given the world the verb **pana po'o**, 'to scratch your head in order to help you remember something you've forgotten'.

Pulling faces

The Arabic **sabaha bi-wajhi** means to begin the day by seeing some-one's face. Depending on their expression, this can be a good or bad omen:

> **sgean** (Scottish Gaelic) a wild look of fear on the face
> **kao kara hi ga deru** (Japanese) a blush (literally, a flame comes out of one's face)

> **verheult** (German) puffy-faced and red-eyed from crying
> **Backpfeifengesicht** (German) a face that cries out for a fist in it

Greek face-slapping

There are several vivid Greek words for being slapped in the face, including **sfaliara**, **hastouki**, **fappa**, **xestrefti**, **boufla**, **karpasia** and **sulta'meremet** ('the Sultan will put you right'). **Batsos** means both 'a slap in the face' and 'a policeman' (from the American use of the word 'cop' to mean 'swipe'). **Anapothi** describes a backhanded slap, while **tha fas bouketo**, 'you will eat a bunch of flowers', is very definitely not an invitation to an unusual meal.

Windows of the soul

Eyes can be our most revealing feature, though the way others see them may not always be quite what we'd hoped for:

makahakahaka (Hawaiian) deep-set eyeballs
mata ego (Rapa Nui, Easter Island) eyes that reveal that a
    person has been crying
ablaq-chashm (Persian) having intensely black and white eyes
jegil (Malay) to stare with bulging eyes
melotot (Indonesian) to stare in annoyance with widened eyes

All ears

English is not terribly helpful when it comes to characterizing ears, unlike, say, Albanian, in which people distinguish between **veshok** ('small ones') or **veshak** ('ones that stick out'). Other languages are similarly versatile:

tapawising (Ulwa, Nicaragua) pointed ears
a suentola (Italian) flappy ears
mboboyo (Bemba, Congo and Zambia) sore ears

Indonesian offers two useful verbs: **nylentik**, 'to flick someone with the middle finger on the ear', and **menjewer**, 'to pull someone by the ear'. While the Russian for 'to pull someone's leg' is **veshat' lapshu na ushi**, which literally translates as 'to hang noodles on someone's ears'.

A real mouthful

In Nahuatl, the language of the Aztecs which is still spoken today in Mexico, **camachaloa** is 'to open one's mouth', **camapaca** is 'to wash one's mouth', and **camapotoniliztli** is 'to have bad breath'.

Getting lippy

Lips can be surprisingly communicative:

zunda (Hausa, Nigeria) to indicate with one's lips
catkhara (Hindi) smacking either the lips or the tongue against the palate
die beleidigte Leberwurst spielen (German) to stick one's lower lip out sulkily (literally, to play the insulted liver sausage)
ho'oauwaepu'u (Hawaiian) to stick the tongue under one's lip or to jut out the chin and twist the lips to the side to form a lump (as a gesture of contempt)

Hooter

Noses are highly metaphorical. We win by a nose, queue nose to tail or ask people to keep their noses out of our business. Then, if they are annoying us, it's that same protuberant feature we seize on:

irgham (Persian) rubbing a man's nose in the dirt
hundekuq (Albanian) a bulbous nose, red at the tip
nuru (Roviana, Solomon Islands) a runny nose
engsang (Malay) to blow the nose with your fingers
ufuruk (Turkish) breath exhaled through the nose

Albanian face fungus

Just below the nose may be found a feature increasingly rare in this country, but popular amongst males in many other societies. In Albania the language reflects an interest bordering on obsession, with no fewer than twenty-seven separate expressions for this fine addition to the upper lip. Their word for moustache is similar to ours (**mustaqe**) but once attached to their highly specific adjectives, things move on to a whole new level:

madh bushy moustache
holl thin moustache
varur drooping moustache
big handlebar moustache
kacadre moustache with turned-up ends
glemb moustache with tapered tips
posht moustache hanging down at the ends
fshes long broom-like moustache with bristly hairs
dirs ur newly sprouted moustache (of an adolescent)
rruar with the moustache shaved off

... to name but ten. The attention the Albanians apply to facial hair they also apply to eyebrows, with another twenty-seven words, including pencil-thin (**vetullkalem**), frowning (**vetullvrenjtur**), plucked (**vetullhequr**), knitted (**vetullrrept**), long and delicately shaped (**vetullgajtan**), thick (**vetullor**), joined together (**vetullperpjekur**), gloomy (**vetullngrysur**), or even arched like the crescent moon (**vetullhen**).

Bearded wonder

The Arab exclamation 'God protect us from hairy women and beardless men' pinpoints the importance of facial hair as a mark of rank, experience and attractiveness:

gras bilong fes (Tok Pisin, Papua New Guinea) a beard
   (literally, grass belonging to the face)
hemigeneios (Ancient Greek) with only half a beard
qarba (Persian) white hairs appearing in the beard
sim-zanakh (Persian) with a silver chin
poti (Tulu, India) a woman with a beard

False friends

willing (Abowakal, Australia) lips
buzz (Arabic) nipple
bash (Zulu) head
thumb (Albanian) teat
finger (Yiddish) toe

Bad hair day

Hair on the top of the head – or the lack of it – remains a worldwide preoccupation:

basribis (Ulwa, Nicaragua) having uneven, poorly cut hair
daberlack (Ullans, Northern Ireland) seaweed or uncontrollable long hair
kudpalu (Tulu, India) a woman with uncombed hair
kucir (Indonesian) a tuft left to grow on top of one's otherwise bald head

. . . not forgetting the Indonesian word **didis**, which means 'to search and pick up lice from one's own hair, usually when in bed at night'.

Teething troubles

Why doesn't English have an expression for the space between the teeth when Malay does – **gigi rongak**? And that's not the only gap in our dental vocabulary:

mrongos (Indonesian) to have ugly protruding upper teeth
angil (Kapampangan, Philippines) to bare the fangs like a dog
laglerolarpok (Inuit) the gnashing of teeth
kashr (Persian) displaying the teeth in laughter
zhaghzhagh (Persian) the chattering of the teeth from the cold or from rage

And that one bizarre word that few of us are ever likely to need:

puccekuli (Tulu, India) a tooth growing after the eightieth year

Getting it in the neck

Although there are straightforward terms for the throat in almost all languages, it's when it comes to describing how the throat is used that things get interesting:

nwik-ga (Wagiman, Australia) to have a tickle in the throat

ngaobera (Pascuense, Easter Island) a slight inflammation of the throat caused by screaming too much

berdaham (Malaysian) to clear the throat, especially to attract attention

kökochöka (Nahuatl, Mexico) to make gulping sounds

jarida biriqihi (Arabic) he choked on but couldn't swallow saliva (from excitement, alarm or grief)

o ka la nokonoko (Hawaiian) a day spent in nervous anticipation of a coughing spell

Armless in Nicaragua

In Ulwa, which is spoken in the eastern part of Nicaragua, no distinction is made between certain parts of the body. So, for example, **wau** means either a thigh or a leg, **ting** is an arm or a hand (and **tingdak** means missing an arm or a hand), **tingmak** is a finger or a thumb, **tibur** is either a wrist or an ankle, and **kungbas** means a beard, a moustache or whiskers.

Safe pair of hands

Other languages are more specific about our extremities and their uses:

sakarlasmak (Turkish) to become butterfingered
lutuka (Tulu, India) the cracking of the fingers
angushti za'id (Persian) someone with six fingers
zastrich' (Russian) to cut one's nails too short
meshetmek (Turkish) to wipe with the wet palm of one's hand
anjali (Hindi) hollowed hands pressed together in salutation

Legging it

Undue attention is put on their shapeliness but the bottom line is it's good to have two of them and they should, ideally, be the same length:

papakata (Cook Islands Maori) to have one leg shorter than the other
baguettes (French) thin legs (literally, chopsticks or long thin French loaves)
x-bene (Afrikaans) knock-knees
bulurin-suq (Persian) with thighs like crystal

Footloose

We don't always manage to put our best one forward:

> **zassledit'** (Russian) to leave dirty footmarks
> **mencak-mencak** (Indonesian) to stamp one's feet on the ground repeatedly, getting very angry
> **eshte thike me thike** (Albanian) to stand toenail to toenail (prior to an argument)

Mind the gap

Several cultures have words to describe the space between or behind limbs: **irqa** (Khakas, Siberia) is the gap between spread legs, and **awawa** (Hawaiian) that between each finger or toe. While **jahja** in Wagiman (Australia) and **waal** in Afrikaans both mean the area behind the knee.

Skin deep

We describe it with just one word but other cultures go much further, whether it's **alang** (Ulwa, Nicaragua), the fold of skin under the chin; **aka'aka'a** (Hawaiian), skin peeling or falling off after either sunburn or heavy drinking; or **karelu** (Tulu, India), the mark left on the skin by wearing anything tight. Another Ulwa word, **yuputka**, records something we have all experienced – having the sensation of something crawling on one's skin.

Covering up

Once it comes to adding clothes to the human frame, people have the choice of either dressing up . . .

> **tiré à quatre épingles** (French) dressed up to the nines (literally, drawn to four pins)
>
> **'akapoe** (Cook Islands Maori) donning earrings or putting flowers behind the ears
>
> **angkin** (Indonesian) a long wide cloth belt worn by women to keep them slim
>
> **Pomadenhengst** (German) a dandy (literally, a hair-cream stallion)
>
> **FHCP** (French) acronym of **Foulard Hermès Collier Perles**, Hermes scarf pearl necklace (a female Sloane Ranger)

or down . . .

> **opgelozen** (Yiddish) a careless dresser
>
> **padella** (Italian) an oily stain on clothes (literally, a frying pan)
>
> **Krawattenmuffel** (German) one who doesn't like wearing ties
>
> **cotisuelto** (Caribbean Spanish) one who wears the shirt tail outside of the trousers
>
> **tan** (Chinese) to wear nothing above one's waist

or just as they feel . . .

> **sygekassebriller** (Danish) granny glasses
>
> **rash** (Arabic) skirt worn under a sleeveless smock
>
> **alyaska** (Russian) anorak or moon-boots
>
> **hachimaki** (Japanese) headbands worn by males to encourage concentration and effort
>
> **ujut'a** (Quechuan, Peru) sandals made from tyres

English clothing

English words for clothes have slipped into many languages. Sometimes the usage is fairly literal, as in **smoking** to describe a dinner jacket in Swedish or Portuguese; or **pants** for a tracksuit in Spanish. Sometimes it's more metaphorical: the Hungarians call jeans **farmer**, while their term for a T-shirt is **polo**. In Barbados the cloth used for the lining of men's clothes is known as **domestic**. Sometimes it's just an odd mix: the Danish for jeans, for example, is **cowboybukser**, while the Japanese **sebiro** means a fashionably cut suit, being their pronunciation of Savile Row, London's famous street of tailors.

Go whistle

On the tiny mountainous Canary Island of La Gomera there is a language called Silbo Gomero that uses a variety of whistles instead of words (in Spanish **silbar** means to whistle). There are four 'vowels' and four 'consonants', which can be strung together to form more than four thousand 'words'. This birdlike means of communication is thought to have come over with early African settlers over 2500 years ago. Able to be heard at distances of up to two miles, the **silbador** was until recently a dying breed. Since 1999, however, Silbo has been a required language in La Gomera schools.

The Mazateco Indians of Oaxaca, Mexico, are frequently seen whistling back and forth, exchanging greetings or buying and selling goods with no risk of misunderstanding. The whistling is not really a language or even a code; it simply uses the rhythms and pitch of ordinary speech without the words. Similar whistling languages have been found in Greece, Turkey and China, whilst other forms of wordless communication include the talking drums (**ntumpane**) of the Kele in Congo, the xylophones used by the Northern Chin of Burma, the banging on the roots of trees practised by the Melanesians, the yodelling of the Swiss, the humming of the Chekiang Chinese and the smoke signals of the American Indians.

Movers and Shakers

mas vale rodear que no ahogar
(*Spanish*)
better go about than fall into the ditch

Shanks's pony

There's much more to walking than simply putting one foot in front of the other:

> **berlenggang** (Indonesian) to walk gracefully by swinging one's hands or hips
> **aradupopini** (Tulu, India) to walk arm in arm or hand in hand
> **uitwaaien** (Dutch) to walk in windy weather for fun

> **murr-ma** (Wagiman, Australia) to walk along in the water searching for something with your feet
> **'akihi** (Hawaiian) to walk off without paying attention to directions

Walking in Zimbabwe

The Shona- speaking people of Zimbabwe have some very specialized verbs for different kinds of walking: **chakwaira**, through a muddy place making a squelching sound; **dowora**, for a long time on bare feet; **svavaira**, huddled, cold and wet; **minaira**, with swinging hips; **pushuka**, in a very short dress; **shwitaira**, naked; **sesera**, with the flesh rippling; and **tabvuka**, with such thin thighs that you seem to be jumping like a grasshopper.

Malaysian movements

The elegant Malaysians have a highly specialized vocabulary to describe movement, both of the right kind, as in **kontal-kontil**, 'the swinging of long earrings or the swishing of a dress as one walks', and the wrong, as in **jerangkang**, 'to fall over with your legs in the air'. Others include:

kengkang to walk with your legs wide apart
tenjack to limp with your heels raised
kapai to flap your arms so as to stay afloat
gayat feeling dizzy while looking down from a high place
seluk to put your hand in your pocket
bongkeng sprawling face down with your bottom in the air

Ups . . .

Sometimes our movements are deliberately athletic, whether this involves hopping on one leg (**vogget** in Cornish, **hinke** in Danish), rolling like a ball (**ajawyry** in the Wayampi language of Brazil), or something more adventurous:

angama (Swahili) to hang in mid-air
vybafnout (Czech) to surprise someone by saying boo
puiyarpo (Inuit) to show your head above water
povskakat' (Russian) to jump one after another
tarere (Cook Islands Maori) to send someone flying through the air
lele kawa (Hawaiian) to jump into the sea feet first

Lele kawa, of course, is usually followed by **curglaff**, Scottish dialect for the shock felt when plunging into cold water.

... and downs

But on other occasions there seems to be a banana skin waiting for us on the pavement:

blart (Ullans, Northern Ireland) to fall flat in the mud

lamhdanaka (Ulwa, Nicaragua) to collapse sideways (as when walking on uneven ground)

tunuallak (Inuit) slipping and falling over on your back while walking

kejeblos (Indonesian) to fall into a hole by accident

apismak (Turkish) to spread the legs apart and collapse

jeruhuk (Malay) the act of stumbling into a hole that is concealed by long grass

False friends

gush (Albanian) to hug each other around the neck

shagit (Albanian) to crawl on one's belly

snags (Afrikaans) during the night

sofa (Icelandic) sleep

purr (Scottish Gaelic) to headbutt

What-d'you-call-it

Just because there is no word for it in English doesn't mean we haven't done it or experienced it:

mencolek (Indonesian) touching someone lightly with one finger in order to tease them

wasoso (Hausa, Nigeria) to scramble for something that has been thrown

idumbulu (Tulu, India) seizing each other tightly with both hands

přesezený (Czech) being stiff from sitting in the same position too long

'alo'alo kiki (Hawaiian) to dodge the rain by moving quickly

honuhonu (Hawaiian) to swim with the hands only

engkoniomai (Ancient Greek) to sprinkle sand over oneself

tallabe (Zarma, Nigeria) to carry things on one's head without holding on to them

gagrom (Boro, India) to search for a thing below water by trampling

chonggang-chongget (Malay) to keep bending forward and then straightening (as a hill-climber)

When it all goes horribly wrong . . .

That sinking feeling, **puangi** (Cook Islands Maori), the sensation of the stomach dropping away (as in the sudden surge of a lift, plane, swing or a tossed boat), is something we know all too well, as are:

dokidoki (Japanese) rapid pounding heartbeats caused by worry or surprise

a'anu (Cook Islands Maori) to sit huddled up, looking pinched and miserable

nggregeli (Indonesian) to drop something due to nerves

bingildamak (Turkish) to quiver like jelly

. . . scarper

baotou shucuon (Chinese) to cover one's head with both hands and run away like a coward

achaplinarse (Spanish, Central America) to hesitate and then run away in the manner of Charlie Chaplin

Learning to relax

In some parts of the world relaxation doesn't necessarily mean putting your feet up:

ongkang-ongkang (Indonesian) to sit with one leg dangling down

naganaga (Rapa Nui, Easter Island) to squat without resting your buttocks on your heels

lledorweddle (Welsh) to lie down while propping yourself up with one elbow

karvat (Hindi) the side of the body on which one rests

Dropping off

Once we start relaxing, snoozing becomes an increasingly strong possibility. Both Danish, with **raevesøvn**, and Russian, with **vpolglaza**, have a word to describe sleeping with one eye open, while other languages describe other similar states of weariness:

aiguttoa (Votic, Estonia) to yawn repeatedly

teklak-tekluk (Indonesian) the head bobbing up and down with drowsiness

utsura-utsura (Japanese) to fluctuate between wakefulness and being half asleep

utouto (Japanese) to fall into a light sleep without realizing it

tengkurap (Indonesian) to lie or sleep with the face downwards

kulubut (Kapampangan, Philippines) to go under the blanket

Out for the count

Having achieved the state the Japanese describe as **guuguu**, 'the sound of someone in a deep sleep accompanied by snoring', we can either have a good night . . .

> **bilita mpash** (Bantu, Zaire) blissful dreams
> **altjiranga mitjina** (Aranda, Australia) the timeless dimensions of dreams
> **ngarong** (Dyak, Borneo) an adviser who appears in a dream and clarifies a problem
> **rêve à deux** (French) a mutual dream, a shared hallucination
> **morgenfrisk** (Danish) fresh from a good night's sleep

. . . or a bad one:

> **menceracan** (Malay) to cry in one's sleep
> **kekau** (Indonesian) to wake up from a nightmare
> **igau** (Malay) to talk while trapped in a nightmare
> **kerinan** (Indonesian) to oversleep until the sun is up

Back as forth

Whatever their length, words have provided excellent material for games from the earliest times. One of the more pleasing arrangements is the palindrome, which is spelt the same backwards as forwards, and can create some bizarre meanings:

neulo taas niin saat oluen (Finnish) knit again, so that you will get a beer

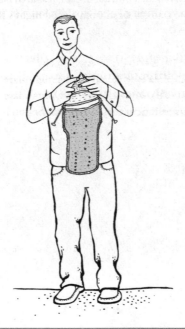

Nie fragt sie: ist gefegt? Sie ist gar fein (German) she never asks: has the sweeping been done? She is very refined

in girum imus nocte et consumimur igni (Latin) we enter the circle after dark and are consumed by fire

nipson anomemata me monan opsin (Ancient Greek) wash (off) my sins, not only my face (written on the edge of a well in Constantinople: NB the 'ps' is a transcription of the Greek letter ψ)

The Finns have three of the world's longest palindromic words:

saippuakivikauppias a soapstone seller
saippuakuppinippukauppias a soap-cup trader
solutomaattimittaamotulos the result from a measurement laboratory for tomatoes

Getting Around

dalu tongtian, ge zou yi bian
(Chinese)
the highway comes out of one's mouth

Thumbing it

Some rides are free:

fara a puttanu (Icelandic) to hitchhike (literally, to travel on the thumb)

usqar (Khakas, Siberia) to take someone on the back of one's horse

radif (Persian) one who rides behind another on the same horse

menggonceng (Indonesian) to have a free ride usually on a friend's bike

plomo (Spanish, Central America) a bus passenger who is just on for the free ride (literally, a lead weight)

Others involve money . . .

ngetem (Indonesian) to stop (of a bus) longer than necessary at unauthorized points along the route to the terminus to look for more paying passengers

ngojek (Indonesian) to earn money by carrying a paying passenger on the rear seat of one's motorbike

. . . or getting your own transport:

essoreuse (French) a noisy motorbike (literally, spindryer)

Warmwassergeige (German) a souped-up motorcycle (literally, warm-water violin)

teplushka (Russian) a heated goods van used for carrying people

bottom-bottom wata wata (African Creole) a submarine

gung gung chi chuh (Chinese) a bus

vokzal (Russian) a railway station (named after Vauxhall in London)

voiture-balai (French) the last train or bus (literally, broom-vehicle as it sweeps up the latecomers)

Set of wheels

One particular form of transport is pre-eminent in the modern world: whether normal, or convertible (**spider** in Italian), or vintage (**oldtimer** in German). What lets most cars down, however, are the people driving them, be it the **viande paraguero** (Caribbean Spanish), the Sunday driver (literally, an umbrella stand); or the **Gurtmuffel** (German), someone who doesn't wear a seat belt. Then, of course, there's the way people drive:

sgasata (Italian) a sudden and violent acceleration
appuyer sur le champignon (French) to put one's foot down
(literally, to stamp on the mushroom)
Geisterfahrer (German), a person driving on the wrong side of
the road

Road rage

Hazards are all too common, whether in the car . . .

desgomarse (Caribbean Spanish) to have bad tyres
ulykkesbilen (Danish) an ill-fated car
Blechlawine (German) a huge traffic jam (literally, a sheet-
metal avalanche)
matadero (Spanish, Central America) a car scrapheap (literally,
a slaughterhouse)

. . . or out of it. The French have the most evocative expressions to describe both the reckless pedestrian – **viande à pneux**, meat for tyres, and the knock suffered by a cyclist – **l'homme au marteau**, literally, the man with the hammer.

Apache cars

The Apache people of the USA name the parts of cars to correspond to parts of the body. The front bumper is **daw**, the chin or jaw; the front fender is **wos**, the shoulder; the rear fender is **gun**, the arm and hand; the chassis is **chun**, the back; the rear wheel is **ke**, the foot. The mouth is **ze**, the petrol-pipe opening. The nose is **chee**, the bonnet. The eyes are **inda**, the headlights. The forehead is **ta**, the roof.

The metaphorical naming continues inside. The car's electrical wiring is **tsaws**, the veins. The battery is **zik**, the liver. The petrol tank is **pit**, the stomach. The radiator is **jisoleh**, the lung; and its hose, **chih**, the intestine. The distributor is **jih**, the heart.

False friends

punk (Japanese) flat tyre
chariot (French) trolley
rower (Polish) bicycle
fly (Danish) aeroplane

escape (Portuguese) car exhaust or gas leak
arrear (Spanish) to drive on
jam (Mongolian) road

Running on time

The Japanese have some fine vocabulary for trains: **gaton gaton** is an electric train; **gotongoton** describes trains rattling along; **shoo shoo po po** is the sound of a steam train; while **kang kang kang** is the noise of the level crossing. **Kakekomi-josha** describes all too vividly rushing onto a train to beat the closing doors, a common sight on Tokyo's underground.

Separatist

Many of the languages around the world are inter-related (for example, Spanish, French and Italian are all Latin languages), but by contrast, 'isolate languages' are those that do not appear to be related to any other at all. Some languages became isolate in historical times, after all their known relatives became extinct; the Piraha language, for example, spoken along a tributary of the Amazon, is the last surviving member of the Mura family of languages. Similar isolates include Burushaski, which is spoken in two Himalayan valleys; the Gilyak and Ket languages of Siberia; and Nivkh, a Mongolian language.

The Basque language Euskara is perplexing. It bears no resemblance at all to the languages of its surrounding countries. Some similarities with Georgian have made linguists think it could be related to languages from the Caucasus. Others have tried to relate it to non-Arabic languages from the north of Africa. A more likely hypothesis argues that Euskara developed where it is still spoken and has always been the language of the Basques, who were gradually surrounded by people speaking other unrelated languages.

It Takes All Sorts

gading yang tak retak *(Indonesian)*
there is no ivory that isn't cracked

Tolerant

When it comes to personality, some people seem to have been put on the planet to make life easier for everyone else:

cooperar (Spanish, Central America) to go along willingly with someone else to one's own disadvantage

abbozzare (Italian) to accept meekly a far from satisfactory situation

ilunga (Tshiluba, Congo) someone who is ready to forgive any abuse the first time, to tolerate it a second time, but never a third time

Flattering

Others take things too far:

vaseliner (French) to flatter (literally, to apply vaseline)

happobijin (Japanese) a beauty to all eight directions (a sycophant)

Radfahrer (German) one who flatters superiors and browbeats subordinates (literally, a cyclist)

Fawning

The Japanese have the most vivid description for hangers-on: **kingyo no funi**. It literally means 'goldfish crap' – a reference to the way that a fish that has defecated often trails excrement behind it for some time.

Egotists

Sweet-talking others is one thing; massaging your own ego can be another altogether:

echarse flores (Spanish) to blow your own trumpet (literally, to throw flowers to yourself)

il ne se mouche pas du pied (French) he has airs above his station (literally, he doesn't wipe his nose with his foot)

yi luan tou shi (Chinese) courting disaster by immoderately overestimating one's own strength (literally, to throw an egg against a rock)

tirer la couverture à soi (French) to take the lion's share, all the credit (literally, to pull the blanket towards oneself)

The awkward squad

But there are worse horrors than the merely conceited:

ataoso (Spanish, Central America) one who sees problems with everything

kibitzer (Yiddish) one who interferes with unwanted advice

nedovtipa (Czech) one who finds it difficult to take a hint

neko-neko (Indonesian) to have a creative idea which only makes things worse

mukzib (Persian) one who eggs on or compels another to tell a lie

iant (Serbian) an attitude of proud defiance, stubbornness and self-preservation, sometimes to the detriment of everyone else – or even oneself

er gibt seinen Senf dazu (German) one who always has something to say even if no one else cares (literally, he brings his mustard along)

Pariah

Some people are able to tough it out whatever happens, imposing their faults on others till the day they die. Others are more sensitive:

scrostarsi (Italian) to remove oneself as if one were a scab (to move or go away because one's presence is not desired)

ulaia (Hawaiian) to live as a hermit because of disappointment

panaphelika (Ancient Greek) to be deprived of all playmates

Lazybones

Others like to spend time alone for altogether different reasons:

kopuhia (Rapa Nui, Easter Island) someone who disappears instead of dedicating himself to his work

linti (Persian) someone who idles his day away lying under a tree

nubie yam (Waali, Ghana) a farmer who points to his farm but does little more (literally, finger farm)

gober les mouches (French) to stand by idly (literally, to gulp down flies)

zamzama (Arabic) to waft along in a relaxed style

goyang kaki (Indonesian) relaxing and enjoying oneself as problems are sorted out by others (literally, to swing one's legs)

kalincak-kelincok (Balinese, Indonesia) the back and forth, here and there or up and down of genuine drifting

Otherwise engaged

Some take idleness to another level:

luftmensch (Yiddish) an impractical dreamer having no definite business or income

viajou na maionese (Portuguese) to live in a dream world (literally, to travel in the mayonnaise)

nglayap (Indonesian) to wander far from home with no particular purpose

umudrovat se (Czech) to philosophize oneself into the madhouse

Situation vacant

Given that many outsiders think of the Japanese as a nation of workaholics, the language has an unusual number of verbs to describe different states of idleness: **boketto** is to gaze vacantly into space without thinking or doing anything; **bosabosa** is to sit around idly not doing what needs to be done; **gorogoro** is to spend time doing nothing (including lolling in a recumbent position); **guzuguzu** is to vacillate, procrastinate or to stretch out a job; while **bura-bura** is to wander around aimlessly, looking at the sights with no fixed destination in mind.

Manic obsessive

No one, as far as we know, died of laziness. Frantic activity, however, is another thing . . .

Putzfimmel (German) a mania for cleaning
samlermani (Danish) a mania for collecting
Grüebelsucht (German) an obsession in which even the
    simplest facts are compulsively queried
muwaswas (Arabic) to be obsessed with delusions
potto (Japanese) to be so distracted or preoccupied that you
    don't notice what is happening right in front of you

. . . and can lead to **karoshi** (Japanese), death from overwork.

The German mindset

A distinguishing feature of the German language is its creation of evocative concepts by linking different words together, useful for depicting not just characters but states of mind. Most of us know **Schadenfreude** (literally, damage joy), which describes what we hardly dare express: that feeling of malicious pleasure in someone else's misfortune. But there are numerous others. We've all had a boss who's suffered from **Betriebsblindheit**: organizational blindness; and who has not worked alongside someone who is **fisselig**: flustered to the point of incompetence? That very same person could be described as a **Korinthenkacker**: one who is overly concerned with trivial details.

False friends

fatal (German) annoying

hardnekkig (Dutch) stubborn

lawman (Aukan, Suriname) crazy person

estúpido (Portuguese) rude

morbido (Italian) soft, tender

xerox (French) unoriginal or robotic individual

extravagans (Hungarian) eccentric

konsekvent (Swedish) consistent

Fools and rogues

There's a rich stream of invective running through the world's languages when it comes to people we regard as less intelligent than ourselves. The Cantonese equivalent to 'you're as thick as two short planks' is the equally graphic **nie hochi yat gau faan gam**, 'you look like a clump of cooked rice', while the German equivalent to 'not quite all there' is **nicht alle Tassen im Schrank haben**, 'not to have all the cups in the cupboard' (not to have all one's marbles).

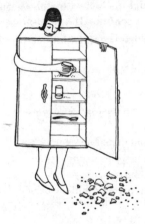

Meanwhile the Maoris of the Cook Islands have the telling word **varevare**, which means 'to be very young and still quite hopeless'.

Schlumps and schleppers

When it comes to insults, few languages can compete with Yiddish. In this wonderfully evocative language, a fool can be not just a **shmutte** or a **schlump** but a **nar**, a **tam**, a **tipesh**, a **bulvan**, a **shoyte**, a **peysi**, a **kuni lemel**, a **lekish**, or even a **shmenge**.

Not content with these, the language gets more specific. A loser is a **schlepper**, a **shmugeggeshnorrer**, a **paskudnik**, a **pisher**, a **yold** or even a **no-goodnik**. A **klutz** is a clumsy, oafish bungler and a **lekish ber schlemiel** is a fool without luck. A fool who is not just stupid but inept is a **schlimazl**. A **farshpiler** is one who has lost all his money gambling. The saddest of all is perhaps the **nisrof**, the burnt-out fool.

Other fine insults in Yiddish have included:

nebbish a nobody
nudnick a yakky, aggressively boring person
putz a simpleton
shlub a clumsy and ill-mannered person
shmegegge a foolish person and a sycophant
shmendrick a timid nonentity
shnook a nice but pathetic gullible person

All talk

Worse than the fool is one of those people who occur in every organization on the planet: the **buchipluma** (Caribbean Spanish), the person who promises but doesn't deliver. The same language has a useful verb for the way such people behave: **culipanear**, which means to look for excuses for not meeting obligations.

Fibbers

Even the infuriating **buchipluma** is surely preferable to the outright liar. And, as Japanese vividly shows, from lying to someone (**nimaijita o tsukau**, to use two tongues), it's just a small step to duping (**hanage o nuku handy**, literally, to pull the hair out of their nostrils) or doublecrossing them (**negaeri o utsu**, literally, to roll them over while sleeping).

Salt of the earth

What a shame that we can't all be uncomplicatedly good: for example, when you're acting with **meraki** (a Greek word) you're doing something with soul, creativity or love, and putting something of yourself into what you're doing:

tubli (Estonian) orderly, strong, capable, hard-working,
    persistent, productive, setting an example to others,
    behaving properly or having will power
ondinnonk (Iroquoian, USA) the soul's innermost benevolent
    desires or the angelic parts of human nature

Indonesian two in one

Indonesian has many words that combine two aspects of character or appearance into a single simple word. So you might well know someone who is **ricuh**, that is, chaotic and noisy; **pandir**, stupid, but innocent and honest; **mungil**, tiny and pretty; **merana**, lonely and miserable; **lencir**, slim and tall; **bangkot**, old and cantankerous; or **klimis**, smooth and shiny.

Tall poppies

Sweden is a country that not only values the concept of a lack of extremes but even has a word for it – **lagom**. In this society, it's generally not thought to be good to stand out too much. Everything and everyone is supposed to be just **lagom** – which is not to say 'boring', so much as 'not too much and not too little', 'not good and not bad', 'okay', 'just right', 'so-so'.

So so similar

The concept of 'so-so' is found in many languages, and often in a similarly repetitive form: it's **tako tako** in Bosnian/Croatian/Serbian, **aixi aixi** in Catalan, **cosi cosi** in Italian, **wale wale** in Chipewyan (Canada), **hanter hanter** in Cornish, **thik thik** in Gujarati (India), **hai hao** in Mandarin, **jako tako** in Polish, **ithin ithin** in Sinhala (Sri Lanka), **soyle boyle** in Turkish, **etsi ketsi** in Greek, **atal atal** in Occitan (France), **asina asina** in Asturian (Spain), **elae belae** in Azeri (Azerbaijan) and **azoy azoy** in Yiddish.

Happy talk

Good or bad, modest or conceited, hard-working or lazy, all of us experience the highs of emotion:

tout baigne dans l'huile (French) hunky-dory (literally, everything is bathing in oil)

ai bu shishou (Chinese) so delighted with something that one can scarcely take one's eyes off it

ichigo-ichie (Japanese) the practice of treasuring each moment and trying to make it perfect

pulaka (Tulu, India) hair that stands on end with ecstasy

bas-bhualadh (Scottish Gaelic) clapping one's hands from joy or grief

tuman (Indonesian) to find something enjoyable and want to have it again

mubshar (Persian) to be exhilarated with good news

zhuxing (Chinese) to add to the fun

Side-splitting

sekaseka (Bemba, Congo and Zambia) to laugh without reason

tergelak (Malay) laughing unintentionally

katahara itai (Japanese) laughing so much that one side of your abdomen hurts

Enraptured

The Japanese have particularly wonderful words for the deep joy that can come as a response to beauty: **uttori** is to be enraptured by the loveliness of something; **aware** describes the feelings created by ephemeral beauty; **yoin** is the reverberating sensation after the initial stimulus has ceased; while **yugen** goes further, describing an awareness of the universe that triggers feelings too deep and mysterious for words.

Down in the dumps

The causes of unhappiness are many, varied and not always easy to put your finger on:

termangu-mangu (Indonesian) sad and not sure what to do
mono-no-aware (Japanese) appreciating the sadness of existence
avoir le cafard (French) to be down in the dumps (literally, to have the cockroach)

litost (Czech) the state of torment created by the sudden realization of one's own misery
kusat' sebe lokti (Russian) to cry over spilt milk (literally, to bite one's elbows)
emakou (Gilbertese, Kiribati) a secret sorrow
bel hevi (Tok Pisin, Papua New Guinea) the heavy sinking feeling that often accompanies extreme sadness (literally, belly heavy)

Weltschmerz

Weltschmerz is another untranslatable German word. It broadly means world-weariness, but carries with it both a sense of sorrow at the evils of the world and a yearning for something better. Aspects of it can be found in the Welsh **hiraeth**, a mingled feeling of sadness, somewhere between homesickness and nostalgia, and the Portuguese **saudade**, the longing for things that were or might have been. Nostalgia also lies at the heart of the Brazilian Portuguese word **banzo**, which describes a slave's profound longing for his African homeland.

In the slough of despond

There are various ways to deal with feelings of despair. Either you can take a philosophical view and try to avoid the Persian concept of **sanud**, that is, the exercise of the mind upon an unprofitable subject; or you can adopt the defeatist attitude inherent in the Indonesian word **jera**, which means 'so scared by a past experience that one will never want to do it again'. Or you can take refuge in **Kummerspeck**, a German word that describes the excess weight you will gain from emotion-related overeating (literally, grief bacon).

Seeing red

Therapists would suggest it's better out than in:

mukamuka (Japanese) feeling so angry one feels like throwing up

geragas (Malay) to comb one's hair in anger

feau (Samoan) to recall good deeds done when one is angry

Survival instincts

Even though some languages are vanishing, in a world less hospitable to aboriginal peoples and more swamped by English, this does not mean it's impossible to keep endangered languages alive. Mohawk, for instance, spoken by indigenous groups in Quebec, was in retreat until the 1970s, when it was first codified and then taught to children in schools. Welsh and Maori have both made a comeback with concerted official help; and Navajo (USA), Hawaiian and several languages spoken in remote parts of Botswana have been artifically revived.

Iceland has managed to keep alive its native tongue, even though it is spoken by no more than 275,000 people; and the ancient Nordic language of Faroese, thought to have been once spoken by the Vikings, was preserved from extinction by the Danish government, who even went as far as putting grammar hints and verb declensions on the sides of milk cartons.

A powerful political purpose is another force for reviving an old language. Resurgent nationalism helped bring Irish back from the Celtic twilight; while the establishment of the nation of Israel has turned Hebrew from a written language into a proudly spoken national tongue.

Falling in Love

nam gawa the wei woe lu yoe;
phung dang si yang they nang
yoe *(Dzongkha, Bhutan)*
fun and pleasure are located below the
navel; dispute and trouble are also
found there

The language of love

In English the language of love is, metaphorically speaking, a violent and disorientating one: we fall in love, are love struck and struggle to avoid heartbreak. It seems things are the same throughout the world:

harawata o tatsu (Japanese) to break one's heart (literally, to sever one's intestines)

coup de foudre (French) love at first sight (literally, a flash of lightning)

mune o kogasu (Japanese) to pine away (literally, to scorch one's chest)

tragado como media de cartero (Colombian Spanish) being hopelessly in love (literally, swallowed like a postman's sock)

The rules of attraction ...

Physical beauty is often the starting point for love:

pichón (Caribbean Spanish) a handsome young man (literally, young pigeon)

qiubo (Chinese) the bright and clear eyes of a beautiful woman
mahj (Persian) looking beautiful after a disease
avoir la frite (French) to be in great shape (literally, to have the French fry)
magandang hinaharap (Tagalog, Philippines) nice breasts (literally, nice future)
dayadrsti (Hindi) compassionate eyes
kemayu (Indonesian) to act like a beauty

Sometimes the basic materials need a little assistance:

slampadato (Italian) a person who gets tanned with an infra-red lamp
zhengrong (Chinese) to tidy oneself up or to improve one's looks by plastic surgery

... and of repulsion

The Japanese have a particular word for a situation in which attraction is all too brief. **Bakku-shan** is a girl who appears pretty when seen from behind but not from the front.

Would like to meet

English is somewhat deficient in words that describe the very early moments of attraction. We need a word like **mamihlapinatapei**, from the Fuegian language found in Chile, meaning that shared look of longing where both parties know the score yet neither is willing to make the first move. Other, more active approaches include:

basabasa (Arabic) to ogle, make sheep's eyes, cast amorous glances

piropo (Spanish) a compliment paid on the street (which ranges from polite to raunchy)

xiyyet (Dardja, Algeria) he is sewing (this is said of someone who is trying to win over a girl, especially by talking)

pulir hebillas (Spanish, Central America) to polish belt buckles (to dance very closely)

The direct approach

The Italians are masters at taking matters to the next level: **pomicione** is a man who seeks any chance of being in close physical contact with a woman; **puntare** is to stare intensely at the one to whom one feels sexually attracted; while **tirino** is the sound made by smacking one's lips together like a loud kiss to indicate attraction. Sometimes a boy will say **cibi cierre** to a girl (**CBCR**). This is an acronym of **cresci bene che ripasso**: 'if you still look like that when you've grown up, I will come and pay you a call' . . .

Dîner à un

. . . while the French have perfected the art of rejection:

poser un lapin à quelqu'un to stand someone up (literally, to lay a rabbit on someone)

Saint-Glinglin a date that is put off indefinitely (**jusqu' à la Saint-Glinglin** means never in a month of Sundays)

Japanese dating

Rainen no kono hi mo issho ni waratteiyoh is one of the country's most successful chat-up lines; it means 'this time next year let's be laughing together'.

Commitment-phobe

The romantic ideal is **Einfühlungsvermögen**, the German word for an understanding so intimate that the feelings, thoughts and motives of one person are readily comprehended by the other; but the route to that happy state can so often be confused by the insincere:

biodegradabile (Italian) someone who falls in love easily and often

capkinlasmak (Turkish) to turn into a skirt chaser

leonera (Spanish, Central America) a bachelor pad (literally, a lion's den)

vieux marcheur (French) an elderly man who still chases women (literally, an old campaigner)

False friends

nob (Wolof, Gambia and Senegal) to love

city (Czech) feelings

dating (Chinese) to ask about, enquire

baron (French) sugar daddy

agony (Rasta Patois) sensations felt during sex

bonk (Afrikaans) lump or thump

song (Vietnamese) to live life

Affairs of the heart

When things can go so sweetly . . .

alamnaka (Ulwa, Nicaragua) to find one's niche, to meet a kindred soul

pelar la pava (Caribbean Spanish) to be alone romancing one's sweetheart (literally, to pluck a female turkey)

andare in camporella (Italian) to go into a secluded spot in the countryside to make love

hiza o majieru (Japanese) to have an intimate talk (literally, to mingle each other's knees)

queesting (Dutch) allowing a lover access to one's bed under the covers for chit-chat

ghalidan (Persian) to move from side to side as lovers, to roll, wallow or tumble

. . . how can they be so bitter at the end?

aki ga tatsu (Japanese) a mutual cooling of love (literally, the autumn breeze begins to blow)

razblyuto (Russian) the feeling for someone once but no longer loved

dejar con el paquete (Spanish) abandoning a woman one has made pregnant (literally, to drop with the parcel)

plaqué (French) dumped (literally, laid flat or rugby-tackled)

cavoli riscaldati (Italian) an attempt to revive a lapsed love affair (literally, reheated cabbage)

Reality check

The Boro people of India have a sophisticated understanding of the complexities of loving: **onsay** means to pretend to love; **ongubsy** means to love deeply, from the heart; and **onsia** signifies loving for the very last time.

Love for sale

Who better than the pragmatic French to construct a precise terminology for love as a business, ranging from a **passe raide**, the basic price for a sex session, to the **kangourou**, a prospective client who hesitates (hops around) before deciding on a girl. When it comes to those who ply their trade, there are many equally specific terms. An **escaladeuse de braguette** is, literally a zipper climber; a **beguineuse** is an unreliable prostitute; a **wagonnière** is a woman who solicits on trains; a **truqueur** means a rentboy who blackmails his clients; while a **cocotte-minute** is a pro who turns many tricks very quickly (literally, a pressure cooker). There is even an expression, **commencer à rendre la monnaie**, to show signs of age, which is said of prostitutes who in better days didn't have to give change for large notes.

Let's talk about sex

The Mosuo people in China have three sacred taboos: it's forbidden to eat dog, to eat cat and to talk about sex. The latter taboo doesn't seem to apply elsewhere:

avoir la moule qui bâille (French) to be horny (literally, to have a yawning mussel)

menggerumut (Indonesian) to approach somebody quietly in the night for sex

jalishgar (Persian) to be addicted to sexual intercourse

carezza (Italian) sexual intercourse in which ejaculation is avoided (literally, caressing or petting)

Penis dialogues

There are many ways to describe **le petit chauve au col roulé** (French), the little baldy in a turtleneck, and the respect with which he's treated:

narachastra prayoga (Sanskrit) men who worship their own sexual organ

enfundarla (Spanish) to put one's penis back in one's pants (or one's sword back in its sheath)

zakilpistola (Basque) a sufferer from premature ejaculation (literally, pistol prick)

koro (Japanese) the hysterical belief that one's penis is shrinking into one's body

camisa-de-venus (Brazilian Portuguese) a condom (literally, shirt of Venus)

The Tagalog speakers of the Philippines take things further with the **batuta ni Drakula** ('Dracula's nightstick'). Added sexual pleasure can be gained from **pilik-mata ng kambing** (goat's eyelashes) or **bulitas** (small plastic balls surgically implanted to enlarge the penises of young Filipinos).

Sex for one ...

The vocabulary is no less specialized when it comes to what the Italians describe as **assolo**, a solo performance. **Up-retiree-hue** (Rapa Nui, Easter Islands) is to touch one's penis with the intention of masturbating, while the Japanese have several graphic terms for the experience. Male masturbation is referred to as **senzuri** (a thousand rubs), with the added refinement of **masu-kagami** (masturbating in front of a mirror). Female masturbation, by contrast, is described as **shiko shiko manzuri** (ten thousand rubs) and **suichi o ireru** (flicking the switch).

... and for many

Similar sensations can be experienced in company:

partousard (French) a participator in group sex

movimento (Italian) a circle of acquaintances who are actual or potential sexual partners

agapemone (Greek) an establishment where free love is practised

sacanagem (Brazilian Portuguese) the practice of openly seeking sexual pleasure with one or more partners other than one's primary partner (during Mardi Gras)

Pacific holiday

On the islands of Ulithi in the Western Pacific, the Micronesian people like to take a holiday from their regular lovemaking. **Pi supuhui** (literally, a hundred pettings) describes a holiday dedicated to mate-swapping. People pair up and go into the woods to share a picnic and make love. Married couples are not allowed to go together and the selection of new partners is encouraged. If there is an unequal number of participants, some couples may become threesomes.

The desired result or the result of desire

The French have a charming expression for this: **voir les anges**, which means to see angels.

Thumbs up

Gestures should be used carefully when abroad for fear of misunderstandings. The cheery thumbs-up used by the English or Americans means 'up yours' in the Middle East and 'sit on this' in Sardinia. In France, pressing a thumb against the fingertips means something is **ooh-la-la parfait** or just right, while in Egypt, the same gesture means 'stop right there'.

An American's sign for 'okay', made by touching the tip of the thumb to the tip of the forefinger, and used internationally by scuba divers, is an insult in Brazil. In some countries, the V sign can be negative, in others positive; in Italy, reversed, it approximates to 'to hell with you'. In some countries, flicking your thumb across the teeth tells the other person he's a cheapskate. Just about everywhere grabbing the crook of your elbow and raising your fist is rude. In the Arab world, the middle finger pointed downwards and moving up and down, with the palm horizontal, equates to a raised middle finger in England.

The Family Circle

bu yin, bu long, bu cheng gu
gong *(Chinese)*
unless one pretends to be stupid or deaf
it is difficult to be a mother-in-law or
father-in-law

Getting hitched

There comes a point, in most societies, where a relationship is formalized in law. As the Romanians say: **dragostea e oarbă, dar căsătoria îi găsește leacul**, love is blind, but marriage finds a cure:

strga (Bulgarian) a survey or visit to the home of a prospective bride

kumoru aluweik (Khowar, Pakistan) to lure a girl into marriage

lobola (Manu Bantu, Zaire) the bride price (which is usually paid in cattle)

casarse de penalti (Spanish) to get married after discovering a pregnancy

dar el braguetazo (Spanish) the marriage of a poor man to a rich woman

skeinkjari (Faroese, Denmark) the man who goes among wedding guests offering them alcohol ('that popular chap')

Trouble and strife

Does one always live happily ever after? The evidence of our global languages suggests that it's not always the case:

desortijarse (Caribbean Spanish) to return the engagement ring

kotsuniku no araso (Japanese) domestic strife (literally, the fight between bones and flesh)

ava (Tahitian) wife (but it also means whisky)

pelotilla (Caribbean Spanish) argument among spouses

ainolektros (Ancient Greek) fatally wedded

talik (Malay) to marry with the stipulation of automatic divorce for a husband's desertion

rujuk (Indonesian) to remarry the wife you've already divorced

Yang

Sometimes, the man is clearly to blame when things go wrong (with the emphasis on infidelity, desertion and gambling):

pu'ukaula (Hawaiian) to set up one's wife as a stake in gambling

qum'us (Persian) one who pimps his own wife

talak (Arabic) a husband who frees himself from his wife

agunah (Hebrew) a woman whose husband has deserted her or has disappeared and who is restrained from remarrying until she shows a bill of divorce or proof of his death

bawusni (Persian) a wife whose husband does not love her and seldom visits

Yin

At other times the fault lies with the woman (with the emphasis on laziness, bullying and antipathy):

farik (Persian) a woman who hates her husband

jefa (Caribbean Spanish) a domineering wife

shiri ni shikareru (Japanese) a husband who is under his wife's thumb (literally, under her buttocks)

polohana'ole (Hawaiian) a woman who refuses to work but lives on her husband's earnings

baulero (Caribbean Spanish) a henpecked husband who cannot go out alone

purik (Indonesian) to return to one's parents' home as a protest against one's husband

Family matters

Once married, man and wife may find that their greatest problem is getting enough time alone. Extending the family can work both ways:

bol (Mayan, Mexico) foolish in-laws

sitike (Apache, USA) in-laws who are formally committed to help during crises

todamane (Tulu, India) entertaining a son-in-law or mother-in-law for the first time

bruja (Spanish, South America) a mother-in-law (literally, a witch)

biras (Malay) the relationship between two brothers' wives or two sisters' husbands

Chercher la femme?

When it comes to the family unit being threatened, why is there is no such thing as an **homme fatal**? Caribbean Spanish differentiates between a woman who prefers married men (**comadreja**, literally, a weasel) and one who lures them into extramarital relationships (**ciegamachos**). Can it really be that women are more predatory than men? Or is it that by luridly painting women as lustful (**aa'amo** in Hawaiian means 'an insatiable woman') and conniving (**alghunjar** is Persian for the feigned anger of a mistress), men the world over have cleverly avoided any blame for their own adulterous behaviour? Even when they're guilty, they try to keep the linguistic upper hand, if the German word **Drachenfutter** is anything to go by. Literally translated as 'dragon fodder' it describes the peace offerings that guilty husbands offer their spouses.

One cure for adultery

Rhaphanidosis was a punishment meted out to adulterous men by cuckolded husbands in Ancient Greece. It involved inserting a radish up their backside.

An avuncular solution

The Western ideal of a monogamous husband and wife is not universal. There is, for example, no word for father in Mosuo (China). The nearest translation for a male parental figure is **axia**, which means friend or lover; and while a child will have only one mother, he or she might have a sequence of **axia**. An **axia** has a series of night-time trysts with a woman, after which he returns home to his mother. Any children resulting from these liaisons are raised in the woman's household. There are no fathers, husbands or marriages in Mosuo society. Brothers take care of their sisters' children and act as their fathers. Brothers and sisters live together all their lives in their mothers' homes.

Polygamy on ice

Other societies replace the complexities of monogamy with those of polygamy, as, for example, the Inuit of the Arctic:

angutawkun a man who exchanges wives with another man or one of the men who have at different times been married to the same woman

areodjarekput to exchange wives for a few days only, allowing a man sexual rights to his woman during that period

nuliinuaroak sharing the same woman; more specifically, the relationship between a man and his wife's lover when the husband has not consented to the arrangement

False friends

dad (Albanian) wet nurse or babysitter

babe (SiSwati, Swaziland) father or minister

mama (Georgian) father

brat (Russian) brother

parents (Portuguese) relatives

loo (Fulani, Mali) storage pot

bang (Albanian) paper bag

sin (Bosnian/Croatian/Serbian) son

Special relations

Whether it's because they have big families, time on their hands in large empty spaces, or for another reason, the Sami people of Northern Scandinavia have highly specific terms for family members and relationships: **goaski** are one's mother's elder sisters, and **sivjjot** is one's older sister's husband; one's mother's younger sisters are **muotta** and one's father's younger sisters are **siessa**; one's mother's brothers are **eanu** and her brothers' wives are **ipmi**; one's brother's wife is a **mangi**. The nearby Swedes exhibit a similar subtlety in their terms for grandfathers and grandmothers: **farfar** is a father's father, **morfar** is a mother's father, **farmor** is a father's mother and **mormor** is a mother's mother.

This pattern of precise names for individual family members had a parallel in an older society. Latin distinguished **patruus** (father's brother) from **avunculus** (mother's brother); and **matertera** (father's sister) from **amita** (mother's sister).

Of even earlier origins, the Australian Kamilaroi **nganuwaay** means a mother's cross-cousin's daughter and also a mother's father's sister's daughter as well as a mother's mother's brother's daughter's daughter as well as a mother's mother's brother's son's daughter.

Tahitian taio

Meanwhile, in the warm climate of Tahiti, the word **taio** (Maohi, French Polynesia) means a formal friendship between people not related by ancestors, which involves the sharing of everything, even sex partners. A **taio** relationship can be male-to-male, female-to-female or male-to-female.

Essential issue

Language testifies to the importance most cultures attach to having children, as well as the mixed emotions the little darlings bring with them. Yiddish, for example, details both extremes of the parental experience, **nakhes** being the mixture of pleasure and pride a parent gets from a child, and **tsuris** the grief and trouble:

izraf (Persian) producing ingenious, witty children

niyoga (Hindi) the practice of appointing a woman to bear a male heir who will be conceived by proxy

menguyel-uyel (Indonesian) to hug, cuddle and tickle someone (usually a child) as an expression of affection

gosh-pech (Persian) twisting the ears of a schoolboy as a punishment

abtar (Persian) one who has no offspring; a loser (literally, a bucket without a handle)

Parental ambitions

In contrast with the paternal indulgence of the French **fils à papa** (a son whose father makes things very easy for him) are some stricter maternal leanings:

kyoikumama (Japanese) a woman who crams her children to succeed educationally

ciegayernos (Caribbean Spanish) a woman who looks for a husband for her daughter

mammismo (Italian) maternal control and interference that continues into adulthood

Home is where the heart is

Not everyone lives in a standard box-like house:

berhane (Turkish) an impractically large mansion, rambling house

angase (Tulu, India) a building where the front part is used as a shop and the back as a residence

vidhvasram (Hindi) a home for widows

And rooms have many uses:

Folterkammer (German) a gym or exercise room (literally, a torture chamber)

ori (Khakas, Siberia) a hole in a yurt to store potatoes

tyconna (Anglo-Indian) an Indian basement room where the hottest part of the day is passed in the hottest season of the year

vomitarium (Latin) a room where a guest threw up in order to empty his stomach for more feasting

Bukumatala

In the Kiriwinian language of New Guinea a **bukumatala** is a 'young people's house', where adolescents go to stay on reaching puberty. As the main aim is to keep brothers and sisters away from the possibility of incestuous sexual contact close relatives will never stay in the same house. The boys return to the parental home for food and may help with the household work; the girls eat, work and occasionally sleep at home, but will generally spend the night with their adolescent sweethearts in one **bukumatala** or another.

On reflection

Him b'long Missy Kween

An urgent need to communicate can create a language without native speakers. Pidgin, for example, has developed from English among people with their own native tongues. Fine examples of pidgin expressions in the Tok Pisin language of Papua New Guinea are: **liklik box you pull him he cry you push him he cry** (an accordion) and **bigfella iron walking stick him go bang along topside** (a rifle). When the Duke of Edinburgh visits Vanuatu, in the Pacific, he is addressed as **oldfella Pili-Pili him b'long Missy Kween**, while Prince Charles is **Pikinini b'long Kween**.

Clocking On

l'argent ne se trouve pas sous le
sabot d'un cheval *(French)*
money isn't found under a horse's hoof

Tinker, tailor ...

The Japanese phrase for 'making a living' is **yo o wataru**, which literally means 'to walk across the world', and it's certainly true that when the chips are down there are some intriguing ways of earning a crust:

folapostes (Spanish) a worker who climbs telephone or
   electrical poles

geshtenjapjeks (Albanian) a street vendor of roast chestnuts

koshatnik (Russian) a dealer in stolen cats

dame-pipi (French) a female toilet assistant

tarriqu-zan (Persian) an officer who clears the road for a prince

kualanapuhi (Hawaiian) an officer who keeps the flies away
   from the sleeping king by waving a brush made of feathers

buz-baz (old Persian) a showman who made a goat and a
   monkey dance together

capoclaque (Italian) someone who coordinates a group of
   clappers

fyrassistent (Danish) an assistant lighthouse keeper

cigerci (Turkish) a seller of liver and lungs

lomilomi (Hawaiian) the masseur of the chief, whose duty it
   was to take care of his spittle and excrement

The daily grind

Attitudes to work vary not just from workplace to workplace, but from one side of the office to the other:

fucha (Polish) to use company time and resources for one's own purposes

haochi-lanzuo (Chinese) to be fond of food and averse to work

aviador (Spanish, Central America) a government employee who shows up only on payday

chupotero (Spanish) a person who works little but has several salaries

madogiwazoku (Japanese) those who have little to do (literally, window gazers)

jeito (Brazilian Portuguese) to find a way to get something done, no matter what the obstacles

Métro-boulot-dodo

This cheery French expression describes life in a none-too-optimistic way. Literally translated as 'tube-work-sleep' it summarizes the daily grind, hinting strongly that it's pointless.

Carrot ...

Motivation is a key factor, and employers who want maximum productivity find different ways of achieving this:

Mitbestimmung (German) the policy in industry of involving both workers and management in decision-making

vydvizhenchestvo (Russian) the system of promotion of workers to positions of responsibility and authority

kaizen (Japanese) the continuous improvement of working practices and personal efficiency as a business philosophy

... and stick

paukikape (Ancient Greek) the projecting collar worn by slaves while grinding corn in order to prevent them from eating it.

German work ethic

The Germans have long had a reputation for working hard. Inevitably, though, alongside the **Urlaubsmuffel**, or person who is against taking vacations, there is also the **Trittbrettfahrer** (literally, running-board rider), the person who profits from another's work. And along with the studious **Technonomade** (someone who conducts most of their business on the road, using laptops and mobiles), you will find the less scrupulous **schwarzarbeiten** (preferring to do work not reported for taxes).

False friends

biro (Arabic) office
adman (Arabic) offering better guaranty
ganga (Spanish) bargain
mixer (Hungarian) barman
slug (Gaulish) servant
fat (Cantonese) prosperity
hot (Romanian) thief
baker (Dutch) nurse

The deal

Others have less noble ways of getting ahead:

zhengquan-duoli (Chinese) to jockey for power and scramble for profit

jinetear el dinero (Spanish, Central America) to profit by delaying payment

tadlis (Persian) concealing the faults of goods on sale

qiang jingtou (Chinese) a fight by a cameraman for a vantage point (literally, stealing the show)

grilagem (Brazilian Portuguese) the old practice of putting a cricket in a box of newly faked documents, until the moving insect's excrement makes the papers look plausibly old and genuine (literally, cricketing)

On the take

If sharp practice doesn't work, then the best thing to do is cast all scruples aside:

bustarella (Italian) a cash bribe (literally, a little envelope)

dhurna (Anglo-Indian) extorting payment by sitting at the debtor's door and staying there without food, threatening violence until your demands are met

sola (Italian) a swindle in which you don't share the loot with your accomplice

sokaiya (Japanese) a blackmailer who has a few shares in a large number of companies and tries to extort money by threatening to cause trouble at the shareholders' annual general meetings

TST (**Tahu Sama Tahu**) (Indonesian) 'you know it, I know it': a verbal agreement between two people, one usually a government official, to cheat the state

Hard cash

In the end, it all comes down to one thing:

lechuga (Caribbean Spanish) a dollar bill (literally, lettuce)

kapusta (Russian) money (literally, cabbage)

mahiyana (Persian) monthly wages or fish jelly

wampum (Algonquian, Canada) strings of beads and polished shells, used as money by native Americans

Spongers

If you don't have much money yourself, there are always ways around the problem:

gorrero (Spanish, Central America) a person who always allows others to pay

piottaro (Italian) one who carries very little cash

Zechpreller (German) someone who leaves without paying the bill

dar mico (Caribbean Spanish) to consume without paying

seigneur-terrasse (French) one who spends much time but little money in a café (literally, a terrace lord)

Neither a borrower nor a lender be

Indonesian has the word **pembonceng** to describe someone who likes to use other people's facilities, but the Pascuense language of Easter Island has gone one step further in showing how the truly unscrupulous exploit friends and family. **Tingo** is to borrow things from a friend's house, one by one, until there's nothing left; while **hakamaroo** is to keep borrowed objects until the owner has to ask for them back.

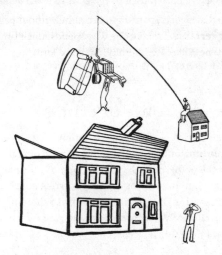

What is yours is mine

It's a short step to outright crime:

mencomot (Indonesian) stealing things of small value such as food or drinks, partly for fun

baderotte (Danish) a beach thief

Agobilles (German) burglar's tools

ajane (Tulu, India) the noise of a thief

pukau (Malay) a charm used by burglars to make people fall asleep

azote de barrio (Spanish, Central America) a criminal who concentrates on a particular neighbourhood

accordéon (French) an extensive criminal record

A life of crime

Italian offers a rich vocabulary for different types of crime and criminal. **Smonta**, for example, is a theft carried out on a bus or train from which the perpetrator gets off as soon as possible, while **scavalco** (literally, climbing over) is a robbery carried out via a window or balcony. A night-time burglary is a **serenata** (literally, a serenade) which may well involve an **orchestra**, or gang of thieves, possibly accompanied by a **palo**, an accomplice who acts as lookout.

Extreme measures

If all else fails one of the following may be necessary:

nakkeskud (Danish) a shot in the back of the head
gusa (Japanese) to decapitate with a sword
rejam (Malay) to execute by pressing into mud

Hiding the evidence

Persian offers a refinement to the crude concept of 'murder'. The expression **war nam nihadan** means to kill and then bury someone, growing flowers over the grave in order to conceal it.

Chokey

As most career criminals would agree, the worst downside to a life of crime is getting caught:

kaush (Albanian) a prison cell or paper bag
squadretta (Italian) a group of prison guards who specialize in beating up inmates (literally, small squad)
fangfeng (Chinese) to let prisoners out for exercise or to relieve themselves
Kassiber (German) a letter smuggled out of jail; a secret coded message
jieyu (Chinese) to break into jail to rescue a prisoner
alba (Italian) the day one leaves prison after serving time

Executive essentials

Conclusions cannot always be drawn about historical connections. Some words are similar in numerous languages. Much linguistic research has led to the theory of an Ur-language (Indo–European) spoken some fifty thousand years ago, from which most other languages have descended. **Papa**, for example, is used for 'father' in seventy per cent of languages across the world.

Meanwhile, essential latterday vocabulary has crossed languages as easily as the jet-setting executive who uses it:

taxi is recognized in French, German, Swedish, Spanish, Danish, Norwegian, Dutch, Czech, Slovak, Portuguese, Hungarian and Romanian

sauna is recognized in Finnish, English, Portuguese, Spanish, Italian, French, German, Dutch, Danish, Lithuanian, Croatian/Bosnian/Serbian, Romanian and Norwegian

bank is recognized in Afrikaans, Amharic (Ethiopia), Bengali, Creole, Danish, Dutch, Frisian (Germany and Holland), German, Gujarati (India), Hungarian, Indonesian, Malay, Norwegian, Polish, Sinhala (Sri Lanka), Swedish and Wolof (Senegal and Gambia)

hotel is recognized in Afrikaans, Amharic, Asturian (Spain), Bulgarian, Catalan, Croatian/Bosnian/Serbian, Czech, Danish, Dutch, Frisian (Germany and Holland), Galician (Spain), German, Icelandic, Polish, Portuguese, Romanian, Slovak, Slovenian, Tswana (Botswana), Ukrainian and Yiddish

Time Off

il giocare non è male, ma è male
il perdere *(Italian)*
*there is no harm in playing but great harm
in losing*

Fun and games

Since the start of time the desire to fill it has resulted in a wide range of recreations. Simplest are the games played by children the world over:

toto (Cook Islands Maori) a shout given in a game of hide-and-seek to show readiness for the search to begin

pokku (Tulu, India) the throwing of pebbles up in the air and catching them as they fall

kabaddi (Pakistan) a game where players take it in turn to hold their breath

bakpi (Ulwa, Nicaragua) a game in which one is swung round in circles until dizzy

cnapan (Welsh) a game where each side tries to drive a wooden ball as far as possible in one direction

kula'i wawae (Hawaiian) the pushing of one's feet against others while seated

kaengurustylte (Danish) a pogo stick (literally, kangaroo stilt)

Frozen walrus carcass

There are games that are highly specific to their culture and environment, such as the Inuit **igunaujannguaq**, which literally means frozen walrus carcass. This is a game where the person in the centre tries to remain stiff and is held in place by the feet of the people who are sitting in a circle. He is passed around the ring, hand over hand. Whoever drops him is the next 'frozen walrus carcass'.

Honing your skills

As we grow up, what we look for in a game becomes increasingly challenging:

shash-andaz (Persian) someone who tries to juggle with six balls so that four are always in the air

antyaksari (Hindi) a pastime in which participants recite verses in turn, the first word of each new verse being the same as the last of the preceding one

kipapa (Hawaiian) to balance on top of a surfboard

waterponie (Afrikaans) a jet ski

elastikspring (Danish) bungee jumping

The beautiful game

One game in particular has achieved international pre-eminence, and a range of closely observed terms to describe it:

armario (Spanish) an awkward or unskilled player (literally, a wardrobe)

wayra jayt'a (Quechuan, Peru) a poor player (literally, an air kicker)

cazar (Spanish) to kick one's opponent and not the ball

ariete (Spanish) a battering ram (centre forward)

verkac (Turkish) passing and running

baile, danze (Spanish) and **melina** (Italian) two players on the same team kicking the ball back and forth to kill time

roligan (Danish) a non-violent supporter

Taking a punt

Sometimes, fun is not enough; chance or expertise has to be made more exciting by speculation:

yetu (Tulu, India) gambling in which a coin is tossed and a bet laid as to which side it will fall on

quiniela (Spanish, USA) a form of betting in which the punter must choose the first and second-place winners in a race, though not necessarily in the correct order

parani (Cook Islands Maori) to put up a stake at poker without examining one's cards

The moral perhaps being that it's better to be the Persian **kuz-baz**, one who lends money to gamblers, than a **mukhtir**, one who risks his property in gambling.

Fingers crossed

Some people are born **lechero**, a Latin American Spanish word for lucky, literally meaning a milkman. Others may be less fortunate:

smolař (Czech) a person dogged by bad luck

apes (Indonesian) to have double bad luck

kualat (Indonesian) to be bound to have bad luck as a result of behaving badly

Break a leg

It's intriguing that wishing people good luck often takes the form of willing ill fortune on them. The German **Hals und Beinbruch**, for example, takes the spirit of the English expression 'break a leg' and goes one step further – it translates as 'break your neck and a leg'. The Italians offer an even more gruesome prospect: the cheery wish **in bocca al lupo** means 'into the mouth of the wolf'.

The competitive streak

Everyone likes to win, but the methods employed to get ahead range from the inventive to the underhand:

chupar rueda (Spanish) running or cycling behind another to benefit from reduced wind resistance (literally, to suck wheel)

kunodesme (Ancient Greek) tying a string round the foreskin to stop the penis getting in the way during athletics (literally, putting the dog on a lead)

sirind (Persian) entangling legs in wrestling to trip your opponent (also a noose for catching prey by the foot)

poki (Cook Islands Maori) to deal cards from the bottom of the pack (i.e. unfairly)

False friends

boghandel (Danish) bookshop

rain (Arabic) viewer, spectator

arse (Turkish) violin bow

jerk (French) praise for an accomplished dancer

pensel (Swedish) paintbrush

catch (French) all-in wrestling

Crooning

For those without sporting interest or prowess, entertainment can be found in the realms of music . . .

iorram (Scottish Gaelic) a rowing song

dizlanmak (Turkish) to keep humming to yourself

Ohrwurm (German) a catchy tune that gets stuck in the brain or rapidly obsesses an entire population (literally, an ear worm)

ngak-ngik-ngok (Indonesian) a derogatory reference to the popularity of rock music in the 1960s (which was much despised by the late President Sukarno)

Twirling

... or of dancing

raspar canillas (Spanish, Central America) to dance (literally, to scrape shins)

zapateado (Spanish) the fast footwork and stamping feet used in dancing

mbuki-mvuki (Bantu, Zaire) to take off one's clothes in order to dance

Ball paradox (German) a ball at which women ask men to dance

verbunkos (Hungarian) a dance performed to persuade people to enlist in the army

Clubbing

The Italians helpfully differentiate between the staff outside and inside a night club: the **buttadentro**, the one who throws you in, is the person in charge of choosing who gets through the door; while the **buttafuori**, the one who throws you out, is the bouncer.

Channel surfing

For those who prefer to stay at home, there's always the television, or **Pantoffelkino** (slippers cinema), as it's described in German. The Romani language of the Gypsies takes a rather sterner view, regarding it as a **dinnilos-dicking-muktar**, or fool's looking-box. Those with extra channels seem to be viewed as a cut-above in France, where **cablé** has now acquired the secondary sense of 'hip and trendy'.

Hi-tech

Having invented numerous machines to give us free time, we now struggle to come up with others to help fill it:

tamagotchi (Japanese) a lovable egg (an electronic device which copies the demands for food or attention of a pet)

khali khukweni (Zulu) a mobile phone (literally, to make a noise in the pocket)

dingdong (Indonesian) computer games in an arcade

toelva (Icelandic) a computer (formed from the words for digit and prophetess)

xiaoxia (Chinese) small lobsters (new internet users)

The arts

There are some pastimes that are elevated, by their practitioners and admirers, onto an altogether higher plane:

sprezzatura (Italian) the effortless technique of a great artist

wabi (Japanese) a flawed detail that enhances the elegance of the whole work of art

ostranenie (Russian) the process by which art makes familiar perceptions seem strange

Verfremdungseffekt (German) a dramatic technique that encourages the audience to preserve a sense of critical detachment from a play (literally, an alienating effect)

Philistines

Those who aren't impressed by artistic claims have coined a different vocabulary:

megillah (Yiddish) an unnecessarily long and tiresome story or
letter
de pacotilla (Spanish) a third-rate writer or actor

Rolling up

In our health-conscious world, can smoking still be regarded as recreation?

segatura (Italian) a cigarette made by mixing cigarette butts
(literally, sawdust)
bakwe (Kapampangan, Philippines) to smoke a cigarette with
the lit end in the mouth
nakurit'sya (Russian) to smoke to one's heart's content
zakurit'sya (Russian) to make oneself ill by excessive smoking

Married in a brothel

Some words must remain a mystery to all except native speakers. You would have had to have lived in these places for quite a while to understand how to use correctly some of the following, which in their simply translated definitions contain what seem to us contradictory meanings:

hay kulu (Zarma, Nigeria) anything, nothing and also everything

irpadake (Tulu, India) ripe and unripe

sitoshna (Tulu, India) cold and hot

merripen (Romani, Gypsy) life and death

gift (Norwegian) poison and married

magazinshchik (Russian) a shopkeeper and a shoplifter

danh t (Vietnamese) a church and a brothel

aloha (Hawaiian) hello and goodbye (the word has many other meanings including love, compassion, welcome and good wishes)

Eating and Drinking

olcsó húsnak híg a leve *(Hungarian)*
cheap meat produces thin gravy

Hunting, shooting ...

In many parts of the world putting together a meal isn't always simply a matter of making a quick trip to the local supermarket:

ortektes (Khakas, Siberia) to hunt together for ducks
geragai (Malay) a hook for catching crocodiles
sumpit (Malay) to shoot with a blowpipe
tu'utu'u (Rapa Nui, Easter Island) to hit the mark time and
    again (shooting with arrows)
ajawy (Wayampi, Brazil) to hit the wrong target

... and fishing

Fishing can be equally labour-intensive:

ta'iti (Cook Islands Maori) to catch fish by encircling a rock
    with a net and frightening them out
kapau'u (Hawaiian) to drive fish into a waiting net by
    splashing or striking the water with a leafy branch
lihnaka inska wauhwaia (Ulwa, Nicaragua) to slap the water
    and cause the fish to jump into a boat
nono (Rapa Nui, Easter Island) fish thrown onto the beach by
    the waves or which jump out of the water into a boat
kusyad (Persian) hard black stone thrown into the water to
    attract fish
fiskevaer (Norwegian) good weather for fishing
ah chamseyah chay (Chorti, Guatemala) someone who fishes
    with dynamite
pau heoheo (Hawaiian) a person who returns from fishing
    without any fish

Global gastronomy

When it comes to the extraordinary things that people around the world enjoy putting in their mouths, it's certainly true that one man's meat is another man's poison:

ptsha (Yiddish) cow's feet in jelly

poronkieli (Finnish) reindeer tongue

kokorec (Turkish) roasted sheep's intestines

nama-uni (Japanese) raw sea urchin

Beuschel (German) stewed calves' lungs

acitron (Mexican Spanish) candied cactus

somad (Sherpa, Nepal) cheese that is old and smelly

calimocho (Spanish) a combination of Coca-Cola and red wine

Gummiadler (German) tough roast chicken (literally, rubber eagle)

marilopotes (Ancient Greek) a gulper of coal dust

ampo (Malay) edible earth

Menu envy

In some cases, though, it's the unfamiliar word rather than the food itself that may alarm the outsider:

flab (Gaelic) a mushroom
moron (Welsh) a carrot
aardappel (Dutch) a potato (literally, earth apple)
bikini (Spanish) a toasted ham and cheese sandwich
gureepufuruutsu (Japanese) a grapefruit

Can't cook . . .

We all know the benefits of **lumur** (Malay), smearing ingredients with fat during cooking. But even that doesn't always prevent **kanzo** (Hausa, Nigeria), burnt food stuck to the bottom of the pot. Perhaps it would help to know the right moment for **nisar-qararat** (Persian), cold water poured into a pot to stop it getting burnt. The only fail-safe way of escaping this is to buy your food **boli boli** (Aukan, Suriname) – already cooked.

Bon appetit

Now we're ready to eat . . .

protintheuo (Ancient Greek) to pick out the dainty bits
beforehand, to help oneself first

muka (Hawaiian) a smacking sound with the lips, indicating
that the food is tasty

pakupaku (Japanese) to eat in big mouthfuls or take quick
bites

parmaklamak (Turkish) to eat with one's fingers

sikkiwok (Inuit) to drink with your chin in the water

nusarat (Persian) crumbs falling from a table which are picked
up and eaten as an act of piety

Boring food

The Japanese are emphatic about how dull food can be: **suna o kamu yo na** means 'like chewing sand'. They even have an evocative term for rehashed food: **nibansenji**, meaning 'brewing tea for the second time using the same tea-leaves'.

Cupboard love

Those who have food on the table will always be popular:

giomlaireachd (Scottish Gaelic) the habit of dropping in at
meal times

aimerpok (Inuit) to visit expecting to receive food

luqma-shumar (Persian) one who attends feasts uninvited and
counts the number of mouthfuls

Snap, crackle, pop!

Is it the way they hear it? Or is it simply what sells the product? The sound of Rice Crispies crackling and popping is very different across Europe:

French: **Cric! Crac! Croc!**
German: **Knisper! Knasper! Knusper!**
Spanish: **Cris! Cras! Cros!**

Rice

In Japan, **gohan** (literally, honourable food) comes in a bowl and means rice that is ready for eating. But it's also a general name for rice and even extends in meaning to 'meal'. At the other end of the spectrum is **okoge**, which is the scorched rice stuck on the bottom of the pan.

False friends

prune (French) plum
gin (Phrygian, Turkey) to dry out
korn (Swedish) barley
sik (Ukrainian) juice
glass (Swedish) ice cream
prick (Thai) pepper
chew (Amharic, Ethiopia) salt

Hawaiian bananas

Hawaii's traditional cuisine is based on quite a restricted list of ingredients: fish (there are 65 words alone for describing fishing nets), sweet potato (108 words), sugarcane (42) and bananas (47). The following are among the most descriptive words for this fruit:

mai'a kaua lau a banana, dark green when young, and yellow and waxy when mature

kapule a banana hanging until its skin has black spots

palaku a thoroughly ripe banana

maui to wring the stem of a bunch of bananas to cause it to ripen

pola the hanging down of the blossom of a banana palm or a bunch of bananas

halane a large bunch of bananas

hua'alua a double bunch of bananas

manila a banana tree not used for fruit but for rope fibre

lele a tall wild banana placed near the altar, offered to the gods and also used for love magic

Replete

As the meal enters its final stages, a sense of well-being descends on the diner – unless, of course, you're suffering from **bersat** (Malay), food that has gone down the wrong way . . .

> **uitbuiken** (Dutch) to take your time at dinner, relaxing between courses (literally, the expansion of the stomach)
> **nakkele** (Tulu, India) a man who licks whatever the food has been served on
> **slappare** (Italian) to eat everything, even to the point of licking the plate
> **'akapu'aki'aki** (Cook Islands Maori) to belch repeatedly

Post-prandial

After it's all over, what are you left with?

> **femlans** (Ullans, Northern Ireland) the remains of a meal
> **sunasorpok** (Inuit) to eat the remains of others' food
> **shitta** (Persian) food left at night and eaten in the morning

Food poisoning

Visitors to Easter Island would be advised to distinguish between the Rapa Nui words **hakahana** (leaving cooked food for another day) and **kai hakahana** (food from the previous day that is starting to rot).

Hunger

Food cannot always be taken for granted. **Homowo** is a Ghanaian word that means 'hooting at hunger'. Local oral tradition recalls a distant past when the rains failed and there was a terrible famine on the Accra Plains, the home of the Ga people. When a good harvest finally came and there was more than enough to eat once again, the Ghanaians celebrated by holding a festival, still celebrated to this day, that ridiculed hunger.

Daily Bread

Food often figures in colloquial sayings and proverbs, as this selection from Spain shows:

quien con hambre se acuesta con pan suena whoever goes to bed hungry dreams of bread (to have a bee in one's bonnet)

agua fría y pan caliente, nunca hicieron buen vientre cold water and hot bread never made a good belly (oil and water never mix)

pan tierno y leña verde, la casa pierde fresh bread and green firewood lose the house (two wrongs do not make a right)

vale bolillo it's worth a piece of bread (it doesn't matter)

con su pan se lo coma may he eat it with bread (good luck to him)

Quenched

After all this talk of food and eating, it's hard not to feel thirsty:

gurfa (Arabic) the amount of water scooped up in one hand

tegok (Malay) the water one can swallow at a gulp

qamus (Persian) [a well] so abundant in water that the bucket disappears

yewh-ma (Wagiman, Australia) to scrape out a hole in the sand to collect fresh water

jabh (Persian) arriving at a well and finding no water

Bakbuk bakbuk bakbuk

Like the English expression 'glug glug glug', the Hebrew word for bottle, **bakbuk**, derives from the sound of liquid being poured from it.

Pythons and sponges

Those who have not experienced **sgriob** (Scottish Gaelic), the itchiness that overcomes the upper lip just before taking a sip of whisky, may have suffered from **olfrygt** (Viking Danish), the fear of a lack of ale. And it's not always a fish the world drinks like:

beber como uma esponja (Portuguese) to drink like a sponge

uwabami no yo ni nomu (Japanese) to drink like a python

geiin suru (Japanese) to drink like a whale

bjor-reifr (Old Icelandic) cheerful from beer-drinking

sternhagelvoll (German) completely drunk (literally, full of stars and hail)

Plastered

To the sober, it's always intriguing to see what drunken people are convinced they can do when under the influence, such as trying to walk in a straight line (**kanale'o** in Hawaiian). Perhaps it's best to bear in mind the Romanian proverb **dacă doi spun că eşti beat, du-te şi te culcă**, if two people say you're drunk, go to sleep.

The morning after

at have tømmermaend (Danish) having a hangover (literally, to have carpenters, i.e. hearing the noise of drilling, sawing, etc.)

Katzenjammer (German) a very severe hangover (literally, the noise made by extremely miserable cats)

A useful excuse

As they say in Aymara (Bolivia and Peru), **umjayanipxitütuwa** – they must have made me drink.

Doormat dandy

Languages are full of traps for the unwary, particularly when it comes to words that sound similar but mean very different things:

Spanish: **el papa** the Pope; **la papa** potato
Albanian: **cubar** ladies' man, womanizer; **cube** proud, courageous girl
Kerja, Indonesia: **aderana** prostitute; **aderòna** perfume
Italian: **zerbino** doormat; **zerbinotto** dandy
Arabic: **khadij** premature child; **khidaj** abortion
Albanian: **shoq** husband; **shog** bald man; **shop** blockhead

Below Par

u miericu pietusu fa la piaga
verminusa *(Calabrian, Italy)*
*the physician with too much pity will cause
the wound to fester*

Ouch!

The exclamation denoting pain has many varieties. If you touch a boiling kettle in Korea you cry **aiya**, in the Philippines **aruy** and in France **aïe**. In Russian you scream **oj**, in Danish **uh** and in German **aua**.

Atishoo!

In Japan one sneeze signifies praise (**ichi home**); two sneezes, criticism (**ni-kusashi**); three sneezes, disparagement (**san-kenashi**),

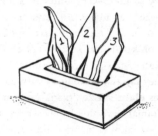

while four or more sneezes are taken to mean, quite reasonably, that a cold is on its way (**yottsu-ijo wa kaze no moto**). Meanwhile, in Mexico, one sneeze is answered with the word **salud** (health); two sneezes with **dinero** (money); three sneezes with **amor** (love); four or more sneezes with **alergías** (allergies); laughter often accompanies four sneezes, because health, money and love are obviously more desirable than allergies.

Bless you!

In response to someone sneezing, the Germans say **Gesundheit**, 'health to you', and the French **à tes souhaits**, literally, 'to your wishes'. In Sierre Leone, Mende speakers say **biseh**, or 'thank you'; in Malagasy, the language of Madagascar, they say **velona**, 'alive', while the Bembe speakers of the Congo say **kuma**, 'be well'. In Tonga a sneeze is often taken to be a sign that your loved one is missing you.

Sneezing protocol

In Brazil, they say **saúde** (health) and the sneezer answers **amen**. In Arabic, the sneezer says **alhumdullilah** ('praise be to God') first, to which the other person responds **yarhamukumu Allah** ('may God have mercy on you'). The sneezer then replies to that with **athabakumu Allah** ('may God reward you'). In Iran, things are more complex. There they say **afiyat bashe** ('I wish you good health') and the sneezer replies **elahi shokr** ('thank God for my health'). After the first sneeze Iranians are then supposed to stop whatever they were doing for a few minutes before continuing. If the sneeze interrupts a decision it is taken as an indication not to go ahead. Ignoring the single sneeze means risking bad luck. However, a second sneeze clears the slate.

Falling ill

The miseries of the sick bed are universally known:

smertensleje (Danish) to toss and turn on your bed in pain
fanbing (Chinese) to have an attack of one's old illness
ruttlin (Cornish) the sound of phlegm rattling in the bronchial
   tubes
miryachit (Russian) a disease in which the sufferer mimics
   everything that is said or done by another

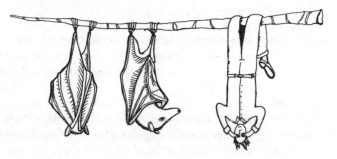

False friends

gem (Mongolian) defect
lavman (Turkish) enema
angel (Dutch) sting
bad (Arabic) amputation
bladder (Dutch) blister
santa (Egyptian Arabic) wart
turd (Persian) delicate or fragile

Bedside manner

Illness demands sympathy, but the Indonesian word **besuk** suggests that this is not always forthcoming. It means to refuse to visit a sick person. Possibly with good reason:

bawwal (Persian) one who pisses in bed
osurgan (Turkish) someone who farts a lot
dobol (Indonesian) to have a swollen anus
ra'ora'oa (Cook Islands Maori) to have swollen testicles
kepuyuh (Indonesian) to have to urinate
jerrkjerrk (Wagiman, Australia) diarrhoea
chiasse (French) runs induced by fear

Impatient?

Perhaps the most telling word in the lexicon of sickness is the Chinese word **huiji-jiyi** – to avoid following your doctor's advice for fear of being recognized as the sufferer of a disease.

Vowelless

The Tashlhiyt dialect of Berber (North Africa) is known for its vowelless words: **tzgr**, she crossed, and **rglx**, I locked. Among the longest are **tkkststt**, you took it off, and **tftktstt**, you sprained it. And if we accept 'r' as a consonant (which is debatable in Czech, as 'l' and 'r' function as sonorants and so fulfil the role of a vowel) then words consisting entirely of consonants are common in their language: **krk**, neck; **prst**, finger or toe; **smrk**, pine tree; **smrt**, death. Words beginning with five consonants are not unknown: **ctvrt**, quarter and **ctvrtek**, Thursday. Likewise in Croatian/Bosnian/Serbian there are: **crkva**, church; **mrkva**, carrot; **trg**, market and **zrtva**, vinegar.

From Cradle to Grave

xian zhang de meimao, bi bu shang hou zhang de huzi *(Chinese)*
the eyebrows that started growing first can't compare with the beard that started growing later

In the family way

Pregnancy can be something of a mixed blessing:

mirkha (Quechuan, Peru) the freckles or spots on a woman's face during pregnancy

waham (Arabic) the craving for certain foods during pregnancy

tafarrus (Persian) the fainting of a pregnant woman

Birth pains

When it comes to childbirth, English tends to be coy. There is no English equivalent for the Inuit word **paggiq**, which describes the flesh torn as a woman delivers a baby, nor for the Japanese **chigo-bami** – bites inflicted on a mother's nipple by a suckling baby. As for the less painful aspects of giving birth, we lack the Indonesian word **uek**, the sound of a baby crying when being born, the very precise Ulwa word from Nicaragua, **asahnaka**, to hold a child on one's hip with its legs straddling the hipbone facing the mother's side, let alone the Persian term **kundamoya**, which is the hair a child is born with.

Birthing partner

The Inuit have a word **tunumiaq** which denotes the person who supports a pregnant woman's back during labour.

First steps in the deep Pacific

In Rapa Nui (Easter Island) there are five detailed words to describe a baby's early progress: **kaukau** is a newborn baby first moving its hands and feet; **puepue** is when it begins to distinguish people and objects; **tahuri** is when it starts to move from side to side; **totoro** is when it's learned to crawl; **mahaga** is when it is able to stand by itself.

Toddling

English is strangely deficient when it comes to observing the many stages of development:

teete (Zarma, Nigeria) to teach a toddler how to walk

menetah (Indonesian) to help a little child walk by holding its hands to keep it in balance

pokankuni (Tulu, India) to learn by looking at others

keke (Hawaiian) a word of caution to children to cover their nakedness

Growing pains

The next few years are crucial:

polekayi (Tulu, India) writing in a large crooked hand as children tend to do

qiangda (Chinese) a race to be the first to answer a question

nylentik (Indonesian) to hit a child's ear with the index finger

paski (Tulu, India) punishing a boy by making him alternate between standing and sitting with his arms crossed and both ears seized by his fingers

zhangjin (Chinese) the progress made in one's intellectual or moral education

Polterabend (German) a stag party for both sexes at which crockery is broken celebrating the end of their single lives

ronin (Japanese) a student who has failed a university entrance examination and is waiting to retake it (adapted from its original sense of a lordless wandering samurai warrior)

Boys and girls

Some cultures go further than merely differentiating between children and adolescents. The Indonesian word **balita** refers to those under five years old; the Hindi term **kumari** means a girl between ten and twelve, while **bala** is a young woman under the age of sixteen. The Cook Islands Maoris continue the sequence with **mapu**, a youth from about sixteen to twenty-five.

False friends

compromisso (Portuguese) engagement

embarazada (Spanish) pregnant

anus (Latin) old woman

chin (Persian) one who catches money thrown at
   weddings

moon (Khakas, Siberia) to hang oneself

bath (Scottish Gaelic) to drown

hoho (Hausa, Nigeria) condolences

Mid-life crisis

Before we know it, the carefree days of our youth are just fading memories:

sanada arba' (Arabic) to be pushing forty
parebos (Ancient Greek) being past one's prime
kahala (Arabic) to be an old fogey at the height of one's life
Torschlusspanik (German) the fear of diminishing
opportunities as one gets older (literally, gate-closing panic);
this word is often applied to women worried about being too
old to have children

Getting older Hawaiian-style

The Hawaiians have a highly specific vocabulary to describe the effects of what the Germans call **Lebensabend**, the twilight of life:

'aua a woman beginning to become wrinkled
ku'olo an old man with sagging cheeks
kani ko'o an aged man who needs to carry a cane
kani mo'opuna the state of old age when one has many
grandchildren
hakalunu extreme old age, as when one is no longer able to
walk
ka'i koko bedridden; so old one needs to be carried in a net
pala lau hala the advanced loss of hair; the last stage of life

Kicking the bucket

Other languages have highly inventive euphemisms for the tricky subject of passing on:

nolikt karoti (Latvian) to put down the spoon
colgar los guantes (Spanish, Central America) to hang up the gloves
het hoek omgaan (Dutch) to go around the corner
bater a bota/esticar a perna (Portuguese) to hit the boot or to stretch the leg
avaler son bulletin de naissance (French) to swallow one's birth certificate

The final reckoning

adjal (Indonesian) the predestined hour of one's death
Liebestod (German) dying for love or because of a romantic tragedy
pagezuar (Albanian) the state of dying before enjoying the happiness that comes with being married or seeing one's children married

Chinese whispers

Chinese has a rich vocabulary when it comes to the last moments of life:

huiguang fanzhao the momentary recovery of someone who is dying

yiyan a person's last words

yiyuan a person's last or unfulfilled wish

mingmu to die with one's eyes closed, to die without regret

txiv xaiv a funeral singer whose songs bring helpful, didactic messages from the dead person to the survivors

Last rites

In the end the inevitable takes its course:

talkin (Indonesian) to whisper to the dying (i.e. words read at
the end of a funeral to remind the dead person of what to say
to the angels of death)

farjam-gah (Persian) the final home (grave)

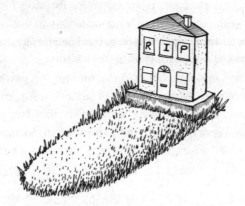

tunillattukkuuq (Inuit) the act of eating at a cemetery

akika (Swahili) a domestic feast held either for a child's first
haircut or for its burial

The long of it

Among languages that build up very long words for both simple and complex concepts are those defined as 'polysynthetic', and many of them are found in Australia or Papua New Guinea. The Aboriginal Mayali tongue of Western Arnhem Land is an example, forming highly complex verbs able to express a complete sentence, such as: **ngabanmarneyawoyhwarrgahganjginjeng**, meaning 'I cooked the wrong meat for them again'. (This breaks down into **nga**: I, **ban**: them, **marne**: for, **yawoyh**: again, **warrgah**: wrongly directed action, **ganj**: meat, **ginje**: cook, **ng**: past tense.) In the Australian language known as Western Desert, **palyamunurringkutjamunurtu** means 'he or she definitely did not become bad'.

Germans are not the only ones who like to create complex compound words as nouns. **Arbejdsløsheds-understøttelse** is Danish for unemployment benefit, while **tilpasningsvanskeligheder** means 'adjustment difficulties'. **Precipitevolissimevolmente** is Italian for 'as fast as possible'. And in the Tupi-Guarani Apiaká language of Brazil, **tapa-há-ho-huegeuvá** means rubber.

But maybe the laurels should go to the Ancient Greek playwright Aristophanes who devised the word **lopado-temacho-selacho-galeo-kranio-leipsano-drim-hu-potrimmato-silphio-karabo-melito-katakechumeno-kichl-epikossuphophatto-perister-alektruon-opto-kephallio-kigklo-peleio-lagoio-siraio-baphe-tragano-pterugon**, a dish compounded of all kinds of dainties, fish, fowl and sauces.

Otherworldly

zig then ma che; dam choe ma ha
(Dzongkha, Bhutan)
do not start your worldly life too late; do not start your religious life too early

Beyond the veil

So what lies beyond the beauties of life, in sight, sound and smell? Do we live for ever? And if so, can any of us ever return?

iwang wayaka (Ulwa, Nicaragua) a spirit that comes out after a person dies, makes noises and yet is never seen

tarniqsuqtuq (Inuit) a communication with a spirit that is unable to ascend

raskh (Persian) the transmigration of the human soul into a plant or tree

hrendi thenok (Sherpa, Nepal) to get in touch with the soul of a dead person

bodach (Scottish Gaelic) the ghost of an old man that comes down the chimney to terrorize children who have been naughty

Spooked in Sumatra

The Indonesians have a particularly varied vocabulary to describe the inhabitants of the spirit world and their attempts to menace the living:

wewe an ugly female ghost with drooping breasts

keblak a ghost cockerel which frightens people at night with the sound of its flapping wings

kuntilanak a ghost masquerading as a beautiful woman to seduce men who are then horrified to find that she actually has a large hole in her back

Looking into the future

A cynical old Chinese proverb offers the thought **ruo xin bu, maile wu; mai gua kou, mei liang dou**: 'if you believe in divination you will end up selling your house to pay the diviners'. But attempting to see into the future has been a constant in all societies for thousands of years:

aayyaf (Arabic) predicting the future by observing the flight of birds

ustukhwan-tarashi (Persian) divination using the shoulder-blade of a sheep

haruspex (Latin) a priest who practised divination by examining the entrails of animals

kilo lani (Hawaiian) an augury who can read the clouds

sortes (Latin) the seeking of guidance by the chance selection of a passage in a book

mandal (Arabic) prophesying while staring into a mirror-like surface

Hide away

Scottish Highlanders formerly had an unusual way of divining the future, known as **taghairm**. This involved wrapping a man in the hide of a freshly butchered bullock and leaving him alone by a water-fall, under a cliff-face, or in some other wild and deserted place. Here he would think about his problem; and whatever answer he came up with was supposed to have been given to him by the spirits who dwelt in such forbidding spots.

False friends

monaco (Italian) monk
fish (Arabic) Easter, Passover
alone (Italian) halo
fall (Breton) bad
lav (Armenian) good
bog (Russian) god

God willing

The French have a term, **bondieuserie**, which means ostentatious piety. But for many the solace of prayer and faith is both necessary and private:

saruz-ram (Persian) the first light breaking upon one committed to a contemplative life

rasf (Persian) the joining together of the feet in prayer (also the joining of stones in pavements)

thondrol (Dzongkha, Bhutan) the removal of sins through the contemplation of a large religious picture

kuoha (Hawaiian) a prayer used to bring a wife to love her husband and a husband to love his wife

tekbir (Arabic) to proclaim the greatness of God, by repeating **allahu akkbar**, 'Allah is great'

pasrah (Indonesian) to leave a problem to God

The short of it

Among single letter words to be found among the world's languages are the following:

u (Samoan) an enlarged land snail
u (Xeta, Brazil) to eat animal meat
u (Burmese) a male over forty-five (literally, uncle)
i (Korean) a tooth
m (Yakut, Siberia) a bear; an ancestral spirit

All Creatures Great and Small

meglio è esser capo di lucertola
che coda di dragone *(Italian)*
*better be the head of a lizard than the tail
of a dragon*

Animal crackers

'Every dog has his day'; 'you can take a horse to water, but you can't make it drink'; 'a cat may look at a king'. Animals crop up left, right and centre in English sayings and phrases, and in those of other languages too:

leben wie die Made im Speck (German) to live like a maggot in bacon (life of Riley)

van een kale kip kan je geen veren plukken (Dutch) you can't pluck feathers from a bald hen (get blood out of a stone)

olla ketunhäntä kainalossa (Finnish) to have a foxtail under your armpits (ulterior motives)

estar durmiendo con la mona (Spanish) to be sleeping with the monkey (be drunk)

eine Kröte schlucken (German) to swallow a toad (make a concession grudgingly)

bhains ke age bansuri bajana (Hindi) to play a flute in front of a buffalo (cast pearls before swine)

vot gde sobaka zaryta (Russian) that's where the dog is buried (the crux of the matter)

avaler des couleuvres (French) to swallow grass snakes (endure humiliation)

karincalanmak (Turkish) to be crawling with ants (have pins and needles)

Dragon's head

The Japanese are particularly fond of animal metaphors:

itachigokko weasels' play (a vicious circle)

gyuho an ox's walk (a snail's pace)

neko no hitai a cat's forehead (a very small area)

yabuhebi ni naru to poke at a bush and get a snake (to backfire)

ryuto dabi ni owaru to start with a dragon's head and end with a snake's tail (to peter out)

dasoku snake legs (excessive or superfluous)

tora ni naru to become a tiger (to get roaring drunk)

unagi no nedoko an eel's bed (a long narrow place)

mushi no idokoro ga warui the location of the worm is bad (in a bad mood)

kirinji a giraffe child (prodigy)

kumo no ko o chirasu yo ni like scattering baby spiders (in all directions)

inu to saru a dog and a monkey (to be on bad terms)

Ships of the desert

As you might expect, the more important an animal is to a particular culture, the more words there are for it. The cattle-herding Masai of Kenya and Tanzania, for example, have seventeen distinct words for cattle; the jungle-based Baniwa tribe of Brazil has twenty-nine for ant (with a range that includes the edible); while in Somali there are no fewer than forty-three words relating to camels of every possible variety. Here are a few:

qoorqab an uncastrated male camel

awradhale a stud camel that always breeds male camels

gurgurshaa a docile pack-camel suitable for carrying delicate items

sidig one of two female camels suckling the same baby camel

guran a herd of camels no longer producing milk that is kept away from dwelling areas

baatir a mature female camel that has had no offspring

gulguuluc the low bellow of a camel when it is sick or thirsty

cayuun camel spit

u maqaarsaar to put the skin of a dead baby camel on top of a living one in order to induce its mother to give milk

uusmiiro to extract drinking water from the stomach of a camel to drink during a period of drought

guree to make room for a person to sit on a loaded camel

tulud one's one and only camel

Persian also has its own detailed camel vocabulary that suggests an even more recalcitrant beast:

nakhur a camel that will not give milk until her nostrils are tickled

wakhd a camel that throws out its feet in the manner of an
   ostrich
munqamih a camel that raises its head and refuses to drink
   any more
zirad a rope tied round a camel's neck to prevent it from
   vomiting on its rider

Horses for courses

Many languages have very specific words to describe not only types
of horse but also its activities and attributes. In the Quechuan language of Peru, **tharmiy** is a horse that stands on its hind legs and
kicks out with its forelegs. The Bulgar **lungur** is an unfit horse, while
the Malay **kuda padi** is a short-legged horse for riding. **Dasparan**,
from the Khowan language of Pakistan, describes the mating of
horses and the Russian **nochoe** means the pasturing of horses for the
night. Persian has an extravagance of equine vocabulary:

zaru a horse that travels nimbly with long steps
mirjam a horse that makes the dirt fly when running
raji a horse returning tired from a journey only to be
   immediately dispatched upon another
rakl to strike a horse with the heel to make it gallop
zau' shaking the horse's rein to quicken the pace
shiyar riding a horse backwards and forwards to show it off to
   a buyer
safin a horse standing on three legs and touching the ground
   with the tip of its fourth hoof

Man's best friend

The Indians of Guatemala have a word, **nagual**, which describes an animal, chosen at birth, whose fate is believed to have a direct effect on the prosperity of its owner.

Hopping mad

The Kunwinjku of Australia use a range of words to describe the way in which kangaroos hop; in part this is because, from a distance, the easiest way to identify a particular type of kangaroo is by the way it moves. Thus **kanjedjme** is the hopping of a wallaroo, **kamawudme** is the hopping of a male Antilopine wallaroo, and **kadjalwahme** is the hopping of the female. **Kamurlbardme** is the hopping of a black wallaroo and **kalurlhlurlme** is the hopping of an agile wallaby.

False friends

ape (Italian) bee

anz (Arabic) wasp

bum (Arabic) owl

medusa (Spanish) jellyfish

slurp (Afrikaans) elephant's trunk

ukelele (Tongan) jumping flea

Shoo!

The Latin American **sape**, the German **husch** and the Pashto (of Afghanistan and Pakistan) **tsheghe tsheghe** are among the many similar-sounding words that mean 'shoo'. Other animal commands refer to particular creatures: Pashto **pishte pishte** is said when chasing cats away; **gja gja** is the Bulgar driving call to horses; **kur** is the Indonesian call to chickens to come to be fed; and **belekisi ontu** (Aukan, Suriname) is an insult hurled at a dog. The Malays are even more specific, with **song**, the command to an elephant to lift one leg, and **soh**, the cry to a buffalo to turn left.

Peacocks' tails

Many languages identify specific parts or attributes of animals for which there is no direct English equivalent. **Kauhaga moa** is the word used by Easter Islanders to designate the first and shortest claw of a chicken, while **candraka** in Tulu (India) is the eye pattern that appears on the feathers of a peacock's tail and **kannu** is the star in the feather. In several languages there are particular words for different types of animal excrement: monkey urine in the Guajá language (Brazil) is **kalukaluk-kaí**; the liquid part of chicken excrement in Ulwa (Nicaragua) is **daraba**; while in Persian the little bit of sweat and dung attached to a sheep's groin and tail is called **wazahat**.

Kissing and hissing

Other words describe the closely observed actions of animals, many of which we can instantly recognize:

mengais (Indonesian) to scratch on the ground with claws in search of food (generally used of a chicken)

apisik (Turkish) any animal holding its tail between its legs

maj u maj (Persian) kissing and licking (as a cat does to her kittens)

greann (Scottish Gaelic) the hair bristling as on an enraged dog

fahha (Arabic) the hissing of a snake

tau'ani (Cook Islands Maori) to squeal at one another while fighting (used of cats)

kikamu (Hawaiian) the gathering of fish about a hook that they hesitate to bite

alevandring (Danish) the migration of the eel

paarnguliaq (Inuit) a seal that has strayed and now can't find its breathing hole

Two Persian tricks

Tuti'i **pas ayina** is a person sitting behind a mirror who teaches a parrot to talk by making it believe that it is its own likeness seen in the mirror which is pronouncing the words. While **kalb** is the practice of imitating barking to induce dogs to respond and thus show whether a particular dwelling is inhabited or not.

Animal magnetism

Some animal words attract other meanings as well. Hausa of Nigeria uses **mesa** to mean both python and water hose, and **jak** both donkey and wheelbarrow. **Wukur** in Arabic signifies a bird of prey's nest

and an aircraft hangar and, intriguingly, **zamma** means both to put a bridle on a camel and to be supercilious. For the Wagiman of Australia **wanganyjarri** describes a green ants' nest and an armpit, while for the French **papillon** is both a butterfly and a parking ticket.

The flying squad

In Hopi, an Amerindian language, **masa'ytaka** is used to denote insects, aeroplanes, pilots; in fact, everything that flies except birds.

Tamed

Humans have rarely been content to let animals run wild and free; using them in one way or another has defined the relationship between two and four legs:

ch'illpiy (Quechuan, Peru) to mark livestock by cutting their ears

bolas (Spanish) two or three heavy balls joined by a cord used to entangle the legs of animals

oorxax (Khakas, Siberia) a wooden ring in the nose of a calf (to prevent it from suckling from its mother)

hundeskole (Danish) a dog-training school

Animal sounds

In Albanian, Danish, English, Hebrew and Polish, to name just a few languages, bees make a buzzing sound, and cats miaow. However, no language but English seems to think that owls go 'tu-whit, tu-woo' or a cockerel goes 'cock-a-doodle-doo'. And not everyone agrees about the birds and the bees either:

Birds
Arabic (Algeria): **twit twit**
Bengali: **cooho'koohoo**
Finnish: **tsirp tsirp**
Hungarian: **csipcsirip**
Korean: **ji-ji-bae-bae**
Norwegian: **kvirrevitt** or **pip-pip**

Bees
Afrikaans: **zoem-zoem**
Bengali: **bhonbhon**

Estonian: **summ-summ**
Japanese: **bunbun**
Korean: **boong-boong** or **wing-wing**

Cats
Indonesian: **ngeong**
Malay: **ngiau**
Nahuatl (Mexico): **tlatzomia**

Chicks
Albanian: **ciu ciu**
Greek: **ko-ko-ko**
Hungarian: **csip-csip**
Indonesian: **cip cip**
Quechuan (Peru): **tojtoqeyay**
Slovene: **čiv-čiv**
Thai: **jiap jiap**
Turkish: **cik cik**

Cockerels
Chinese: **gou gou**
French: **cocorico**
Italian: **chicchirichí**
Portuguese: **cocorococo**
Thai: **ake-e-ake-ake**

Cows
Bengali: **hamba**
Dutch: **boeh**
Hungarian: **bú**
Korean: **um-muuuu**
Nahuatl (Mexico): **choka**

Crows
French: **croa-croa**
Indonesian: **gagak**
Korean: **kka-ak-kka-ak**
Spanish: **cruaaac, cruaaac**
Swedish: **krax**
Thai: **gaa gaa**
Turkish: **gaaak, gaak**

Cuckoos
Japanese: **kakkou kakkou**
Korean: **ppu-kkook-ppu-kkook**
Turkish: **guguk, guguk**

Elephants
Finnish: **trööt** or **prööt**
Spanish (Chile): **prraaahhh, prrraaaahhh**
Thai: **pran pran**

Frogs
Afrikaans: **kwaak-kwaak**
Estonian: **krooks-krooks**
Munduruku (Brazil): **korekorekore**
Spanish (Argentina): **berp**

Goats
Nahuatl (Mexico): **choka**
Norwegian: **mae**
Quechuan (Peru): **jap'apeyay**
Russian: **mee**
Ukrainian: **me-me**

Hens
Turkish: **gut-gut-gudak**
Arabic (Algeria): **cout cout cout**
Rapa Nui (Easter Island): **kókokóko**

Owls
Korean: **buung-buung**
Norwegian: **uhu**
Russian: **ukh**
Swedish: **hoho**
Thai: **hook hook**

Pigs
Albanian: **hunk hunk**
Hungarian: **röf-röf-röf**
Japanese: **buubuu, boo boo boo**
Dutch: **knor-knor**

Sheep
Mandarin Chinese: **mieh mieh**
Portuguese: **meee meee**
Slovene: **bee-bee**
Vietnamese: **be-hehehe**
French: **bêê (h)**

Spellcheck nightmare

If only Scrabble allowed foreign words how much greater our wordscores could be:

3 consecutive vowels: **aaa** (Hawaiian) a lava tube

4 consecutive vowels: **jaaaarne** (Estonian) the edge of the ice; **kuuuurija** (Estonian) a moon explorer

6 consecutive vowels: **zaaiuien** (Dutch) onions for seeding; **ouaouaron** (Quebecois French) a bullfrog

7 consecutive vowels: **hääyöaie** (Finnish) – counting 'y' as a vowel – a plan for the wedding night

8 consecutive vowels: **hooiaioia** (Hawaiian) certified; **oueaiaaare** (Estonian) the edge of a fence surrounding a yard

5 consecutive consonants (and no vowels): **cmrlj** (Slovenian) a bumblebee

7 consecutive consonants: **razzvrkljati** (Slovenian) preparing the egg for baking, or making omelettes; **opskrbljivač** (Croatian) a supplier; **ctvrtkruh** (Czech) a quadrant

8 consecutive consonants: **angstschreeuw** (Dutch) a cry of fear; **varldsschlager** (Swedish) a worldwide music hit; **gvbrdgvnit** (Georgian) you tear us into pieces

11 consecutive consonants: **odctvrtvrstvit** (Czech) to remove a quarter of a layer

Whatever the Weather

chuntian hai'er lian, yi tian
bian san bian (*Chinese*)
*spring weather is like a child's face, changing
three times a day*

And the forecast is ...

Despite our obsession with the weather, the English language doesn't cover all the bases when it comes to precise observations of the natural world ...

serein (French) fine rain falling from a cloudless sky
imbat (Turkish) a daytime summer sea breeze
'inapoiri (Cook Islands Maori) a moonless night
wamadat (Persian) the intense heat of a still, sultry night
gumusservi (Turkish) moonlight shining on water
tojji (Tulu, India) the scum of water collected into bubbles
efterarsfarver (Danish) autumn colours

... though, inevitably, there are some local phenomena that we have to struggle harder to imagine:

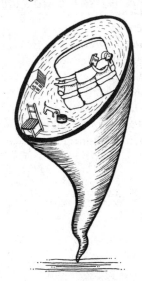

wilikoi (Hawaiian) substances that are gathered up in the centre of a whirlwind

isblink (Swedish) the luminous appearance of the horizon caused by reflection from ice

Meteorological metaphors

Our descriptions of the weather often use metaphors, such as raining cats and dogs, but some languages use the weather itself as the metaphor:

Schnee von gestern (German) yesterday's snow (water under the bridge)

huutaa tuuleen (Finnish) to shout to the wind (to do something that has no use)

aven solen har fläckar (Swedish) even the sun has got spots (no one is perfect)

snést někomu modré z nebe (Czech) to bring the blue down from the sky for someone (do anything to please them)

chap phar kah chap jil pa chu kha ray (Dzongkha, Bhutan) the rain falls yonder, but the drops strike here (indirect remarks hit the target)

xihuitl barq (Arabic) lightning without a downpour (a disappointment, a disillusionment or an unkept promise)

Those words for snow

The number of different Inuit words for snow has been the subject of endless debate, few people taking into account the fact that the now-offensive group name 'Eskimo' (from the French **Esquimaux**, derived from North American Algonquian and literally meaning 'eaters of raw flesh') covers a number of different language areas: Inuit in Greenland and Canada, Yupik in Eastern Siberia and Aleut in Alaska. Here is a selection of words for snow from some Inuit languages:

snow, **kaniktshaq**; no snow, **aputaitok**; to snow, **qanir**, **qanunge**, **qanugglir**; snowy weather, **nittaatsuq**, **qannirsuq**; to get fine snow or rain particles, **kanevcir**; first falling, **apingaut**; light falling, **qannialaag**; wet and falling, **natatgo naq**; in the air, falling, **qaniit**; feathery clumps of falling snow, **qanipalaat**; air thick with snow, **nittaalaq**; rippled surface of snow, **kaiyuglak**; light, deep enough for walking, **katiksugnik**; fresh without any ice, **kanut**; crusty, **sillik**; soft for travelling, **mauyasiorpok**; soft and deep where snowshoes are needed for travel, **taiga**; powder, **nutagak**; salty, **pokaktok**; wind-beaten, **upsik**; fresh, **nutaryuk**; packed, **aniu**; sharp, **panar**; crusty that breaks under foot, **karakartanaq**; rotten, slush on sea, **qinuq**; best for building an igloo, **pukaangajuq**; glazed in a thaw, **kiksrukak**; watery, **mangokpok**; firm (the easiest to cut, the warmest, the preferred), **pukajaw**; loose, newly fallen which cannot be used as it is, but can provide good building material when compacted, **ariloqaq**; for melting into water, **aniuk**; that a dog eats, **aniusarpok**; that can be broken through, **mauya**; floating on water, **qanisqineq**; for building, **auverk**; on clothes, **ayak**; beaten from clothes, **tiluktorpok**; much on clothes, **aputainnarowok**; crust, **pukak**; cornice, formation about to collapse, **navcaq**; on the boughs of trees, **qali**; blown indoors, **sullarniq**; snowdrift overhead and about to fall, **mavsa**; snowdrift that blocks something, **kimaugruk**; smoky drifting snow, **siqoq**; arrow-shaped snowdrift, **kaluto-ganiq**; newly drifting snow, **akelrorak**; space between drifts and obstruction, **anamana**, **anymanya**; snowstorm, **pirsuq**, **pirsirsursuaq**, **qux**; violent snowstorm, **igadug**; blizzard, **pirta**, **pirtuk**; avalanche, **sisuuk**, **aput sisurtuq**; to get caught in an avalanche, **navcite**.

There are also a large number of Inuit words for ice, covering everything from icicles through 'solidly frozen slush' to 'open pack ice in seawater'.

False friends

air (Indonesian) water, liquid, juice
blubber (Dutch) mud
shit (Persian) dust
nap (Hungarian) sun
sky (Norwegian) cloud
pi (Korean) rain

Highland mist

Either there is more weather in the cold, wet places of the world or people have more time to think about and define it. The Scots may not have as many words for snow as the Inuits, but they have a rich vocabulary for their generally cool and damp climate.

Dreich is their highly evocative word for a miserably wet day. Gentle rain or **smirr** might be falling, either in a **dribble** (drizzle) or in a **dreep** (steady but light rainfall). **Plowtery** (showery) weather may shift to a **gandiegow** (squall), a **pish-oot** (complete downpour), or a **thunder-plump** (sudden rainstorm accompanied by thunder and lightning). Any of these is likely to make the average walker feel **dowie** (downhearted) as they push on through the **slaister** (liquid bog) and **glaur** (mire), even if they're not yet **drookit** (soaked to the skin). The track in front of them will probably be covered with **dubs** (puddles), as the neighbouring **burn** (stream) grows into a fast-flowing **linn** (torrent).

The very next day the weather may be different again, and the walker beset by **blenter** (gusty wind). Or if it's **grulie** (unsettled), there's always the hope that it might turn out **leesome** (fair) with a lovely **pirl** (soft breeze). And then, after the next **plype** (sudden heavy shower), there may even be a **watergow** (faint rainbow). In deepest winter it will generally be **snell** (piercingly cold), and sometimes **fair jeelit** (icily so) among the **wreaths** (drifts) of snow.

For a precious few fair days in summer, there may even be a **simmer cowt** (heat haze), though the more austere will be relieved that the likelihood of discomfort remains high on account of the fierce-biting **mudges** (midges).

My underground oven

Riddles are found the world over. Here are some intriguing ones from Hawaii:

1 **ku'u punawai kau i ka lewa** my spring of water high up in the clouds

2 **ku'u wahi pu ko'ula i ka moana** my bundle of red sugarcane in the ocean

3 **ku'u wahi hale, 'ewalu o'a, ho'okahi pou** my house with eight rafters and one post

4 **ku'u imu kalua loa a lo'ik'i** my long underground oven

Answers

1 **niu** a coconut

2 **anuenue** a rainbow

3 **mamula** an umbrella

4 **he** the grave

Hearing Things

quien quiere ruido, compre un
cochino *(Spanish)*
he that loves noise must buy a pig

Sound bites

The sounds of most of the words we use have little to do with their meanings. But there are exceptions in other languages, too. For best results try saying the words out loud:

ata-ata (Rapa Nui, Easter Island) to laugh
ba'a (Hausa, Nigeria) ridicule, mockery
baqbaq (Arabic) garrulous
bulubushile (Bemba, Congo and Zambia) a stammer or lisp
capcap (Maltese) to clap
chopchop (Chamorro, Guam, USA) to suck
cizir cizir (Turkish) with a sizzling noise
karkara (Arabic) to rumble (of a stomach)
kekek-kekek (Malay) to giggle
kitikiti (Tulu, India) the ticking of a watch; or giggling, tittering

pes pes (Pashto, Afghanistan and Pakistan) whispering
pshurr (Albanian) to urinate, to wet one's clothes
raxxax (Maltese) to drizzle
ringongo (Gilbertese, Kiribati) to snore
taptap (Maltese) to patter

yuyurungul (Yindiny, Australia) the noise of a snake sliding through the grass

xiaoxiao (Chinese) the whistling and pattering of rain or wind

zonk zonk (Turkish) to throb terribly

Making a splash

Local experience shapes local language. The Tulu people of India, for example, have a fine array of evocative, specific words to do with water: **gulum** describes a stone falling into a well; **gulugulu** is filling a pitcher with water; **caracara** is spurting water from a pump; **budubudu** is bubbling, gushing water; **jalabala** is bubbling or boiling water; **salasala** is pouring water; while **calacala** describes the action of children wading through water as they play.

Ding dong

The sound of an altogether noisier culture can be heard in Indonesian: **kring** is the sound of a bicycle bell; **dentang**, cans being hit repeatedly; **reat-reot**, the squeaking of a door; **ning-nong**, the ringing of a doorbell; **jedar-jedor**, a door banging repeatedly. But there are gentler moments, too: **kecipak-kecipung** is hands splashing water in a rhythm, while **desus** is a quiet and smooth sound as of someone farting but not very loudly.

Chirping cuckoos

The Basques of the Pyrenees also use highly expressive words. You might recognize such terms as **kuku** (a cuckoo), **miau** (miaou), **mu** (moo), **durrunda** (thunder), **zurrumurru** (a whisper) and **urtzintz** (to sneeze), but could you guess the meaning of these?

thu	to spit
milikatu	to lick
tchiuka	to chirp
chichtu	to whistle
uhurritu	to howl
chehatu	to chew
karruskatu	to gnaw

False friends

rang (Chinese) to yell, shout

boo (Latin) to cry out, resound

hum (Ainu, Japan) sound, feeling

rumore (Italian) noise

bum (Turkish) bang

Sounds Japanese

The Japanese can be equally imitative: **shikushiku** is to cry continuously while sniffling, and **zeizei** is the sound of air being forced through the windpipe when one has a cold or respiratory illness. We can hear perhaps a gathering of Japanese women in **kusukusu**, to giggle or titter, especially in a suppressed voice; and of men in **geragera**, a belly laugh. Moving from the literal to the more imaginative, the Japanese have **sa**, the sound of a machine with the switch on, idling quietly; **sooay sooay**, fish swimming; **susu**, the sound of air passing continuously through a small opening.

Gitaigo describes a more particular Japanese concept: words that try to imitate not just sounds, but states of feeling. So **gatcha gatcha** describes an annoying noise; **harahara** refers to one's reaction to something one is directly involved in; and **ichaicha** is used of a couple engaging in a public display of affection viewed as unsavoury by passers-by. Mimicry of feelings extends to descriptions of the way we see: so **jirojiro** is to stare in fascination; **tekateka** is the shiny appearance of a smooth (often cheap-looking) surface; **pichapicha** is splashing water; and **kirakira** is a small light that blinks repeatedly.

Sounds familiar

Not all words about sound are imitative; or perhaps it's just that things strike the ear differently in other parts of the world:

bagabaga (Tulu, India) the crackling of a fire
desir (Malay) the sound of sand driven by the wind
faamiti (Samoan) to make a squeaking sound by sucking air
    past the lips in order to gain the attention of a dog or
    children
riman (Arabic) the sound of a stone thrown at a boy

ghiqq (Persian) the sound made by a boiling kettle
kertek (Malay) the sound of dry leaves or twigs being trodden
    underfoot
lushindo (Bemba, Congo and Zambia) the sound of footsteps
nyangi (Yindiny, Australia) any annoying noise
yuyin (Chinese) the remnants of sound which remain in the
    ears of the hearer

Top ten

In terms of numbers of speakers, the top ten world languages are as follows:

1 Mandarin 1,000+ million
2 English 508 million
3 Hindi 497 million
4 Spanish 342 million
5 Russian 277 million
6 Arabic 246 million
7 Bengali 211 million
8 Portuguese 191 million
9 Malay–Indonesian 159 million
10 French 129 million

Seeing Things

cattiva è quella lana che non si
puo tingere *(Italian)*
it is a bad cloth that will take no colour

Colourful language

We might well think that every language has a word for every colour, but this isn't so. Nine languages distinguish only between black and white. In Dan, for example, which is spoken in New Guinea, people talk in terms of things being either **mili** (darkish) or **mola** (lightish).

Twenty-one languages have distinct words for black, red and white only; eight have those colours plus green; then the sequence in which additional colours are brought into languages is yellow, with a further eighteen languages, then blue (with six) and finally brown (with seven).

Across the spectrum

As with colours, so with the rainbow. The Bassa language of Liberia identifies only two colours: **ziza** (red/orange/yellow) and **hui** (green/blue/purple) in their spectrum. The Shona of Zimbabwe describe four: **cipsuka** (red/orange), **cicena** (yellow and yellow-green), **citema** (green-blue) and **cipsuka** again (the word also represents the purple end of the spectrum). It is just Europeans and the Japanese who pick out seven colours: red, orange, yellow, green, blue, indigo and violet.

Welsh blues

The Welsh for blue is **glas**, as in the expression **yng nglas y dydd**, in the blue of the day (the early morning). But **glas** is a hard-working word. It's also used in the expression **gorau glas** (blue best), to mean to do one's best, and, changing tack rather dramatically, it appears as **glas wen** (blue smile), a smile that is insincere and mocking. In Welsh literature, **glas** is a colour that is somewhere between green, blue and grey; it also has poetic meanings of both youth and death.

False friends

blank (German) shiny
hell (German) clear, bright, light
cafe (Quechuan, Peru) brown

Thai dress code

Thais believe that if they dress in a certain colour each day it will bring them good luck. The code is: Monday, yellow (**lueang**); Tuesday, pink (**chom poo**); Wednesday, green (**kiaw**); Thursday, orange (**som**); Friday, blue (**nam ngem**); Saturday, purple (**muang**); Sunday, red (**daeng**). Black (**dam**) is not lucky for conservative people and is reserved for funerals; unless you are young, in which case it's seen as edgy and sophisticated.

Colour-coded

We can be green with envy, see red, or feel a bit blue. Colours have a strong symbolic force, but not everyone agrees on what they stand for:

Red

makka na uso (Japanese) a deep red (outright) lie
aka no tannin (Japanese) a red (total) stranger
film a luci rosse (Italian) a red (blue) film
romanzo rosa (Italian) a pink (romantic) story
vyspat se do červena/růžova (Czech) to sleep oneself into the red (have had a good night's sleep)

Yellow

jaune d'envie (French) yellow (green) with envy
gelb vor Eifersucht werden (German) to become yellow with jealousy
kiroi koi (Japanese) a yellow (particularly screeching) scream
gul och blå (Swedish) yellow and blue (black and blue)

Black

svartsjuk (Swedish) black ill (jealousy)

hara guroi (Japanese) black stomach (wicked)

être noir (French) to be black (drunk)

mustasukkainen (Finnish) wearing black socks (jealous)

White

andare in bianco (Italian) to go into the white (to have no success with someone romantically)

ak akce kara gun icindir (Turkish) white money for a black day (savings for a rainy day)

un mariage blanc (French) a white marriage (a marriage of convenience)

obléci bílý kabát (archaic Czech) to put on the white coat (to join the army)

Blue

aoiki toiki (Japanese) sighing with blue breath (suffering)

blau sein (German) to be blue (drunk)

en être bleu (French) to be in the blue (struck dumb)

aoku naru (Japanese) blue with fright

blått öga (Swedish) blue eye (black eye)

modré pondělí (Czech) blue Monday (a Monday taken as holiday after the weekend)

Green

al verde (Italian) in the green (short of cash)

vara pa gron kvist (Swedish) as rich as green (wealthy)

langue verte (French) green language (slang)

darse un verde (Spanish) to give oneself greens (to tuck into one's food)

aotagai (Japanese) to buy green rice fields (to employ college students prematurely)

Polyglossary

Two countries, Papua New Guinea with over 850 languages and Indonesia with around 670, are home to a quarter of the world's languages. If we add the seven countries that each possess more than two hundred languages (Nigeria 410, India 380, Cameroon 270, Australia 250, Mexico 240, Zaire 210, Brazil 210), the total comes to almost 3,500; which is to say that more than half of the world's spoken languages come from just nine countries.

If we look at it in terms of continents, North, Central and South America have around one thousand spoken languages, which is about 15 per cent; Africa has around 30 per cent; Asia a bit over 30 per cent; and the Pacific somewhat under 20 per cent. Europe is by far the least diverse, having only 3 per cent of the world's languages.

Number Crunching

c'est la goutte d'eau qui fait
déborder le vase *(French)*
*it's the drop of water that makes the vase
overflow*

Countdown

You might expect words to get longer as numbers get bigger, so perhaps it's a surprise to find that in some languages the words for single digits are a real mouthful. In the Ona-Shelknam language of the Andes, for example, eight is **ningayuneng aRvinelegh**. And in Athabaskan Koyukon (an Alaskan language) you need to get right through **neelk'etoak'eek'eelek'eebedee'oane** to register the number seven.

Vital statistics

The world's vocabulary of numbers moves from the precise . . .

parab (Assyrian, Middle East) five-sixths
halvfemte (Danish) four and a half
lakh (Hindustani) one hundred thousand

. . . to the vague:

tobaiti (Machiguengan, Peru) any quantity above four
mpusho (Bemba, Congo and Zambia) any unit greater than the number ten
birkacinci (Turkish) umpteen

Counting in old China

From the very biggest to the very smallest, the Ancient Chinese were highly specific in their delineation of numbers, from:

tsai 100 trillion
cheng 10 trillion
chien a trillion
kou 100 billion
jang 10 billion
pu / tzu a billion
kai 100 million
ching 10 million

right down to:

ch'ien one tenth
fen one hundredth
li one thousandth
hao one ten-thousandth
ssu one hundred-thousandth
hu one millionth
wei one ten-millionth
hsien one hundred-millionth
sha one billionth
ch'en one ten-billionth

Double-digit growth

Counting in multiples of ten probably came from people totting up items on their outspread fingers and thumbs. Some cultures, however, have approached matters rather differently. The Ancient Greeks rounded things off to sixty (for their low numbers) and 360 (for their high numbers) and speakers of old Germanic used to say 120 to mean many. The Yuki of Northern California counted in multiples of eight (being the space between their two sets of fingers) and rounded off high numbers at sixty-four. Some Indian tribes in California based their multiples on five and ten; others liked four as it expressed North, South, East and West; others six because it added to those directions the worlds above and below ground.

Magic numbers

Different cultures give different significance to different numbers. Western traditions offer the five senses and the seven sins, among other groupings. Elsewhere we find very different combinations. The following list is drawn from the Tulu language of India unless otherwise stated:

Three
tribhuvara the three worlds: heaven, earth and hell
trivarga the three human objects: love, duty and wealth

Four
nalvarti the four seasons

Five
pancabhuta the five elements: earth, air, fire, water and ether
pancaloha the five chief metals: gold, silver, copper, iron and
   lead

pancavarna the five colours: white, black, red, yellow and green

pancamahapataka the five greatest sins: murdering a Brahman, stealing gold, drinking alcohol, seducing the wife of one's spiritual mentor, and associating with a person who has committed such sins

pancavadya the five principal musical instruments: lute, cymbals, drum, trumpet and oboe

Six

liuqin (Chinese) the six relations (father, mother, elder brothers, younger brothers, wife and children)

Seven

haft rang (Persian) the seven colours of the heavenly bodies: Saturn, black; Jupiter, brown; Mars, red; the Sun, yellow; Venus, white; Mercury, blue; and the Moon, green

Eight

ashtabhoga the eight sources of enjoyment: habitation, bed, clothing, jewels, wife, flower, perfumes and betel-leaf/areca nut

Nine

sembako (Indonesian) the nine basic commodities that people need for everyday living: rice, flour, eggs, sugar, salt, cooking oil, kerosene, dried fish and basic textiles

Ten

dah ak (Persian) the ten vices – named after the tyrant Zahhak who was notorious for ten defects of body or mind: ugliness, shortness of stature, excessive pride, indecency, gluttony, scurrility, cruelty, hastiness, falsehood and cowardice

Expressed numerically

Specific numbers are also used in some colloquial phrases:

mettre des queues aux zeros (French) to add tails to noughts
(to overcharge)
siete (Spanish, Central America) seven (a right-angled tear)
Mein Rad hat eine Acht (German) my bike has an eight (a
buckled wheel)
se mettre sur son trente et un (French) to put yourself on
your thirty-one (to get all dressed up)
ein Gesicht wie 7 Tage Regenwetter haben (German) to
have a face like seven days of rain (a long face)

Kissing time

The adult understanding of the French number **soixante-neuf**
(69) is well known. Less familiar is the other meaning of **quatre-
vingt-huit** (88) – a kiss.

Take your time

Not everyone sees time in terms of past, present and future. The Kipsigis of the Nile region have three types of past tense: today's past, yesterday's past and the distant past. Several American Indian languages divide the past tense into the recent past, remote past and mythological past; other languages have different definitions:

pal (Hindi) a measure of time equal to twenty-four seconds
ghari (Hindi) a small space of time (twenty-four minutes)
tulat (Malay) the third day hence
xun (Chinese) a period of ten days (in a month) or a decade (in someone's life)
jam karet (Indonesian) rubber time (an indication that meetings may not necessarily start on time)

Can't say exactly when

In Hindi, the word for yesterday, **kal**, is the same as that for tomorrow (only the tense of the attached verb tells you which). And in Punjabi **parson** means either the day before yesterday or the day after tomorrow.

Time of day

Around the world different cultures have created highly specific loosely clock-related vocabulary that divides up the day. The Zarma people of Western Africa use **wete** to cover mid-morning (between nine and ten); the Chinese **wushi** is from eleven to one; and the Hausa (of Nigeria) **azahar** takes in the period from one-thirty to around three. The Samoan word **afiafi** covers both late afternoon and evening, from about 5 p.m. till dark. They call the period right after sunset **afiafi po**; this is then followed after a couple of hours by **po**, the dead of night. Of the various expressions for dusk, perhaps the most evocative is the French **entre chien et loup** – literally, between the dog and the wolf.

Elevenses

Dutch (and other Germanic languages) confusingly uses **half twaalf** for 11.30. While in Africa they are more long-winded for this specific time of day:

baguo gbelleng pie ne yeni par miti lezare ne pie (Dagaari Dioula, Burkina Faso)

isikhathi yisigamu emva kwehora leshumi nanye (Zulu)

metsotso e mashome a meraro ka mora hora ya leshome le motso e mong (Sesotho, Southern Africa)

Shouting the distance

Krosa is Sanskrit for a cry, and thus has come to mean the distance over which a man's call can be heard, roughly two miles. In the central forests of Sri Lanka calculations of distance are also made by sound: a dog's bark indicates a quarter of a mile; a cock's crow something more; and a **hoo** is the space over which a man can be heard when shouting the word at the highest pitch of his voice. While in the Yakut language of Siberia, **kiosses** represents a specific distance calculated in terms of the time it takes to cook a piece of meat.

Tip to toe

Parts of the body have long been used to define small distances – the foot in the imperial system of measuring, for example. The Zarma people of Western Africa find the arm much more useful: **kambe kar** is the length of the arm from the elbow to the tip of the middle finger and **gande** is the distance between two outstretched arms. Elsewhere we find:

dos (Hmong, China) from the thumb tip to the middle-finger tip

muku (Hawaiian) from the fingers of one hand to the elbow of the opposite arm when it is extended

sejengkal (Malay) the span between the tips of the stretched thumb and little finger

dangkal (Kapampangan, Philippines) between thumb and forefinger

The Micmac calendar

The Mikmawisimk language of the Micmac Indians is spoken by some eight thousand people in Canada and the USA. Their twelve months all have highly evocative names:

English	Mikmawisimk	Literal translation
January	**Punamujuikús**	the cod are spawning
February	**Apunknajit**	the sun is powerful
March	**Siwkewikús**	maple sugar
April	**Penamuikús**	birds lay eggs
May	**Etquljuikús**	frogs are croaking
June	**Nipnikús**	foliage is most verdant
July	**Peskewikús**	birds are moulting
August	**Kisikwekewikús**	it's ripening time
September	**Wikumkewikús**	it's moose-calling time
October	**Wikewikús**	our animals are fat and tame
November	**Keptekewikús**	the rivers are about to freeze
December	**Kiskewikús**	chief moon

False friends

fart (Turkish) excess or exaggeration
dim (Welsh) zero
age (Hindi and Urdu, Pakistan) in the future
beast (Persian) twenty
slut (Swedish) end or finish
tilt (Cantonese) one-third

Caribou calendar

Similar charmingly named months make up the various Inuit calendars. January is **siqinnaarut**, the month when the sun returns; February is **qangattaarjuk**, referring to the sun getting higher and higher in the sky; March is **avunniit**, when premature baby seals are born: some make it, some freeze to death; April is **natsijjat**, the proper month for seal pups to be born; May is **tirigluit**, when bearded seals are born; June is **manniit**, when the birds are laying eggs; July is **saggaruut**, the sound of rushing water as the rivers start to run; August is **akulliruut**, when the summer has come and the caribous' thick hair has been shed; September is **amiraijaut**, when the caribou hair is neither too thin nor too thick but just right for making into clothing; October is **ukialliruut**, when the caribou antlers lose their covers; November is **tusaqtuut**, when the ice forms and people can travel to see other people and get news; December is **taujualuk**, a very dark month.

Tea time

Tea is a fundamental part of Chinese culture, so it's no surprise to find that there's an elaborate calendar relating to the growth and preparation of it:

Chinese	Literal translation	Western Calendar
Li Chun	spring starts	5 February
Yushui	the rains come	19 February
Jingzhe	insects wake up	5 March
Chunfen	spring equinox	20 March
Qingming	clear and bright	5 April
Guyu	grain rain	20 April
Lixia	summer starts	5 May

Chinese	Literal translation	Western Calendar
Xiaoman	grains fill out	21 May
Mangzhong	the grain is in ear	6 June
Xiazhu	summer solstice	21 June
Xiaoshu	little heat	7 July
Dashu	big heat	23 July
Liqiu	autumn starts	7 August
Chushu	limit to food	23 August
Bailu	white dew	8 September
Qiufen	autumn equinox	23 September
Hanlu	cold dew	8 October
Shuangjiang	frost descends	23 October
Lidong	winter starts	7 November
Xiaoxue	little snow	22 November
Daxue	big snow	7 December
Dongzhi	winter solstice	21 December
Xiohan	little cold	6 January
Dahan	big cold	26 January

Halcyon days

In 2002 President Saparmurat Niyazov of Turkmenistan decided to rename both the months of the year and the days of the week. Some months were to take the names of heroes of Turkmenistan's past, but January was to become **Turkmenbashi**, after the president's official name ('Head of all the Turkmen'). In response to his suggestion that April should become known as 'Mother', one of his supporters suggested that instead it should be named after the president's mother, **Gurbansoltan-eje**. The president heeded this advice.

The days of the week were also renamed: Monday became Major (main or first) Day; Tuesday, Young Day; Wednesday, Favourable Day; Thursday, Blessed Day; Friday remained as it was; but Saturday became Spiritual Day; and Sunday, Rest Day.

Revolutionary

Turkmenistan is not the only country to consider changing the months of the year at a single stroke. In 1793 the newly established French republic abandoned the Gregorian calendar in favour of a new, 'rational' calendar. It lasted thirteen years, until abolished by Napoleon in 1806.

Each season was divided into three months, and the name of the months in each season shared a common word ending.

Printemps *(spring)*
Germinal seeds sprouting

Floréal flowering
Prairial meadow

Eté *(summer)*
Messidor harvest
Thermidor heat
Fructidor fruit

Automne *(autumn)*
Vendémiaire vintage
Brumaire fog
Frimaire sleet

Hiver *(winter)*
Nivôse snow
Pluviôse rain
Ventôse winds

These months quickly became nicknamed by the British as Showery, Flowery, Bowery, Wheaty, Heaty, Sweety, Slippy, Nippy, Drippy, Freezy, Wheezy and Sneezy.

Stages of the Hawaiian moon

The Hawaiians in earlier times named each of the thirty nights of a lunar month. The first night was called **hilo**, to twist, because the moon was like a twisted thread. The second was **hoaka**, a crescent. The third was **ku-kahi**, the day of a very low tide. The subsequent days described rough seas, light after moonset or days suitable for fishing with a torch. On the eleventh night, **huna**, the sharp points of the crescent were lost. On the twelfth, **mohalu**, the moon began to round. This was a favoured night for planting flowers; it was believed they would be round too. The thirteenth night was **hua**, the egg; the fourteenth, **akua**, the night of the perfectly rounded moon. On the sixteenth night, **mahea-lani**, the moon began to wane. More named days of rough seas followed until the twenty-ninth night, **mauli**, meaning that the last of the moon was visible. **Muku**, the thirtieth night, literally meant 'cut off' as the moon had disappeared.

A time for celebration

njepi (Balinese, Indonesia) a national holiday during which everyone is silent

Process of elimination

Not just words, but languages themselves change endlessly, some to the point where they go out of use altogether (on average one language a fortnight). Out of the (roughly speaking) 6,800 languages that comprise the global range, some recent victims have included Catawba (Massachusetts), Eyak (Alaska) and Livonian (Latvia). Many are from the jungles of Papua New Guinea, which still has more languages than any other country.

Others that run an imminent risk of extinction are: Abkhaz (Turkey/Georgia); Aleut (Alaska); Archi (Daghestan); British Romany; Apurina/Monde/Purubora/Mekens/Ayuru/Xipaya (Brazil); Brapu (Papua New Guinea); Southern Chaco/Chorote/Nivacle/Kadiweu (South America); Diyari (South Australia); Eastern Penan (Sarawak and Brunei); Gamilaraay (New South Wales); Goemai (Nigeria); Guruntum (Nigeria); Iquito (Peru); Jawoyn (Southern Arnhem Land); Jiwarli/Thalanji (Western Australia); Khumi Chin (Western Myanmar); Sandaun (Papua New Guinea); Sasak (Eastern Indonesia); Lakota (The Plains, America); Maku (East Timor); Ngamini (South Australia); Rongga (Flores, Indonesia); Uspanteko and Sakapulteko (Guatamala); Takana and Reyesano (Bolivia); Tofa (Siberia); Tundra Nenets (Arctic Russia and Northwestern Siberia); Uranina (Peru); Vedda (Sri Lanka); Vures (Vanuatu).

What's in a Name?

ming bu zheng; yan bu shun
(Chinese)
if the name is not right, the words cannot be appropriate

Angry bumblebees

Most first names, if not derived from myth, place, flower or surnames, have a specific meaning. **Patrick**, for example, means noble, from the Latin **patricius**. **Naomi** means 'pleasant' in Hebrew, while the Irish Gaelic **Kevin** literally means 'comely birth'. More unusual meanings of names from around the world include the following (m stands for a male name; f for female):

Astell (m)	sacred cauldron of the gods (Manx)
Delisha (f)	happy and makes others happy (Arabic)
Ebru (f)	eyebrow (Turkish)
Farooq (m)	he who distinguishes truth from falsehood (Arabic)
Fenella (f)	fair shoulder (Manx)
Lama (f)	with dark lips (Arabic)
Matilda (f)	strength in battle (German)
Xicohtencatl (m)	angry bumblebee (Nahuatl, Mexico)
Xiao-Xiao (f)	morning sorrow (Chinese)

Eyes like hard porridge

A number of particularly evocative names are to be found in different parts of Africa. Sometimes they refer to pregnancy or birth:

U-Zenzo (m)	things happened in the womb (Ndebele, Southern Africa)
Anindo (m)	mother slept a lot during pregnancy (Luo, Kenya)
Arogo (m)	mother nagged a lot during pregnancy (Luo, Kenya)
Ige (f)	born feet first (Yoruba, Nigeria)
Amadi (m)	seemed destined to die at birth (Yoruba, Nigeria)
Haoniyao (m)	born at the time of a quarrel (Swahili)

... to prophecy or destiny:

Amachi (f)	who knows what God has brought us through this child (Ibo, Nigeria)
U-Linda (f)	mind the village until the father's return (Ndebele, Southern Africa)
Nnamdi (m)	my father is alive (when thought to be a reincarnation of his grandfather) (Ibo, Nigeria)
Sankofa (f)	one must return to the past in order to move forward (Akan, Ghana)

... to appearance or behaviour:

Chiku (f)	chatterer (Swahili)
Masopakyindi (m)	eyes like hard porridge (Nyakyusa, Tanzania)
Masani (f)	has a gap between the front teeth (Buganda, Uganda)

... or to the parental reaction:

U-Thokozile (f)   we are happy to have a child (Ndebele,
                        Southern Africa)

Abeni (f)   we asked for her and behold we got her
                        (Yoruba, Nigeria)
Guedado (m)   wanted by nobody (Fulani, Mali)
Anele (f)   enough (given to a last born) (Xhosa, South
                        Africa)

Silent foreigners

Czechs describe people from outside their country in intriguing caricature. Originally all foreigners were called **Němec** (from the adjective **němý** meaning 'mute'); now the suggestion that outsiders are deprived of speech applies specifically to Germans, whose country is known as **Německo**. Hungary in Czech used to be **Uhersko**, and a Hungarian **Uher**, literally, a pimple.

The Italians, meanwhile, are called **makaróni**, for obvious reasons; while Australians are known as **protinožcí**, meaning 'legs placed in an opposite direction', as they would be on the other side of the globe. Other cheerfully frank generalizations include: **opilý jako Dán**, to be as drunk as a Dane; **zmizet po anglicku**, to disappear like an Englishman; and when the Czechs *really* don't understand something, they say **to pro mně španělská vesnice**, it's all a Spanish village to me.

False friends

handel (Polish and Dutch) trade

liszt (Hungarian) flour

berlin (Wagiman, Australia) shoulder

bengal (Malay) temporarily deaf or stubborn

malta (Italian) mortar

bach (Welsh) cottage

pele (Samoan) pack of playing cards

Skin and buttocks

Just for the record, and to avoid confusion abroad, here are the meanings of a variety of English names when written in other languages:

adam (Arabic) skin
alan (Indonesian) comedian
alf (Arabic) thousand, millennium
anna (Arabic) moans and groans
calista (Portuguese) chiropodist
camilla (Spanish) stretcher

cilla (Zarma, Nigeria) basket
doris (Bajan, Barbados) police van

eliza (Basque) church
eve (Rapa Nui, Easter Island) buttocks
fay (Zarma, Nigeria) divorce
fred (Swedish, Danish and Norwegian) peace
jim (Korean) baggage
kim (Ainu, Japan) mountain
kylie (Dharug, Australia) boomerang
laura (Greek) group of monks' huts
luke (Chinese) traveller
marianna (Italian) accomplice who tells a gambler the cards
held by other players
sara (Hausa, Nigeria) snakebite
sid (Arabic) plaster
susan (Thai) cemetery
vera (Italian) wedding ring

First person singular

Ben in Turkish, **Ami** in Bengali, **Fi** in Welsh, **Jo** in Catalan, **Mimi** in Swedish, **Mama** in Sinhala (Sri Lanka) and **Man** in Wolof (Senegal and Gambia) all mean I.

Speaking in tongues

British first names crop up as the names of languages, too:

Alan (Georgia); Ali (Central Africa); Dan (Ivory Coast); Dido (Russia); Karen (Myanmar and Thailand); Kim (Chad); Laura (Indonesia); Mae (Vanuatu); Maria (Papua New Guinea and India); Pam (Cameroon); Ron (Nigeria); Sara (Chad); Sonia (Papua New Guinea); Uma (Indonesia); Zaza (Iran).

And equally intriguing to English ears may be:

Afar (Ethiopia); Alas (Indonesia); Anus (Indonesia); Bare (Venezuela); Bats (Georgia); Bench (Ethiopia); Bile (Nigeria); Bit (Laos); Bum (Cameroon); Darling (Australia); Day (Chad); Doe (Tanzania); Eton (Vanuatu/Cameroon); Even (Russia); Ewe (Niger-Congo); Fang (Western Africa); Fox (North American); Fur (Sudan); Ham (Nigeria); Hermit (Papua New Guinea: extinct); Logo (Congo); Mango (Chad); Miao (South-East Asia); Moore (Burkina Faso); Mum (Papua New Guinea); Noon (Senegal); Pear (Cambodia); Poke (Congo); Puma (Nepal); Quiche (Guatemala).

Grand capital of the world

The capital of Thailand is abbreviated by all Thais to Krung Thep, and referred to as Bangkok, meaning literally 'grove of the wild plums'. But, bearing in mind that there are no spaces between words in written Thai, its full correct name is:

Krungthephphramahanakhonbowonratanakosinmahinthara yuthayamahadilokphiphobnovpharadradchataniburiromudo msantisug

meaning: City of Angels, Great City and Residence of the Emerald Buddha, Impregnable City of the God Indra, Grand Capital of the World, Endowed with Nine Precious Gems, Abounding in Enormous Royal Palaces which resemble the Heavenly Abode where reigns the Reincarnated God, a City given by Indra and built by Vishnukarm.

It rather leaves the Welsh

Llanfairpwllgwyngyllgogerychwyrndrobwillantysilioogofgoch

(meaning St Mary's Church by the pool of the white hazel trees, near the rapid whirlpool, by the red cave of the Church of St Tysilio) in the shade.

A to Y

At the other end of the scale are three places called **A** (in Denmark, Norway and Sweden), and two more, in Alaska and France, called **Y**.

Toujours Tingo

I.
Getting Acquainted

bie shi rongyi; jian shi nan (*Chinese*)
parting is easy but meeting is difficult

Hamjambo

However good or bad we're feeling inside, we still have to communicate with each other. We come out of our front door, see someone and adopt the public face. 'How are you?' 'Awright, mate?' we ask at home. Abroad, greetings seem somehow more exotic:

stonko?	Muskogee (Oklahoma and Florida, USA)
ah chop?	Aramaic (Maaloula, Syria)
oli?	Koyo (Congo)
hamjambo?	Kiswahili (South East Africa)

'Fine, thanks!' we reply. They say:

bare bra	Norwegian
dagu dad	Adyghe (North Caucasus, Russia)
bash	Kurdi (Iran, Iraq)

How is your nose?

The Onge of the Andaman Islands don't ask 'How are you?' but 'How is your nose?' The correct response is to reply that you are 'heavy with odour'. Around the world there are numerous other ways to meet and greet:

cead mile failte (Irish) one hundred thousand welcomes

añjalikā (Pali, India) the raising of the hands as a sign of greeting

inga i moana (Gilbertese, Oceania) to greet with open arms but soon tire of

er-kas (Pahlavi, Iran) hands under the armpits in respectful salutation

abruzo (Latin American Spanish) the strong hug men give each other whenever they meet

lamuka usalali (Mambwe, Zambia) to greet somebody lying down on one's back (a salute generally given to chiefs)

'And this is ...'

The Scots have a useful word, **tartle**, which means to hesitate in recognizing a person or thing, as happens when you are introducing someone whose name you can't quite remember. They are not the only ones to suffer from this infuriating problem:

ciniweno (Bemba, Zambia) a thing, the name of which one does not remember

joca (Portuguese) thingumajig, thingumabob

Tongue-tied

That little dilemma solved, not everyone finds it easy to continue:

byatabyata (Tsonga, South Africa) to try to say something but fail for lack of words

vóvôhetâhtsenáotse (Cheyenne, USA) to prepare the mouth before speaking (for example, by moving or licking one's lips)

dabodela (Malagasy, Madagascar) one in the habit of opening his mouth so as to show his tongue projecting and rolling a little beyond the teeth, and yet not able to speak

bunhan bunahan (Boro, India) to be about to speak and about not to speak

Chatterbox

With others you sometimes wish they found self-expression harder:

láu táu (Vietnamese) to talk fast and thoughtlessly

hablar hasta por los codos (Spanish) to talk non-stop (literally, to talk even through the elbows)

mae hi'n siarad fel melin bupur (Welsh) she talks non-stop (literally, she talks like a pepper mill)

hinikiza (Swahili) to out-talk a person by making a noise

kumoo musu baa (Mandinka, West Africa) to jump into a conversation without knowing the background

nudnyi (Russian) someone who, when asked how they are, tells you in detail

chovochovo (Luvale, Zambia) the tendency to carry on talking after others have stopped

gnagsår i ørene (Norwegian) blisters in your ears: what someone who talks a lot gives you

What's in a name?

First impressions are important, particularly to the people visiting a place for the first time. The name of the Canary Islands (Islands of the Dogs) derives from the wild dogs (**canes**) that barked savagely at the Romans when they first arrived on Gran Canaria.

Cities

Cuzco (Quechuan, Andes) navel of the earth
Khartoum (Arabic) elephant's trunk
Topeka, Kansas (Sioux Indian) a good place to grow potatoes

Countries

Anguilla: from the Spanish for eel, so named by Columbus due to its elongated shape
Cameroon: from the Portuguese **Rio de Camarões**, River of Shrimps
Faroe Islands: from the Faroese **Føroyar**, Sheep Islands
Barbados: from the name **Os Barbados**, the Bearded Ones: the island's fig trees sported long roots resembling beards

Keeping in touch

Advances in technology have ensured that we are always on call, but whether that improves the quality of our lives is somewhat debatable:

yuppienalle (Swedish) a mobile phone (literally, yuppie teddy: as they were like security blankets for yuppies when they first came out)

proverka sloukha (Russian) an expression used in telephone conversations, meaning 'I have nothing special to say – I just called to say hello' (literally, a hearing test)

telebabad (Tagalog, Philippines) talking on the phone for a long time

prozvonit (Czech and Slovak) to call someone's mobile from your own to leave your number in their phone's memory, without the intention of the other person picking up

Tower of Babble

Not that we should ever take communication of any kind for grant-ed. At whatever pace, misunderstandings are all too easy:

geop (Gaelic) fast talk which is mostly unintelligible
beròhina (Malagasy, Madagascar) to be spoken to in a strange dialect, to be perplexed by hearing provincialisms
betenger (Manobo, Philippines) to speak another language with a pronunciation that reflects one's own native language
tener papas en la boca (Chilean Spanish) to speak in a stuffy or incomprehensible manner (literally, to have potatoes in the mouth)

False friends

Those who learn languages other than their own will some-times come across words which look or sound the same as English, but mean very different things:

dating (Tagalog, Philippines) arrival
phrase (French) sentence
dating (Chinese) to ask about, enquire
Handy (German) mobile phone

Baloney

And sometimes people just speak rubbish anyway:

höpöhöpö (Finnish) nonsense

prietpraat (Dutch) twaddle

botalo (Russian) a chatterbox, a babbler (literally, a cowbell)

poyipoyi (Tsonga, South Africa) a person who talks at length but does not make sense

bablat (Hebrew) baloney (an acronym of **Beelbool Beytseem Le-Io Takhleet**: bothering someone's testicles for no reason)

ich verstehe nur Wortsalat (German) I don't understand a thing you are saying (literally, all I hear is the word salad)

Q and A

Information is power, they tell us; but finding out what we need to know isn't always as straightforward as we'd like. Sometimes we have to adopt special methods:

> **candrānā** (Hindi) to make an enquiry with a feigned air of ignorance
>
> **antsafa** (Malagasy, Madagascar) enquiries about things of which one is fully cognisant beforehand

... although of course two can play at that game:

> **gadrii nombor shulen jongu** (Tibetan) giving an answer that is unrelated to the question (literally, to give a green answer to a blue question)
>
> **kinkens** (Scots) an evasive answer to an inquisitive child
>
> **iqsuktuq** (Iñupiat, Inuit) to respond negatively by wrinkling the nose

Mhm mmm

So sometimes it's 'yes' …

mhm	Lithuanian
hooo	Agua Caliente (California, USA)
ow	Amharic (Ethiopia)
eeyee	Setswana (Botswana)
uh-uh-huh	Tamashek (West Africa)

… and other times 'no':

mmm	Pulawat (Micronesia)
uh uh	Shimasiwa (Comoros, Indian Ocean)
yox	Azerbaijani
bobo	Bété (Cameroon)
doo-yee	Kato (California, USA)
halo	Chinook (North America)
pepe	Chitonga (Zambia)
hindi	Tagalog (Philippines)
yuk	Tatar (Russia)

Just be sure you know which m(h)mm is which.

It's all Greek to me

People fail to understand each other all the time it seems. The English idiom 'it's all Greek to me' has counterparts throughout the languages of Europe. To the Germans it's 'Spanish', to the Spanish and Hungarians it's 'Chinese', to the French it's 'Hebrew', to the Poles it's 'a Turkish sermon'. And, more unusually still, the Germans say

ich verstehe nur Bahnhof I only understand station

2.
The Human Condition

ge ru-wa nhagi mo choe
(*Dzongkha, Bhutan*)
the nose doesn't smell the rotting head

Tightwad

However much we like to think that all those odd-looking, strange-speaking people around the world are different from us, the shocking evidence from language is that we are all too similar. Don't most of us, whether we live in city, shanty-town or rural bliss, know one of these?

hallab el-nammleh (Syrian Arabic) a miserly person (literally, ant milker)

krentenkakker (Dutch) one who doesn't like spending money (literally, someone who shits currants)

kanjus makkhichus (Hindi) a person so miserly that if a fly falls into his cup of tea, he'll fish it out and suck it dry before throwing it away

yaalik (Buli, Ghana) sponging, always expecting help or gifts from others without being willing to offer help

False friends

ego (Rapanui, Easter Island) slightly soiled
hiya (Tagalog, Philippines) bashful
incoherent (French) inconsistent
liar (Malay) undomesticated
um (Bosnian) mind, intellect
slug (Swedish) astute

Big-hearted

Fortunately, those are not the only kind of people on our beautiful and fragile planet:

pagad (Manobo, Philippines) to show consideration for a slow-walking person by also walking slowly, so that he can keep up

manàra-drìmitra (Malagasy, Madagascar) to involve oneself in another's calamity by seeking to extricate him

elunud (Manobo, Philippines) to go deliberately to someone's aid and share in his misfortune, regardless of the obviously ill-fated outcome

Ulterior motive

If only people displaying such fine qualities were always pure of heart. But the Italians are not the only ones who understand **carita pelosa**, generosity with an ulterior motive:

mutakarrim (Persian) one who makes pretensions to generosity

Tantenverführer (German) a young man of excessively good manners whom you suspect of devious motives (literally, aunt seducer)

uunguta (Yamana, Chile) to give much more to one than to others

Obligation

Then again, sometimes the totally sincere can be altogether too much:

Bärendienst (German) an act someone does for you thinking they are doing you a favour, but which you really didn't want them to do

arigata-meiwaku (Japanese) an act someone does for you thinking they are doing you a favour, but which you really didn't want them to do; added to which, social convention now requires you to express suitable gratitude in return

Watching the English

In Greek **megla** (derived from 'made in England') denotes elegance and supreme quality and **jampa** (derived from 'made in Japan') means very cheap. Other languages use rather different standards of Englishness in their idioms:

s kliden Angličana (Czech) as calm as an Englishman
ubbriaco come un marinaio inglese (Italian) as drunk as an English sailor
filer à l'anglaise (French) to slip away like the English

Hat over the windmill

Rather than being a sucker who takes consideration for other people's feelings too far, perhaps it would be better to be one of those enviable individuals who simply doesn't give a damn?

menefreghista (Italian) a person who has an 'I don't care' attitude

piittaamaton (Finnish) unconcerned about other people's feelings

i v oos nye doot (Russian) not to give a damn (literally, it doesn't blow in one's moustache)

no me importa un pepino (Spanish) I don't care two hoots (literally, I don't care a cucumber)

jeter son bonnet par-dessus les moulins (French) to throw caution to the winds (literally, to throw one's hat over the windmills)

Number one

On second thoughts, perhaps not. For the line between self-confidence and self-centredness is always horribly thin:

szakbarbár (Hungarian) a crank who can think of nothing but his/her subject

iakićagheća (Dakota, USA) one who is unreasonable in his demands, one who keeps asking for things after he should stop

kverulant (Czech) a chronic complainer, a litigious person

hesomagari (Japanese) perverse or cantankerous (literally, bent belly button)

Warm showerer

The Germans have pinpointed some particularly egotistic types:

Klugscheisser someone who always knows best (literally, smart shitter)

Warmduscher someone who is easy on himself (literally, warm showerer)

Nose in the clouds

And it's another short step from egotism to conceit:

péter plus haut que son cul (French) to think highly of
yourself (literally, to fart higher than your arse)

creerse la ultima Coca-Cola en el desierto (Central
American Spanish) to have a very high opinion of oneself
(literally, to think one is the last Coca-Cola in the desert)

nosom para oblake (Serbian) he's conceited, puffed up (literally, he's ripping clouds with his nose)

khenh khang (Vietnamese) to walk slowly like an important
person, to put on airs

cuello duro (Spanish) a snob, stuck-up (literally, hard or stiff
neck – from keeping one's nose in the air)

Impressing

Almost as irritating as the conceited and the pompous are those
who fail to see that, as they say in the Kannada language of Southern
India, **'Tumbida koDa tuLukuvudilla'**, the pot which is full does
not splash:

farolero (Spanish) a show-off (literally, a lantern maker)

m'as-tu-vu (French) a show-off (literally, one who constantly
asks other people 'Did you see me?')

Spesenritter (German) someone who shows off by paying the
bill on the firm's money (literally, expense knight)

poshlost (Russian) ostentatious bad taste

jor-joran (Indonesian) to compete in showing off one's wealth

elintasokilpailu (Finnish) keeping up with the Joneses

Sucking up

And yet, despite their obvious failings, both snobs and show-offs are often surrounded by the human equivalent of a benign parasite. As the Spanish say, '**La lisonja hace amigos, y la verdad enemigos**', flattery makes friends and truth makes enemies:

chupamedias (Chilean Spanish) a sycophant (literally, sock sucker)

banhista (Portuguese) someone who soft-soaps another

digdig (Manobo, Philippines) to praise a person for the quality which he lacks in order to encourage him to develop that quality

jijirika (Chichewa, Malawi) to curry favour by doing more than expected, but not necessarily well

Eejit

Can it get worse? Unfortunately it can:

lū-lū (Hindi) an idiot, nincompoop

gugbe janjou (Tibetan) a stupid person trying to be clever

kaptsn (Yiddish) one who does not amount to anything and never will

eldhus-fifi (Old Icelandic) an idiot who sits all day by the fire

el semaforo de medianoche (Venezuelan Spanish) a person no one respects and of whom everyone takes advantage, a pushover (literally, traffic light at midnight)

Salt in the pumpkin

'It is foolish to deal with a fool,' say the practical Japanese, though the Chinese wisely observe that 'He who asks is a fool for five minutes, but he who does not ask remains a fool forever.' Such observations reveal what the Catalans call **seny**, a canny common sense. Others value such qualities too:

> **ha sale in zucca** (Italian) he has common sense (literally, he's got salt in the pumpkin)
> **baser** (Arabic) one with great insight or one who is blind

Idiot savant

In Italy you are **stupido come l'acqua dei maccheroni**, as stupid as macaroni water; in Lithuania, **kvailas kaip žąsis**, as silly as a goose; while in France you can be as stupid as **une cruche** (a pitcher), **un pot** (a pot) or **un chou** (a cabbage). But even idiots are not necessarily all they seem:

> **adalahendry** (Malagasy, Madagascar) a person ignorant yet wise in some things
> **Spruchkasper** (German) a fool full of wise sayings
> **apo trelo kai apo pedi mathenis tin aletheia** (Greek proverb) from a crazy person and from children you learn the truth

Pregnant birds

Although the very young can delight us with their wonderful and surprising remarks, naivety is not, sadly, a state of mind that will work for a lifetime:

creer en pajaritos preñados (Venezuelan Spanish) to be credulous (literally, to believe in pregnant birds)

yelang zida (Chinese) ludicrous conceit stemming from pure ignorance

lolo (Hawaiian Pidgin) someone who would be glad to give you the time of day, if he knew how to read a clock

A piece of bread

How wonderful it is when we meet that rare person who just gets it right all the time:

katundu (Chichewa, Malawi) a person with outstanding positive qualities

Lieblingsstück (German) the favourite item of a collection (said of someone special)

para quitar el hipo (Latin American Spanish) very impressive; astonishing (literally, enough to cure the hiccups)

es un pedazo de pan (Spanish) he/she's a good person/it's a good thing (literally, he/she/it is a piece of bread)

A leopard cannot change its spots

chassez le naturel, il revient au gallop (French) chase
away the natural and it returns at a gallop

**aus einem Ackergaul kann man kein Rennpferd
machen** (Swabian German) you cannot turn a farm horse
into a racehorse

dhanab al kalb a 'waj walaw hattaytu fi khamsin galib
(Arabic) the dog's tail remains crooked even if it's put in
fifty moulds

vuk dlaku mijenja ali æud nikada (Croatian) a wolf changes his coat but not his attitude

die Katze lässt das Mausen nicht (German) the cat will not
abandon its habit of chasing mice

chi nasce quadrato non muore tondo (Italian) if you are
born square you don't die round

karishkirdi kancha baksang dele tokoigo kachat
(Kyrgyz) no matter how well you feed a wolf it always looks
at the forest

gorbatogo mogila ispravit (Russian) only the grave will
cure the hunchback

3.
Emotional Intelligence

wie boter op zijn hoofd heeft,
moet niet in de zon lopen (*Dutch*)
*those who have butter on their head should
not run around under the sun*

Happy valley

Whatever kind of character we've been blessed with, we all still experience similar highs and lows of emotion. Pure happiness is a wonderful thing; and we should never take it for granted, for who knows how long it may last?

kusamba (Ngangela, Angola) to skip, gambol, express uninhibited joy

sungumuka (Luvale, Zambia) to experience transitory pleasure in the novel

faly ambonindoza (Malagasy, Madagascar) delight before the danger is passed, premature joy

choi lu bù (Vietnamese) to have round after round of fun

alegria secreta candela muerta (Spanish proverb) unshared joy is an unlighted candle

In the coal cellar

The opposite emotion is rarely sought, but it arrives all the same:

at være i kulkælderen (Danish) to be very sad or depressed
(literally, to be in the coal cellar)

lalew (Manobo, Philippines) to grieve over something to the
extent that one doesn't eat

dastehen wie ein begossener Pudel (German) to look
depressed (literally, to stand there like a soaked poodle)

mal ikke fanden på veggen (Norwegian) to be very pessi-
mistic (literally, to paint the devil on the wall)

dar lástima (Latin American Spanish) to be in such a bad way
that people feel sorry for you

False friends

bang (Dutch) afraid

blag (Haitian Creole) joke

puke (Rotuman, South Pacific) to come strongly over one (of
feelings)

drift (Dutch) passion

job (Mongolian) correct, good

meal (Gaelic) to enjoy

Boo-hoo

Sometimes the best course is just to let it all hang out:

kutar-atugutata (Yamana, Chile) to get hoarse from much crying

gegemena (Rukwangali, Namibia) to mutter while sobbing

sekgamatha (Setswana, Botswana) the dirtiness of the face and eyes from much crying

dusi (Malay) to be perpetually crying (of young children)

āpaddharm (Hindi) a conduct permissible only in times of extreme distress

Crocodile

Though even tears are never as straightforward as we might like them to be:

ilonkyynelet (Finnish) tears of joy

miangòtingòtim-bòninàhitra (Malagasy, Madagascar) to weep in order to get something

chantepleurer (French) to sing and weep simultaneously

Smiley

'Cheer up!' we tell each other. And hopefully this brings the right results:

elmosolyodik (Hungarian) to break into a smile

sogo o kuzusu (Japanese) to smile with delight (literally, to demolish one's face)

cười khì (Vietnamese) to laugh a silly laugh

German Blues

The idioms of the world are full of colour. But in Germany 'blue' has a rich range of uses:

blaue vom Himmel herunter lügen to lie constantly (literally, to lie the blue out of the sky)

grün und blau ärgern sich to see red (literally, to anger oneself green and blue)

blau machen to take a day off (literally, to make blue)

blau sein to be drunk (literally, to be blue)

mit einem blauen Auge davon kommen to get off unscathed (literally, to get away with a blue eye)

ein blaues Auge a black eye (literally, a blue eye)

die blaue Stunde the time before dusk especially during winter (literally, the blue hour)

Tee-hee

Sometimes, indeed, more than the right results:

bungisngís (Tagalog, Philippines) one who giggles at the slightest provocation

ngisngis (Manobo, Philippines) someone who cannot control his laughter

latterkrampe (Norwegian) convulsive laughter

mengare (Gilbertese, Oceania) a forced laugh, to laugh on the wrong side of one's mouth

tirebouchonnant (French) extremely funny (literally, like a corkscrew – as one takes in air repeatedly to laugh)

mémêstátamaò'o (Cheyenne, USA) to laugh so hard that you fart

No potato

In the Arab world they distinguish between those who are good-humoured, **damak khafeef**, literally, their blood is light, and the opposite, **damak tieel**, their blood is heavy. But however well-meaning, humour always carries the risk of failure:

pikun (Kapampangan, Philippines) one who cannot take a joke

nye kartoshka (Russian) no joking matter (literally, no potato)

jayus (Indonesian) someone who tries to make a joke which is so unfunny that you laugh anyway

Pulling your nose

The different expressions for 'pulling someone's leg' reveal subtle distinctions in approaches to teasing. For the Germans it's **jemandem einen Bären aufbinden**, literally, to fasten a bear onto someone; for the French it's **mettre en boite**, to put someone in a box. The Spanish pull your hair (**tomar el pelo**), the Finns pull your nose (**vetää nenästä**), while the Czechs go one further and hang balls on your nose (**věšet bulíky na nos**).

Worry-wart

But better, surely, to laugh at your troubles than live on your nerves:

> **bēi gōng shé yǐng** (Chinese) worrying about things that aren't there (literally, seeing the reflection of a bow in a cup and thinking it's a snake)
>
> **qaquablaabnaqtuq** (Iñupiat, Inuit) to be tense because of an impending unpleasantness
>
> **doki doki** (Japanese) the feeling of great anxiety when someone is about to do or doing something very nerve-racking
>
> **hira hira** (Japanese) the feeling you get when you walk into a dark and decrepit old house in the middle of the night
>
> **como cocodrilo en fabrica de carteras** (Puerto Rican Spanish) to be extremely nervous (literally, to be like a crocodile in a wallet factory)

No balls

We all aspire to **zanshin** (Japanese), a state of relaxed mental alertness in the face of danger; but for most of us our reactions are all too human when bad things really do happen:

les avoir à zéro (French) to be frightened (literally, to have one's testicles down to zero)

ngua mat (Vietnamese) unable to stand something shocking

khankhanana (Tsonga, South Africa) to fall backwards rigid (as in a fit or from extreme fright)

jera (Indonesian) so scared by a past experience that one will never want to do it again

Spider on the ceiling

Then again, rather be healthily scared than driven round the bend:

keçileri kaçırma (Turkish) to lose one's marbles (literally, to kidnap the goats)

avoir une araignée au plafond (French) to be crazy (literally, to have a spider on the ceiling)

lud ko struja (Serbian) crazy as electricity

más loco que un plumero (Spanish) crazier than a feather duster

vrane su mu popile mozak (Croatian) he's crazy (literally, cows have drunk his brain)

A sandwich short of a picnic

šplouchá mu na maják (Czech) it's splashing on his lighthouse

hij heeft een klap van de molen gehad (Dutch) he got a blow from the windmill

ne pas avoir inventé le fil à couper le beurre (French) not to have invented the cheese wire to cut butter

hu khay beseret (Hebrew) he lives in a movie; his whole life is like a movie

non avere tutti i venerdì (Italian) to be lacking some Fridays

tem macaquinhos no sotão (Portuguese) he has little monkeys in the attic

udaren mokrom čarapom (Serbian) hit with a wet sock

ikke at være den skarpeste kniv i skuffen (Danish) not to be the sharpest knife in the drawer

4.
Social Animals

ui mai koe ki ahau he aha te mea nui
o te ao, māku e kī atu he tangata, he
tangata, he tangata! (*Maori*)
*ask me what is the greatest thing in the world,
I will reply: it is people, it is people, it is people!*

Most of us are sociable creatures, unable to avoid relying on those around us to keep us happy:

bukaladza (Tsonga, South Africa) to dispel boredom by doing something such as paying a visit

buren (Dutch) to look in upon one's neighbours

lishashamana (Lozi, Niger-Congo) the habit of running out to see anything that happens

gezellig (Dutch) an atmosphere of cosiness, of being with good friends, and spending time together laughing and having fun; the kind of moments that create memories

Hermit

Better that than being the odd one out:

lappsjuka (Swedish) a state of melancholy through being so isolated

encontrarse como un pulpo en un garaje (Spanish) to be like a fish out of water (literally, to be like an octopus in a garage)

nkunkula pansi (Mambwe, Zambia) an orphan who has no one to look after him and passes his time playing in the dust

Whacking aunt

When we do get together, are our conversations as morally improving as they might be?

gigirhi-gigirhi (Tsonga, South Africa) to go from village to village exchanging gossip

Klatschbase (German) a person who always gossips (literally, whacking aunt)

ngasngás (Tagalog, Philippines) a scandal caused by gossip

Bären aufbinden (German) to tell false tales (literally, to tie a bear onto someone)

False friends

sober (Estonian) male friend
drug (Russian) good friend
fun (Yoruba, Nigeria, Benin and Togo) to give
host (Czech) guest

Party spirit

For some the urge to socialize can get the better of their wiser instincts:

mawadishiweshkiwin (Ojibway, North America) the habit of making visits too often

mit der Tür ins Haus (German) failing to take someone by surprise, to be too direct, to be too forward (literally, to fall with the door into the house)

paglaguma (Tagalog, Philippines) the act of joining others in a party although uninvited

paracaidista (Central American Spanish) a freeloader, gate-crasher; also someone who jumps into a discussion without knowing anything about the subject (literally, parachutist)

Storm-free shack

But then who can resist a really good bash?

parapetowka (Polish) the first party in someone's new apartment (literally, a windowsiller – as there's no furniture yet)

ipeje (Yoruba, Nigeria, Benin and Togo) an invitation to a banquet

ponkal (Tamil) a boiling, a bubbling-up; a great festival in honour of the sun entering the sign Capricorn (the name comes from the cooking of the celebratory rice)

eine sturmfreie Bude (German) a flat without the parents, thus allowing the children to throw a party (literally, a storm-free shack)

nachspil (Swedish) a follow-up party

After-parties

In Japan, the second, sometimes spontaneous gathering that happens after you have left the main party is called **nijikai**. If you move on after a while to a third place, it's called **sanjikai**.

Looking over the fence

Some guests are obviously more welcome than others:

partigangare (Swedish) a fanatical partygoer
laumaeläin (Finnish) a gregarious animal
Zaungast (German) a guest who looks over the fence to get at least the music of the party (literally, fence guest)
aguafiestas (Spanish) a killjoy, one who throws water on a party (literally, water party)

The sound of yoghurt

A little music often helps ...

kanariom (Yoeme, USA and Mexico) the first tune played or danced
dorremifassolar (Portuguese) to play scales on the piano
yaourt (French) English pop music sung without any understanding of the meaning; singing to create something that sounds like English pop music but actually isn't (literally, yoghurt)
accharika (Pali, India) to make heavenly music

Wiggle your bucket

... and then things can really kick off:

gida (South Africa Township) to jump up and down constantly
  in one place (as a form of dance)
menear el bote (Mexican Spanish) to dance (literally, to
  wiggle your bucket)

chachula (Tsonga, South Africa) a dance with the rhythmic
  quivering of the body
kundáy (Tagalog, Philippines) dance movements made by the
  wrist

Duck feet

Or not, as the case may be:

hávêsévôhomo'he (Cheyenne, USA) to dance badly
asiqtuq (Iñupiat, Inuit) nodding with the head while others dance
pamutas-silya (Tagalog, Philippines) ladies who go to dances but do not dance
paton (Cuban Spanish) duck feet (i.e. can't dance)

Keeping their bottle

Sometimes you just have to call in the professionals:

binasohan (Bikol, Philippines) a dance in which three glasses partially filled with wine are balanced, one on the head and one on each hand
danza de la botella (Paraguayan Spanish) a bottle dance in which each dancer balances a flower-filled bottle on his head
gamadj (Ojibway, North America) dancing with a scalp in one's hands, in order to receive some presents

National anthems

The title of a country's officially chosen anthem can be very revealing about its history: the Czech **Kde domov můj** (Where is My Home) reflects many years of shifting borders and invasions. Other interesting titles include:

Burkina Faso: **Une seule nuit** (Just One Night)

Israel: **Hatikvah** (The Hope)

Kurdistan: **Ey Reqîb** (Hey Enemy or Hey Guardian)

Netherlands: **Het Wilhemus** (The William)

Norway: **Ja, vi elsker dette landet** (Yes, We Love This Country)

Romania: **Deşteaptă-te, Române** (Wake Up, Romanian)

Tuva, Siberia: **Tooruktug Dolgay Tangdym** (The Forest is Full of Pine Nuts)

Time, please

Always be wary of overstaying your welcome. As the Italians say, **'L'ospite è come il pesce: dopo tre giorni puzza'**, the guest is like a fish: after three days he smells bad:

desconvidar (Portuguese) to withdraw an invitation

il est comme un cheveu dans la soupe (French) he is not welcome; he has come at an awkward time (literally, he is like a hair in the soup)

pudyapudya (Tsonga, South Africa) to go away because one is shown one is not wanted

ngloyor (Indonesian) to go without saying goodbye

apagavelas (Caribbean Spanish) the last person to leave a party

Have your cake and eat it

auf zwei Hochzeiten tanzen (German) to dance at two
  weddings

aam ke aam, guthliyon ke daam (Hindi) you can have
  mangoes and sell the seeds as well

dikasih hati minta jantung (Indonesian) given the liver
  and demands the heart

avoir le beurre, argent du beurre et la crémière avec
  (French) to have butter, money from butter, and the woman
  who makes the butter

non si puo avere la botte piena è la moglie ubriaca
  (Italian) you can't have a full cask of wine and a drunken
  wife

5.
Having an
Argument

casa onde não há pão, todos ralham
e ninguém tem razão (*Portuguese*)
*in a breadless home, everyone complains and
nobody is right*

Cold porridge

One downside to socializing is all the enforced jollity, often with people you might not choose to spend that much time with otherwise:

metepatas (Spanish) a person who always does or says the wrong thing

yokogamiyaburi (Japanese) an obstinate person (literally, to be difficult to tear paper sideways)

elle coupe les cheveux en quatre (French) she is a difficult person (literally, she cuts hair into four pieces)

kashi nye svarit (Russian) to be impossible to get along with (literally, the porridge can't be boiled)

Being difficult

The German expression **Fisimatenten machen**, meaning to make things unnecessarily difficult, is a mangling of the French **visiter ma tante** (visit my aunt). It originates in the difficulty of imposing a curfew on occupied France during the Second World War. **Visiter ma tante** was the general excuse used by people arrested on the streets at night by French soldiers.

On the edge

Watch out for those snappy exclamations. They're generally a sign of rapidly fading patience:

kalter Kaffee (German) that's old hat (literally, cold coffee)
dang-geun i-ji (Korean) it's obvious (literally, it's a carrot)

da lachen die Hühner (German) you must be joking
(literally, this makes the chickens laugh)
heso de cha o wakasu (Japanese) don't make me laugh
(literally, I boil tea in my navel)
nu tog fan bofinken (Swedish) now that's done it (literally,
the devil took the chaffinch)
ne cui hui v chai (Russian) don't mess things up (literally,
don't stir the tea with your penis)

Looking for the hair

And some people just can't help but provoke you:

bamp (Scots) to harp on the same topic constantly, to nag about the same thing

chercher un poil aux oeufs (French) to nit-pick (literally, to look for a hair on eggs)

juubakonosumi o (yoojide) tsutsuku (Japanese) to split hairs (literally, to pick at the corners of a food-serving box with a toothpick)

no tener pelos en la lengua (Latin American Spanish) to be very outspoken (literally, to have no hairs on your tongue)

napleiten (Dutch) to discuss might-have-beens, go over old ground again, keep on arguing after a thing has been decided

Pig's ribbon

Sometimes you can feel it all getting too much:

la moutarde me monte au nez (French) to begin to lose one's temper (literally, mustard is climbing up my nose)

akaspa (Dakota, USA) to be provoked beyond endurance

poner como lazo de cochino a (alguien) (Mexican Spanish) to jump down someone's throat (literally, to make someone look like a pig's ribbon)

Cracking up

We must, of course, do our very best to be tactful and discreet, relying on our wits to keep us out of trouble:

mijèry àrina an-tàva (Malagasy, Madagascar) not to tell a person his faults (literally, to notice a blotch on the face but not mention it)

dar(le) el avión a (alguien) (Mexican Spanish) to say yes or agree, without really meaning it or paying attention (literally, to give the aeroplane)

tumodisa (Setswana, Botswana) to shut a person's mouth to prevent him from speaking

ad-hoc-Bildungen (German) making up a new word on the spot in a moment of need

adin' andriana (Malagasy, Madagascar) a quarrel in which both parties show great respect for each other

Hell is other people(s)

It's always easier to describe unpleasant things or experiences in foreign terms; it makes them less immediate and it's a good way of having a dig at another culture at the same time. When we can't understand someone's English we call it Double Dutch; while the Danes call a grey cloudy day Swedish Sunshine:

spaans benauwd (Dutch) lack of air when you are dead nervous (literally, Spanish lack of air)

une querelle d'Allemand (French) a quarrel started for no obvious or good reason (literally, a German argument)

kitaiskyi televizor (Russian) the manual examination of baggage at customs (literally, Chinese television)

mandras kaip prancūzų šuo (Lithuanian) proud as a French dog

avoir l'oeil americain (French) to have a sharp eye (literally, an American eye)

doccia scozzese (Italian) a shower that goes from very hot to very cold (literally, Scottish shower)

schwedische Gardinen (German) prison bars (literally, Swedish curtains – the Swedish had a reputation for fine quality steel)

Mexican rage

Mexican Spanish has expressions for each stage of losing your patience with someone. **Alucinar a alguien** is to be fed up with someone's constant and not very welcome presence; **estar como agua para (pa') chocolate**, to be absolutely furious (literally, to be as hot as the water needed to melt chocolate); and finally **parar(se) de pestañas** describes losing it completely (literally, to stand on your eyelashes).

Picking a fight

The typically polite Japanese use few insults and those they do use tend to be indirect. **Baka** (fool) is a combination of the words for 'horse' and 'deer', with the implication that anyone who cannot tell a horse from a deer is obviously a fool.

Get lost !

Other cultures get straight to the point:

vai à fava (Portuguese) go to the fava bean!
sukse kuuseen (Finnish) ski into a spruce!
ej bekot (Latvian) go mushrooming!
skatertyu droga (Russian) table cloth to the road!

... especially in the Spanish-speaking world:

banarse take a bath!
buscar berros find watercress!
freir bunuelos fry doughnuts!
freir esparragos fry asparagus!
hacer gargaras gargle!
a la goma as far as rubber stretches!

Dumb as bread

The rest of the world is not short of colourful verbal insults. 'May the fleas of a thousand camels infest your armpits,' they say in Arabic; and many other languages compare people to animals when being rude. In French your object of scorn is a **chameau** (camel) or **vache** (cow); in Swahili, a **punda** (zebra); while in Vietnam you call the offender **do cho de**, literally, you dog birth. Other expressions of abuse have clearly exercised the full imagination of the truly upset:

du bist doch dumm wie Brot (German) you are as dumb as bread

korinttiaivot (Finnish) an insult to describe the old (literally, currant brains)

du kannst mir mal in die Schuhe blasen (Swiss German) kiss my arse (literally, you can blow into my shoes)

du kannst mir gern den Buckel runterrutschen und mit der Zunge bremsen (Austrian German) you can slide down my hunchback using your tongue as a brake

Anger-hair

Now things are in danger of getting seriously out of control:

tener una cara de telefono ocupado (Puerto Rican
Spanish) to be angry (literally, to have a face like a busy
telephone)

Gesicht wie ein Feuermelder (German) to be so angry that
one's face turns red (literally, a face like a fire alarm)

mencak-mencak (Indonesian) to stamp one's feet on the
ground repeatedly, getting very angry

dohatsu-ten o tsuku (Japanese) to be beside oneself with
rage (literally, anger-hair points to heaven)

mouton enragé (French) maddened sheep (said of an angry
person who is usually calm)

wašihdaka (Dakota, USA) one who gets angry at everything

False friends

twist (Dutch) quarrel, dispute, altercation, wrangle
batman (Turkish) thrust
pee (Dutch) to be annoyed
hot (Swedish) threat

The blame game

The blame game

When the blood is boiling things can get increasingly complicated:

togogata (Yamana, Chile) to turn one's attention and anger from one person to another

fijoo (Mandinka, West Africa) anger at someone other than the one who caused the anger

babit (Malay) to implicate third parties in a dispute

hewula (Tsonga, South Africa) to shout down one who keeps on arguing after the evidence has shown him to be guilty

Macho moment

Pray God, it doesn't turn physical:

imbang (Malay) reluctant but prepared to fight

makgatlha (Setswana, Botswana) challengers who show their wish to fight by throwing down a handful of earth

dii-konya (Ndebele, Southern Africa) to destroy your own property in anger

lusud (Manobo, Philippines) to go into someone's house to fight them

parandhu parandhu adikkaradhu (Tamil) to fight by jumping and flying in the air

langola (Mambwe, Zambia) to repeatedly throw a man very hard to the ground

sugun (Malay) seizing the hair or throat to force down your adversary

cisanan (Yamana, Chile) a canoe with an avenger of blood in it coming to exact vengeance

The female is the deadlier ...

The Finnish have a wonderful word, **knapsu**, for anything that's not male behaviour. Other cultures are quick to notice the gender-specific:

Stutenbeißen (German) the special behaviour of women in a rivalry situation (literally, mare biting)

dzinana (Tsonga, South Africa) to pummel one another with the side of the fists, away from the thumb, as fighting women do)

vongola (Tsonga, South Africa) to expose the buttocks (which is done by women as the ultimate insult when they run out of invective)

agarrar(se) del chongo (Latin American Spanish) to brawl, to fight – applied to women (literally, to grab each other by the bun of the hair)

The flapping of wings

Whatever sex we are, we sometimes can't resist having the last word:

>
> **kulumbana** (Tsonga, South Africa) to follow a person who left a meeting in disgust and shout insults and reproaches after him
>
> **dar patadas de ahogado** (Latin American Spanish) to fight a losing battle (literally, to thrash around uselessly when you'll drown anyway)
>
> **aleteo** (Caribbean Spanish) the last words in a lost argument (literally, flapping of wings)

The pot calling the kettle black

c'est l'hôpital qui se moque de la Charité (French) it's the hospital that mocks Charity

bagoly mondja a verébnek, hogy nagyfejű (Hungarian) the owl calls the sparrow big-headed

rugala se sova sjenici (Croatian) the owl mocked the tit

il bue che dice cornuto all'asino (Italian) the ox saying 'horned' to the donkey

rîde ciob de oală spartă (Romanian) the splinter laughs at the broken pot

al jamal ma yishuf sanamu (Arabic) the camel cannot see its own hump

ein Esel schimpft den anderen Langohr (German) a donkey gets cross with a rabbit

6.
The Rules of Attraction

a tola e à lettu alcunu rispettu
(*Corsican*)
have no respect at the table and in bed

The Russian word for falling in love, **oupast'**, also means to be at a loss, to understand nothing. Other languages stress the magic of the early stages of the romantic encounter:

koi no yokan (Japanese) a sense on first meeting that something is going to evolve into love

ong buóm (Vietnamese) bees and butterflies, flirtations, love-making

anhimmeln (German) to look enraptured at someone (literally, as if they were the sky)

No-pan kissa

On summer evenings, in little towns in Italy, young men and women **fare la passeggiata**, perambulating the central square sizing each other up and flirting, or, as they say in that country, **fare il galletto**, to do like the rooster. Other societies offer other options:

blyazh (Russian) a beach where girls can be picked up

kamáki (Greek) the young local guys strolling up and down beaches hunting for female tourists (literally, harpoons)

no-pan kissa (Japanese) coffee shops with mirrored floors to allow customers to look up waitresses' skirts

tyčovka (Czech) a woman who hangs on to the pole next to the bus driver and chats him up

Like a motorway

In Indonesia, they have a word for falling in love at first sight: **kepincut**. But when it comes to what's most attractive in a woman, there seems to be no accounting for tastes:

rombhoru (Bengali) a woman having thighs as well-shaped as
   banana trees
autostrada (Italian) a very slender girl without pronounced
   sexual attributes (literally, a motorway)
e thamba (Oshindonga, Namibia) a big, fat and clean girl
baffona (Italian) an attractive moustachioed woman

at have både til gården og til gaden (Danish) a woman
   well equipped both at the front and the rear (literally, to
   have both to the courtyard and to the street)

Double take

Certainly, caution is advised in the early stages:

layogenic (Tagalog, Philippines) someone good-looking from afar but not up close

daburu bikkuri (Japanese) women who, as they are approaching a stall, look so attractive that they give the vendor a shock, but when they finally arrive at his counter they give him another shock as the scales fall from his eyes (literally, double shock)

A face only a mother could love

And one should always be wary of a blind date:

kakobijin (Japanese) the sort of woman who talks incessantly about how she would have been thought of as a stunner if she had lived in a different era, when men's tastes in women were different (literally, bygone beauty)

kimangamanga (Gilbertese, Oceania) a person with a ridiculous walk and defective bottom

sjøstygg (Norwegian) being so ugly that the tide won't come in if you're on the shore (literally, sea ugly)

skreeulelik (Afrikaans) scream ugly (i.e. so frightening as to make the viewer scream)

être moche à caler des roués de corbillard (French) to be extremely ugly (literally, to be ugly enough to stop the wheels of a hearse)

Diving fish, swooping geese

In China, many hundreds of years ago, a poet said of the great beauty Hsi Chi that when she went for a walk fish dived deeper, geese swooped off their course, and deer ran into the forest before her beauty. Therefore, instead of saying a woman is as beautiful as Hsi Chi, in Chinese one simply says the four words **ch'en yü, le yen**, diving fish, swooping geese.

You beautiful creature

In other languages the comparison with animals may be even more direct. In Arabic, a beautiful woman is spoken of as having **yoon al ghrazaali**, the eyes of the gazelle. Similar metaphorical expressions abound:

miyulesa (Sinhala, Sri Lanka) a woman with eyes like a deer's
omïrïghlïgh (Khakas, Siberia) a person having a beautiful
    bearing in the same way that a horse has a strong chest
kati-keharī (Hindi) having the waist of an elegant lion (used
    of an attractive woman)

And what do women want?

The men of the Wodaabe (a nomadic tribe of Central and East Africa) perform the **yaake**, a competition of charm and personality judged by young women. Performing the yaake, a man who can hold one eye still and roll the other is considered particularly alluring by the judges.

karlakarl (Swedish) a real man
bellone (Italian) a hunk who's rather too pleased with himself
tarzan (Hebrew) a dandy
armoire à glace (French) a great hulking brute (literally, a wardrobe of ice cream)

Double Valentine

In Japan, Valentine's Day is celebrated on two different dates: 14 February, when girls are allowed to express their love to boys by presenting chocolate; and 14 March, known as White Day, when the male has to return the gift he received. Chocolates given sincerely on these days are **honmei-choko**, true-feeling chocolates. However, women are also obliged to give chocolates to all the men in their lives, meaning large numbers of co-workers, bosses, etc. These are known as **giri-choko**, obligatory chocolates.

My Japanese prints

The Hindi language has **sandesh-kāvya**, describing a poetic form where the lover sends his message of love and yearning to his beloved through clouds or birds. The Mailu language of Papua New Guinea has **oriori**, a boy's song to attract a girl. Aspiring Western Romeos often prefer a more basic approach:

war dein Vater ein Dieb? Weil er die Sterne vom Himmel gestohlen hat um sie dir in die Augen zu setzen (German) Was your father a thief? Because he stole the stars from the sky and put them in your eyes

scusa, baci gli sconosciuti? No? Allora, mi presento … (Italian) Excuse me, do you kiss strangers? No? Well, let me introduce myself …

venez voir mes estampes japonaises (French) Why don't you come up and see my Japanese prints

Hit by a basket

Not all approaches are necessarily welcome:

echar(le) los perros a alguien (Latin American Spanish) to flirt with, make a pass at someone (literally, to set the dogs on someone)

oshi no itte (Japanese) to pursue someone aggressively; to not take no for an answer (literally, pushing and pushing alone)

dostat košem (Czech) to flirt with or hit on somebody who isn't interested and turns you down (literally, to be hit by a basket)

dikupu (Setswana, Botswana) stubs or stumps of hands or legs (said teasingly by women to a man who shows no interest in them)

Octopussy

And there are some guys who just don't get the message at all:

atracador (Latin American Spanish) a person who feels up a woman; someone whose sexual advances are heavy-handed and unwelcome (literally, mugger)

ozhappu edukkaradhu (Tamil) an act of sexual harassment perpetrated against female passengers in a crowded bus or train

el pulpo (Spanish) someone who is 'all hands', who likes to touch women inappropriately (literally, octopus)

Gooseberry

However well or badly it's going, in matters of romance, two's company, but three is very definitely a crowd:

tocar el violin (Chilean Spanish) a person who uncomfortably accompanies an amorous couple (literally, to play the violin)

segurando a vela (Portuguese) to be the third wheel on a date (literally, holding the candle)

False friends

sleep (Afrikaans) girlfriend or boyfriend
titì (Tagalog, Philippines) penis
poluzzione (Italian) semen
Puff (German) brothel
spunk (Scots) a spark of fire
bite (French) penis
chain (Yiddish) charm

See-you-home wolf

Beware those for whom the habit has become more important than the object:

Schuerzenjaeger (German) someone who chases after women (literally, a hunter of aprons)

amoureux d'une chèvre coiffée (French) a man who is attracted to every woman he sees (literally, a lover of a goat whose fur is combed)

buaya darat (Indonesian) a man who fools women into thinking he's a very faithful lover when in fact he goes out with many different women at the same time (literally, land crocodile)

okuri-okami (Japanese) a man who feigns thoughtfulness by offering to see a girl home only to try to molest her once he gets in the door (literally, a see-you-home wolf)

tlazolmiquiztli (Aztec) the stench which emanates from adulterers

No sweat

For the less sophisticated, courtship can be full of confusing obstacles and hard work:

castigar (Latin American Spanish) purposely to ignore your boyfriend or girlfriend in order to heighten their yearning for you

janeleiro (Portuguese) said of one who spends a lot of time at the front window, especially a young woman who is something of a coquette

talisuyò (Tagalog, Philippines) the work done by a man to win a lady's hand

shvitzer (Yiddish) someone who sweats a lot (especially a nervous seducer)

otenkiya (Japanese) someone who blows hot and cold (literally, weatherman)

Peppery-hot

So we can only hope that sincere feeling will win the day:

cay (Vietnamese) to be peppery-hot; to have a passion for

an jemandem einen Affen gefressen haben (German) to be infatuated with someone (literally, to have eaten a monkey in someone)

ciğerimin köşesinden (Turkish) to love someone from the bottom of your heart (literally, from the corner of your liver)

avoir des atomes crochus (French) to really hit it off (literally, to have hooked atoms)

Mouth relaxation

Comes the magic moment when the mental can at last become physical:

oxsanïstïr (Khakas, Siberia) to let oneself be kissed

conk (Hindi) the imprint of a kiss

smirikin (Scots) a stolen kiss

şap şap öpmek (Turkish) to kiss by making a smacking noise with the lips

csókolgat (Hungarian) to shower with kisses

cupang (Indonesian) a love bite (literally, Siamese fighting fish)

Spider feet

Then how easy life can be:

afilar (Argentinian Spanish) to chat with your sweetheart

gemas (Indonesian) a feeling of finding something or somebody so cute that you want to squeeze or pinch it

cafuné (Brazilian Portuguese) the loving, tender running of one's fingers through the hair of one's mate (from the act of a favoured slave who picked lice out of the slavemaster's child's hair)

cwtch (Welsh) to hug and snuggle up in a loving way

faire des pattes d'araignée (French) to touch lightly with the fingertips (literally, to make spider feet)

The Paraguayan way

One thing leads to another and soon events move to a whole new level. As the Russians say, '**Snyavshi shtany, po volosam ne gladyat**', once you've taken off your pants it's too late to look at your hair:

zulana (Mambwe, Zambia) to undress one another
lapóng (Tagalog, Philippines) sexual foreplay with the breasts
ikibari (Japanese) a lively needle, if a man is willing but
  under-endowed
Notstandt (German) an emergency erection
hacerlo a la paraguaya (Chilean Spanish) to have sex standing up (literally, the Paraguayan way)
voir la feuille à l'envers (French) to have sex under a tree
  (literally, to see the leaf from underneath)
rabu hoteru (Japanese) hotels especially for making love

The little death

The Maguindanaon language of the Philippines uses the same word, **lembu**, to describe both an orgasm and the fat of animals, whereas descriptions in other languages dwell on the intensity of the experience:

şiddetli heyecan (Turkish) literally, drastic excitement
höchste Wallung (German) literally, maximum bubbling

Secrets and lies

Such compelling activity brings with it, in some societies, a whole new set of excitements and problems:

Fensterln (German) the act of climbing a ladder to a woman's window, bypassing the parents and chaperones, to have sex in the night

besengkayau (Iban, Sarawak and Brunei) to hang by the hands from a beam and move along it hand over hand (done by young men courting at night to avoid walking on the springy and creaking floor)

miàla màndry (Malagasy, Madagascar) to spend the night away from home and yet be back in the early morning as if never having been away

un petit cinq-à-sept (French) a quick five to seven o'clock (an afternoon quickie with your lover before going home to your spouse)

In Rome love will come to you suddenly

Palindromes – words and sentences that read the same forwards and backwards – have been popular since ancient times. The Germans have even come up with a palindromic word – **Eibohphobie** – that means a fear of palindromes:

a dyma'r addewid diweddar am y da (Welsh) and here is
   the recent promise about the livestock
socorram-me, subi no onibus em Marrocos (Portuguese)
   help me I took a bus in Morocco
Selmas lakserøde garagedøre skal samles (Danish)
   Selma's salmon red garage doors must be assembled
ein Neger mit Gazelle zagt im Regen nie (German) a
   Negro with a gazelle never despairs in the rain
Roma tibi subito motibus ibit amor (Latin) in Rome love
   will come to you suddenly

Thanks for the treat

In Japan, **norokeru** means to boast in an annoying way about your great relationship, while **gochisosama** is a sarcastic reply (literally, thanks for the treat). But good, bad or too-perfect-to-be-true, in reality relationships come in all varieties:

sarbo (Dutch) a person who regularly sleeps with the same partner while living separately

nanoua (Gilbertese, Oceania) a heart divided between two loves

kutzwagers (Dutch) two or more men who have slept with the same woman

stroitel' (Russian) a man who likes to have sex with two women at the same time

Fried fish enthusiasm

The Germans have come up with some very useful descriptions of the nuances of modern love:

die Bettgeschichte a one-night stand (literally, bedtime story)

das Bratkartoffelverhältnis someone who cooks and cleans in exchange for occasional affection (literally, home-fries affair)

Lückenfüller the person one dates between two serious relationships (literally, hole-filler)

Backfischschwärmerei the crush young teenage girls get for older men (literally, fried fish enthusiasm)

Faded tomatoes

Relationships come in all lengths too. If it's not going to end in marriage or a seemly long-term partnership without legal ties, there inevitably must come the brutal moment when one has to tell the other that things are no longer rosy in the garden of love:

Trennungsagentur (German) a man hired by women to break the news to their men that they are dumped (literally, separation agent)

dejar clavado a alguien (Spanish) to dump someone, to stand them up (literally, to leave someone nailed)

dostat kopačky (Czech) to be dumped (literally, to get football boots)

dar calabazas (Spanish) to jilt, ignore or stand someone up; to reject a marriage proposal (literally, to give pumpkins)

il due di picche (Italian) to be dumped (literally, the two of spades, as in the card you are given)

proshla mlyubov' zavyali pomidory (Russian) the love affair is over (literally, love is gone, the tomatoes have faded)

Once bitten, twice shy

el gato escaldado del agua caliente huye (Spanish) the cat
that has been scalded runs away from hot water

sütten ağizi yanan yoğurdu üfleyerek yer (Turkish) if hot
milk burns your mouth, you'll blow the yoghurt before you
eat it

brændt barn skyer ilden (Danish) a burned child is shy of
fire

**puganaya vorona kusta/telezhnogo skripa/sobstvennoj
teni/boitsya** (Russian) a spooked crow is afraid of a bush/a
carriage wheel's squeak/its own shadow

mtafunwa na nyoka akiona unyasi hushtuka (Swahili)
one who has been bitten by a snake startles at a reed

cão picado por cobra, tem medo de linguiça (Portuguese)
a dog that has been bitten by a snake fears sausages

7.
Family Ties

žena se plaši prvog muža, a muž
se plaši druge žene (*Serbian*)
a wife is frightened of her first husband;
a husband is frightened of his second wife

Matchmaking

Until relatively recently in the West, open relationships of a pre-marital kind were not the norm. The Dutch described unmarried couples who lived together as **hokken**, literally, living in a pigsty together. In many other parts of the world such a set-up still wouldn't even be considered. The aim of society is to get a man and woman up the aisle, round the fire, or over the threshold:

> **gökyüzünde düğün var deseler, kadınlar merdiven kurmaya kalkar** (Turkish proverb) if they say there is a wedding in the sky, women will try to put up a ladder

giftekniv (Norwegian) a person trying to get two people married

xem mat (Vietnamese) to see a candidate bride before deciding on the marriage

dulang (Manobo, Philippines) to arrange an auspicious marriage, especially between members of two opposing factions in order to bring about peace

sunkiya (Pali, India) the price paid for a wife

Objecting

Not that the young people in question always agree:

tlatlavala (Tsonga, South Africa) to refuse to marry the person selected for one by the family

kestë'shâétkë' (Mingo, USA) to object to a marriage

luyam (Manobo, Philippines) to hide one's true intentions in order to throw someone off guard so that one's real wishes can be carried out (for example, a girl who has resisted efforts to have her married then seems to change her mind so that she will not be watched, and she is thus able to run away)

Camel life

For women, at least, society could always hold the threat that they would end up alone:

ntingitihomu (Tsonga, South Africa) a girl that nobody wishes to marry

momá'kó'éné (Cheyenne, USA) having red eyes from crying because one's boyfriend got married to someone else

kurisumasu keiki (Japanese) leftover Christmas cake (traditionally applied to women over twenty-five years old)

quedar(se) a (para) vestir santos (Latin American Spanish) to be left unmarried (literally, to be left to dress figures of saints)

radudaraifu (Japanese) single women who spend much of their weekends cooking food and deep-freezing it so that it can be reheated in a hurry when they return late from work (literally, camel life)

gattara (Italian) a woman, often old and lonely, who devotes herself to stray cats

Old hat

In France the expression for an unmarried woman was even backed up by a festival. **Coiffer Sainte Catherine** meant to remain single after the age of twenty-five (literally, to put a headdress on St Catherine). From the Middle Ages, St Catherine has traditionally been the patron saint of young girls. On 25 November each year, girls would make beautiful headdresses to decorate statues of the saint. Unmarried women over twenty-five would attend a dance, wearing hats that they had made specially for the occasion, while everyone around wished them a rapid end to their spinsterhood.

Bare branches

However, since the implementation of the Chinese 'one child' policy things are changing in one part of the world at least:

> **gagung** (Cantonese) a man who has no woman because of the inequality of the gender ratio (literally, bare branches)

False friends

chosen (Yiddish) bridegroom
dig in (Armenian) wife
fear (Irish) man
he (Hebrew) she
mama (Hindi) uncle
self (Egyptian Arabic) brother-in-law
that (Vietnamese) wife

Stalker

Of course, in all societies there have always been determined suitors:

baling (Manobo, Philippines) the action of an unmarried woman who, when she wants to marry a certain man, goes to his house and refuses to leave until the marriage is agreed upon

nusukaaktuat (Iñupiat, Inuit) grabbing a wife, ensuring marriage by capturing her

Regular footing

There are all kinds of reasons why people want to tie the knot:

se ranger (French) to get married for domestic comfort and put life on a regular footing

ikabaebae (Gilbertese, Oceania) to be engaged from childhood

damoz (Amharic, Ethiopia) a temporary marriage arrangement, usually for pay, between a man who is away on his travels and a woman who is his companion or cook

casar(se) con hombre en base (Latin American Spanish) to get married when you're already pregnant

Wedding lists

Female relatives of the Swahili groom perform a ritual called **kupeka begi** (send a bag) in which they bring to the bride gifts from her husband. In response, the bride's female relations perform **kupeka mswaki** (bring the chewsticks), whereby they deliver to the groom a tray of toiletries. This is particularly important because the bride and groom are forbidden to meet before marriage.

The bride wore black

In the Tsonga language of South Africa **qanda** refers to the traditional bringing of an ox along with the bride as a symbol or guarantee of her future progeny. The ox is then eaten by her new husband's family. She is not allowed to see any part of it; if she does she should say, 'They killed my child.' If language is our evidence, this is by no means the weirdest wedding event in the world:

trá-hôn (Vietnamese) to substitute another girl for the bride
faanifin maanoo (Mandinka, West Africa) a bride wearing black (signifying that she had sex with her future husband before the ceremony)
ii/fuya (Ndonga, Namibia) strips of meat from the wedding ox wound around the arm of the bridesmaid
infar-cake (Scots) a cake broken over the bride's head as she crosses the threshold of her new home

Apron strings

Wives come in all styles:

ntshadi (Setswana, Botswana) a dear little wife

mon cinquante-pour-cent (French) wife (literally, my fifty per cent)

sokozuma (Japanese) a woman who settles for a so-so marriage just to get it out of the way

minekokon (Japanese) a woman who gives up a high-powered job in the city for a dull life in the country with a quiet husband

As do husbands:

mandilon (Mexican Spanish) a hen-pecked, oppressed husband (from **mandil** meaning apron)

stroin (Bengali) a married man who does everything and anything his wife says

tøffelhelt (Norwegian) someone who has nothing to say in a marriage or at home (literally, slipper hero)

mariteddu tamant'è un ditu lèddu voli essa rivaritu (Corsican proverb) a husband must be respected, even if he's very short

Green hat

We can only hope that neither of them has an urge to misbehave:

piniscar la uva (Chilean Spanish) to seduce a woman who's
    already taken (literally, to grab the grape)

fanifikifihana (Malagasy, Madagascar) a charm for making
    another man's wife disliked by her husband, or the hus-
    band by the wife

dài lümào (Chinese) implies that someone's wife is unfaith-
    ful (literally, wearing a green hat)

kentenga (Tsonga, South Africa) to find oneself suddenly
    without some vital item (said of a man whose only wife has
    run away, or when the roof of a hut has blown off)

Recognized

Though sometimes such potentially destructive liaisons can be
defused by being formalized:

kutua-na (Yamana, Chile) to give the second wife the place of
    the first in the wigwam

cicisbeo (Italian) an acknowledged lover of a married woman

chandek (Malay) a recognized concubine of a prince (as dis-
    tinct from **gundek**, an inferior wife, or **jamah-jamahan**, a
    casual mistress)

antis (Manobo, Philippines) a father's action, after his
    daughter's adultery, when he gives his son-in-law another
    daughter as a second wife

Three's a crowd

In some societies, of course, monogamy doesn't even exist as an ideal, throwing up a whole new set of complications:

lefufa (Setswana, Botswana) the jealousy between the wives of one man

elungan (Manobo, Philippines) to divide one's time equally between two wives who live in separate households

gintawan (Manobo, Philippines) the energy and industry of the first wife (when her husband takes an additional wife) as a result of the competition from the second wife

allupaareik (Iñupiat, Inuit) the return of a woman after a wife exchange

Hope springs eternal

In these days of **rikonmiminenzo** (Japanese), the divorce-promotion generation, things are never that simple in any case:

manàntom-bàdy (Malagasy, Madagascar) to put away a wife without divorcing her altogether

gila talak (Malay) a husband or wife who are divorced yet wishing very much to reunite

ebpamituanen (Maguindanaon, Philippines) a divorced person who keeps their figure in the hope of a future marriage

china buta (Malay) the intermediate husband a divorced Muslim woman must have before remarriage to her original husband

Workbox or housewife

Various languages have words with surprising double meanings, creating some thought-provoking associations:

mjall (Swedish) dandruff or tender
varik (Buli, Ghana) castrated or huge and strong
váram (Tamil) friendship or a week
dánamu (Telugu, India) a gift or elephant semen
ola (Samoan) fishing basket or life
panjitkori (Korean) workbox or housewife
turba (Italian) crowd or trouble
toil (Mongolian) mirror or dictionary
rooie (Dutch) carrots or ginger
saje (Hausa, Nigeria) side whiskers or a sergeant
hege' (Hebrew) steering wheel or murmur

Relative values

Let's look on the bright side. Though often derided in our fickle age, family life can bring many and varied benefits:

agusto (Latin American Spanish) the cosiness felt when snuggling with a relative

onimagu (Yamana, Chile) to feel such pity as relatives do towards each other when hurt

ka-otaba (Gilbertese, Oceania) to preserve the beauty and freshness of a daughter-in-law

dyadya (Russian) a rich relative abroad, considered as a source of money (literally, an uncle)

bombela (Tsonga, South Africa) to make free with another's belongings (especially with those of one's maternal uncle)

Dirt on the nest

Although those who hold up the family as the answer to all things are probably sadly deluded:

butika roko (Gilbertese, Oceania) a brother-in-law coming around too often

kyodai-genka (Japanese) a fight or argument between siblings

mātrigāmī (Hindi) one who commits incest with his mother

Nestbeschmutzer (German) someone ruining the reputation of the family or community (literally, someone who puts dirt on the nest)

rihorhabodo (Tsonga, South Africa) an irresponsible man who does not care for his family, but just roams around, generally in town

wićawokha (Dakota, USA) a man who lives with his wife's relations (literally, a buried man)

bayram değil (seyran değil enişte beni niye öptü?) (Turkish proverb) there must be something behind this (literally, it's not festival time, it's not a pleasure trip, so why did my brother-in-law kiss me?)

Congo confusion

As every son-in-law knows, you've got to be very careful what you say about one particular family member. In the Lokele language of the Congo there is only a tonal difference (shown by the capital letters) between **aSOolaMBA boili**, I'm watching the riverbank, and **aSOoLAMBA boIli**, I'm boiling my mother-in-law.

Auntie

In the Pakistani language of Urdu a woman is addressed in the following way:

apa (or **baji**)	by her younger sisters or brothers
khala	by her sister's children
mani (or **momani**)	by the children of her husband's sisters
ch' hachi	by the children of her husband's younger brothers
ta'i	by the children of her husband's elder brothers
p' huppi	by the children of her brother
bahu	by her parents-in-law
nani	by the children of her daughters
dadi	by the children of her sons
bhabi	by her sisters-in-law and brothers-in-law
patiji	by her aunts and uncles
sas	by her daughter-in-law
nand	by her brother's wife
sali	by the husband of her sister

Prodigal son

In Fiji, they observe the custom of **vasu** which gives a son certain powers over his mother's native place. He may take anything he covets from the houses, tear down the fruit trees, and generally behave in such a way that if he were a stranger he would be clubbed to death.

Family tree

Of course, however much you try to escape the familial bond, there's really no getting away from who you are and where you're from:

asal pagasal (Maguindanaon, Philippines) to trace family relationships among people newly acquainted with each other

anestolt (Norwegian) proud of one's ancestors

progonoplexia (Greek) bragging about one's ancestors

kupu (Hawaiian) one whose ancestors were born where he himself was born

kacang lupakan kulit (Malay) a man who refuses to acknowledge his background and forgets his family or friends once he has made a fortune for himself

Between the devil and the deep blue sea

telan mati emak, luah mati bapa (Malay) if you swallow it
your mother will die, if you throw it up your father will die

estar entre a espada e a parede (Portuguese) to be between
the sword and the wall

tussen twee vuren staan (Dutch) to be between two fires

byt mezhdu molotom i nakovalnyei (Russian) between
hammer and anvil

wählen zwischen Hölle und Fegefeuer (German) to choose
between hell and purgatory

se correr o bicho pega e se ficar o bicho (Portuguese) if
you run, the animal will catch you, if you stay it will eat you

eddyr daa stoyl ta toyn er laare (Manx, Isle of Man) between
two stools your arse is on the floor

8.
Kids

ogni scarafone è bello a mamma sua
(*Italian*)
every mother likes her own beetle

Pragmatic future

When it comes to the prospect of having children, the Japanese have brought the vocabulary firmly into the twenty-first century:

kondoumukeikaku the way in which some women over thirty-five have unprotected sex with strangers to have children

nakayoshi ninpu (buddy pregnancy) describes the act of two women deliberately getting pregnant at the same time so that they can experience childbirth together (literally, pregnancy-now plan)

shoshika a future society without children

Warped

From the moment a woman conceives, a new life has begun – for the one in the womb, obviously, but also for the mother. French metaphors take particular notice of her difference in appearance: she has **tombée sur un clou rouillé**, fallen on a rusty nail, and thus swollen; or, to put it another way, she has begun **gondoler sur la devanture**, to warp from the display window:

 ubháya-siras (Sanskrit) two-headed, a pregnant female
 ajamonarse (Spanish) used to describe a pregnant woman's
  increase in size (literally, to be like a ham)
 proglotit' arbouz (Russian) to become pregnant (literally, to
  swallow a watermelon)

Longings

She starts to feel differently too:

> **dohada** (Sanskrit) the longing of a pregnant woman for particular objects
>
> **afa-dratsiaina** (Malagasy, Madagascar) the condition of a pregnant woman who has eaten what she had a great longing for

A mark of frustration

When a Maltese pregnant woman has a wish, one should try to satisfy her, or else the baby will be born with a large mole on its face; this is known as **it-tebgħa tax-xewqa**, the wish mark.

Paternity leave

In some African tribes the men will take to their beds for the entire duration of their wife's pregnancy, while the women continue to work as usual until a few hours before giving birth. This is called **couvade** (from the French word meaning, literally, brooding or hatching). The men believe that they are cleverer and stronger than women and so are better able to defend unborn children against evil spirits. Prone in his bed, the husband simulates the pains that the wife actually undergoes. Following the birth of the child, he keeps to his bed and receives all the attentions which in other societies are bestowed upon the mother. Variations of this behaviour have been seen in such diverse places as Papua New Guinea, Bolivia and the Basque districts of Northern Spain and South-West France.

Those who comes divided

The Fon people of Benin are particularly enthusiastic about twins. All twins are regarded as separate parts of a single being so their birth signals the arrival of **mabassa**, those who comes divided. They also believe that some babies may refuse to be born. Just before birth, the elder of a set of twins is said to peek out of the womb to survey the outside world. If it determines that the world is unsafe, it returns to the womb to report to its sibling. The twins may then refuse their delivery. If one twin dies, a small wooden image of the deceased must be carried by the mother and cared for at all times. All gifts to the survivor must be duplicated: one for the living twin and one for the dead.

kœmœ (Chewa, South East Africa) the firstborn twin
embangurane (Kiga Nkore, Niger-Congo) twins of different sex

Breast water

Caring for a helpless baby has inspired some charming words around the world:

komvya (Mambwe, Zambia) to feed a child with one's finger

namaonga (Gilbertese, Oceania) to taste a little portion and chew it for a baby

ukkun (Sinhala, Sri Lanka) an expression of fondness used to infants when breastfeeding

anoka (Malagasy, Madagascar) the perfect contentment in sucking or drinking (used primarily of children or the young of animals at the breast)

ngibá (Tagalog, Philippines) a baby's tendency to cry when held by a stranger

We will rock you

In Southern Africa they certainly have ways and means of keeping a baby quiet:

kolopeka (Mambwe, Zambia) to appease a child, stop him from crying by amusing him

vundzata (Tsonga, South Africa) to turn a child's head sideways when on its mother's back or when put to sleep

pakatika (Mambwe, Zambia) to place one's own child on the lap of a companion

khan'wetela (Tsonga, South Africa) to rock a child to sleep on one's back by nudging with the elbows

halalata (Tsonga, South Africa) to throw a baby up into the air, at a ceremony of the first new moon after its birth

wo-mba (Bakweri, Cameroon) the smiling in sleep by children

Babygrow

All too soon the little creature wants to go its own way:

  abula (Setswana, Botswana) the attempt of a baby to move
    when lying on its belly
  toto-toto (Setswana, Botswana) a term of endearment to en-
    courage a baby to stand or walk
  a'matiti (Rotuman, South Pacific) to accustom a baby to cool-
    er temperatures by taking it on a walk in the early morning
  dede (Swahili) to stand uncertainly, as a child just beginning
    to walk stands when not held
  sparkedragt (Danish) a pair of rompers (literally, kicking
    suit)
  kopisata (Yamana, Chile) to get thin, like a fat baby when it
    gets older

Draggling

Despite its best intentions, it's still a long way from being
independent:

  ma-ma (Car, Nicobar Islands) 'father', 'daddy', the child's cry
    for its father
  po-po (Car, Nicobar Islands) 'mother', 'mummy', the child's
    cry for its mother
  upuss-eata (Yamana, Chile) to draggle after one, as a child, a
    long line or anything tied to a string
  pobi (Buli, Ghana) to wrap or to tie a child on one's back
  n-velekula (Kerewe, Tanzania) to swing a child round from
    the back to hip, preparatory to putting it down or feeding it

A desk job

In Malta, the baby's first year is regarded as dangerous, so the first birthday – **Il-Quccija** – is a happy event. On this day the child's future is suggested when a tray of small objects is carried in and placed on the floor. The baby is then put down and allowed to crawl in any direction it wants. What it picks up from the tray signifies its future. The traditional objects include an egg (**bajda**) for an abundance of happiness, a pen (**pinna**) for a desk job, some coins (**muniti**) for wealth, a ball (**ballun**) for sport, rosary beads (**kuruna**) for the church, scissors (**mqass**) for tailoring, a book (**ktieb**) for a lawyer, a hammer (**martell**) for a carpenter, and these days other items such as a stethoscope (for a doctor) or a CD (for a disc jockey).

Mother love

As the Nigerian saying goes, **nwanyi umu iri o dighi ihe mere nabali o naghi ama**, when a woman has ten children there is nothing that happens in the night that she does not know about:

wahdećapi (Dakota, USA) the sympathy that is said to exist between a mother and her absent children, producing peculiar sensations in the breast

songkom (Malay) to bury the face in a mother's lap (as a child)

xilandzalandza (Tsonga, South Africa) a child constantly staying close to its mother

Cuckoo

With all this vulnerability at stake, one can only pray for decent parents ...

kukushka (Russian) a mother who gives up her child to be raised by others (literally, a cuckoo)

kaelling (Danish) a woman yelling obscenities at her kids

Kinderfeindlichkeit (German) an intense dislike or disregard of children

False friends

taxi (Greek) classroom

Gymnasium (German) grammar school, high school

son (Vietnamese) to be still childless

Daughter in a box

… but not to the point where they overdo it:

onba-higasa (Japanese) a wealthy family's pampered child (literally, wet nurse and parasol)

curlingforeldre (Danish) parents who do anything to sweep the road of life ahead of their children to ensure that it is free of obstacles (literally, curling parents)

hakoiri-musume (Japanese) a young woman who has always been protected from the harsh realities of life by doting parents (literally, daughter in a box)

ser flor de estufa (Spanish) overprotected, not allowed to become independent (literally, to be a hothouse flower)

Impossible child

'The child who is one night old,' say the Arabs, 'has already learned to annoy its parents.' It doesn't stop there:

lundaezi (Lozi, Niger-Congo) to walk in the manner of a disrespectful angry child

riu' (Iban, Sarawak and Brunei) rushing about and getting in the way (especially of children)

upuk'anaana (Yamana, Chile) to throw away anything cooked, as a naughty child might throw away a fish its mother gave it to eat

bunget (Manobo, Philippines) as a child, to want something one can't have, get angry and then refuse it when it is finally offered

Dolls' house

Distractions must be found; and the Yamana speakers of Chile have several delightfully specific words to describe the making of toys for children and how they play with them:

tukau-iyana to put a foot or feet on a doll or a picture of one

utellana to make or put eyes in the head of a figure one carves or draws

tumusgaia to put down with the face upwards, as with some dolls on a table

kaiyena-na to play quietly, as a little child with a toy

manax-soatekana to play with someone else's toys

Junken a munken

But who needs toys when kids are so delightfully inventive anyway?

goagoana (Setswana, Botswana) to shout at each other in play
chottu (Tamil) a slap on the head with both hands in play
ha-lo-po (Car, Nicobar Islands) to have practical jokes played
   on one
junken a munken, a sucka sucka po, wailuku wailuku,
   bum bum show (Hawaiian Pidgin) a kids' way of deciding
   who goes first: eeny meeny miney mo

Cheese head

The years race by; things seem to change so fast:

propanach (Gaelic) a well-built boy, beginning to run about
botshegangangatswane (Setswana, Botswana) little boys
   when still at a stage when they are unabashed by their
   nakedness
kaaskop (Dutch) a very blond, rosy-cheeked child (literally,
   cheese head)
timtum (Yiddish) a beardless youth with a high-pitched voice

My sister's toenails look like my grandfather's

From 'Around the rugged rock, the ragged rascal ran' to 'red leather, yellow leather', a key part of learning a language is being able to master its tongue-twisters. They are always decidedly odd sentences. One French example featuring the s sound focuses on food:

Combien de sous sont ces saucissons-ci? Ces saucissons-ci sont six sous (How much are these sausages here? These sausages here are six cents.)

While a German tongue-twister that offers a lot of practice in the pronunciation of sch portrays a rather dangerous situation:

Zwei schwartze schleimige Schlangen sitzen zwischen zwei spitzigen Steinen und zischen (Two black slimy snakes sit between two pointed stones and hiss.)

Other favourites include:

Kuku kaki kakak kakak ku kayak kuku kaki kakek kakek ku (Indonesian) My sister's toenails look like my grandfather's.

Méla babka v kapse brabce, brabec babce v kapse píp. Zmáčkla babka brabce v kapse, brabec babce v kapse chcíp (Czech) Grandma had a sparrow in her pocket and the sparrow made a sound. Grandma pressed the sparrow and it died.

Als vliegen achter vliegen vliegen, vliegen vliegen vliegensvlug (Dutch) If flies fly behind flies, flies will fly like lightning.

Król Karol kupił Królowej Karolinie korale koloru koralowego (Polish) King Karl bought Queen Caroline a coral-coloured bead.

Saya sebal sama situ sebab situ suka senyum-senyum sama suami saya saya sehingga sekarang suami saya suka senyum-senyum sendiri sembari sama (Indonesian) I hate you because you used to smile at my husband; now he likes to smile for no obvious reason when he is with me.

Far, får får får? Nej, inte får får får, får får lamm (Swedish) Father, do sheep have sheep? No, sheep don't have sheep, sheep have lambs.

Kan-jang-kong-jang kong-jang-jang-eun kang kong-jang-jang-ee-go, dwen-jang-kong-jang kong-jang-jang-eun kong kong-jang-jang-ee-da (Korean) The president of the soy-sauce factory is president Kang and the president of the bean-paste factory is president Kong.

Learning curve

Soon enough it's time to start getting to grips with the ways and means of the adult world ...

kinder-vraag (Dutch) a childish question

ABC-Schuetze (German) a pupil in the first year of school (literally, ABC shooter)

skolplikt (Swedish) compulsory school attendance

managòana (Malagasy, Madagascar) to go over a list of names to see if all are there

ageographetos (Greek) useless at geography

katapádama (Sinhala, Sri Lanka) a lesson committed to memory

chongak (Malay) to raise the head and the chin or to do mental arithmetic in class

daoshu (Chinese) to count backwards

sonkkopta (Korean) to count on one's fingers

mushtiya (Sinhala, Sri Lanka) a fist, a closed hand (also applied to the behaviour of a teacher who withholds some knowledge from his pupils through fear that they may surpass him)

Target practice

... with all the unpleasant ordeals that that entails:

quemarse las pestanas (cejas) (Spanish) to study hard
(literally, to burn one's eyelashes (eyebrows)
nochnoe (Russian) late-night studying, as before exams
acordeón (Mexican Spanish) a crib sheet used to cheat in a
test or exam (literally, an accordion)
ponchar (Cuban Spanish) to fail an exam (literally, to get a
flat tyre)
vo chuoi (Vietnamese) to fail an exam (literally, to slip on a
banana skin)
kvarsittare (Swedish) a pupil who has not been moved up
suberidome (Japanese) a school one applies to in case one
isn't accepted elsewhere (literally, skid stopper)

Hanging out

What every parent fears is **slynaldern** (Swedish), the awkward
age, when their once innocent and biddable child starts rebelling
against their authority:

kutu embun (Malay) on the streets constantly; young people
who roam the streets at night
hangjongeren* (Dutch) groups of teenagers with nothing
to do but hang around in groups, making strange grunting
noises at passers-by (literally, hanging youth)
katoro buaka (Gilbertese, Oceania) neglectful of one's
parents or grandparents

---

* Obviously, not to be confused with **hangouderen** (Dutch), pensioners who have nothing
to do but hang around in considerable numbers in shopping malls and hamburger bars
(literally, hanging elderly)

Filial

The good parent can only hope that all their love and hard work is reciprocated:

matteyyatā (Pali, India) filial love towards one's mother

tindi (Tsonga, South Africa) to express joy at seeing one's parents (of children)

chengqi (Chinese) to grow up to be a useful person

IDIOMS OF THE WORLD

Like father like son

kakov pop takov i prikhod (Russian) like priest like church

æblet falder ikke langt fra stamen (Danish) the apple doesn't fall far from the trunk

ibn al bat 'awwam (Arabic) the son of a duck is a floater

filho de peixe sabe nadar (Portuguese) a fish's child knows how to swim

de tal palo tal astilla (Spanish) from such stick comes such splinter

hijo de tigre sale rayado (Central American Spanish) the son of the tiger turns out striped

barewa tayi gudu danta ya yi rarrafe? (Hausa, Nigeria) how can the offspring of a gazelle crawl when its mother is a fast runner?

9.
Body Beautiful

kozla boysya speredi, konya — szadi, a likhogo cheloveka — so vsekh storon
(*Russian*)
beware of the goat from its front side, of the horse — from its back side, and the evil man — from any side

Mugshot

Our face is our fortune, they say, but some are undeniably more fortunate than others:

chimmurui no kao (Japanese) a face that would stop a clock
kwabbig (Dutch) flabby pendulous cheeks
oriiti (Anywa, Nilo-Saharan) wrinkles on the forehead
papada (Spanish) a double chin
boirg (Gaelic) a small screwed-up mouth
busachd (Gaelic) the deformity of blubber-lips
bemandromba (Malagasy, Madagascar) having a large and
   ill-looking head
**avoir un oeil qui joue au billard et l'autre qui compte
   les points** (French) said of someone who is cross-eyed (literally, to have one eye that's playing billiards while the other
   is off counting the points)

False friends

ache (Bashgali, India) eye
flint (Swedish) bald head
glad (Dutch) smooth, sleek
groin (French) snout
honk (Armenian) eyebrow
mute (Latvian) mouth
pea (Estonian) head
pong (Khowar, Pakistan) foot

Gobstruck

Of course it's all too easy to spoil the appearance of what we've been given ...

vaaye-nokke (Malayalam) to stare at somebody with your mouth open (literally, mouth-see)

gaillseach (Gaelic) a large mouthful which makes the cheeks bulge out

... especially if we're putting it to good use:

kecomak-kecamik (Indonesian) to move the mouth around when eating something or saying a prayer

fújtat (Hungarian) to pant, puff and blow

menggonggong (Malay) to carry something in your mouth

ayapsun (Dakota, USA) to pull something out by the roots using the mouth

raspakhivat' varezhky (Russian) to drop one's jaw in surprise or amazement (literally, to open someone's mitten)

Lippy

With the fleshiest part of that useful opening, emotion can easily get the better of appearance:

maiskuttaa (Finnish) to smack one's lips

bibidia (Swahili) to thrust out and turn down the lower lip as a sign of derision or contempt

Tsk tsk

In many parts of the world, the tongue is not used just for speaking or eating:

tam-tac (Vietnamese) to smack the tongue as a sign of admiration

mitimiti (Rapa Nui, Easter Island) to click one's tongue as a sign of disagreement or of annoyance (tsk, tsk)

auau (Bugotu, Solomon Islands) to stick the tongue out

lamz (Persian) rolling the tongue about the mouth to pick the teeth

imel-es (Ik, Nilo-Saharan) to move the tongue in and out like a snake

Trouble gum

Americans talk disparagingly of 'English teeth', but England is not the only country in the world where dental radiance could be improved:

kasyápa (Sanskrit) having black teeth

kadadat (Sinhala, Sri Lanka) possessing only half of your original teeth

wahdatepa (Dakota, USA) to wear one's own teeth short

si gwa pau (Cantonese) someone with buck teeth (literally, watermelon shoveller)

Smiling, squirting, stripping

The Italians say, 'Teeth placed before the tongue give good advice'; and whatever your gnashers look like, you can always put them to good use:

gigil (Tagalog, Philippines) the gritting of the teeth when controlling emotion

n'wayin'wayi (Tsonga, South Africa) to smile showing the teeth

ntseka (Tsonga, South Africa) to squirt forcibly through the teeth

ki'it (Manobo, Philippines) to bite off something with the front teeth (as when eating corn on the cob)

yigul-a (Yamana, Chile) to pull out stitches with the teeth

eeti (Rapanui, Easter Island) to strip off bark or hard skin with the teeth

dona (Yamana, Chile) to take out lice from a person's head and squash them between one's teeth

dentilegus (Latin) one who picks up his teeth after they have been knocked out

Long teeth

When the French talk of aiming for the impossible, they say they are trying to **prendre la lune avec les dents**, literally, to seize the moon with one's teeth; to be very ambitious, likewise, is **avoir les dents qui rayent le parquet**, to have teeth that scratch the floor. For the Finns, to do something unwillingly is **pitkin hampain**, with long teeth; while for the Spanish, **andar con el diente largo**, walking around with long teeth, means to be very hungry.

Copping an eyeful

'The eyes are the mirror of the soul,' say the Japanese, echoing an English saying. But often it's the more mundane aspects of these organs that people worry about:

xitsavatsava (Tsonga, South Africa) the involuntary twitching of an eyelid or eyebrow

bitlisisa (Setswana, Botswana) a sore eye that has been rubbed

kuseng (Manobo, Philippines) to rub one's eyes with the back of the hand

rabun ayam (Malay) poor eyesight, especially during sunset

Bewitching

As with the teeth, our peepers are at their best when they're put to use:

gwilgat (Breton, France) to watch from the corner of one's eye
langut (Malay) to look upwards longingly
pangangalumbabà (Tagalog, Philippines) a pensive look
   (with the head supported by the palm)
ingikaranawá (Sinhala, Sri Lanka) to wink significantly
vekaveka (Luvale, Zambia) the shiftiness of eyes, looking here
   and there with madness or evil intent
temuna (Luvale, Zambia) to pull down an eyelid in mockery
embila (Maguindanaon, Philippines) to pretend to be
   cross-eyed

Cyrano

The French say that 'a big nose never spoiled a handsome face', a charitable judgement, perhaps influenced by the many fine probosci to be found in that country. But others have more serious problems than mere size:

khuranásá (Sinhala, Sri Lanka) one having a nose like a
   horse's hoof
tapíl (Tagalog, Philippines) flat-nosed
bapp-nose (Scots) a nose threatening to meet the chin
ngongò (Tagalog, Philippines) one who talks with a twang
   due to a nasal disorder
patināsikā (Pali, India) a false nose

Lughole

Big or small, flat or sticky-out, our final external organs on the head are also closely observed by our worldwide languages:

anak telinga (Malay) the external gristly portion of the ear

budálu (Telugu, India) the place where the top of the ear meets the head

ukkanna (Pali, India) having the ears erect

n'wii (Tsonga, South Africa) to have buzzing in the ears, as when under water

parece Volkswagen con las puertas abiertas (Latin American Spanish) big-eared (literally, he looks like a Volkswagen with the doors open)

Grass belong head

In the Tok Pisin language of Papua New Guinea, they call hair **gras bilong het**. Such grass may take different forms, quite apart from appearing in all the wrong places:

kesuir (Malay) hairy nostrils

gejigeji-mayuge (Japanese) bushy eyebrows (literally, centipede eyebrows)

giri-giri (Hawaiian Pidgin) the place where two or three hairs stick up no matter what

mas (Hindi) soft hair appearing above a lad's upper lip, heralding the imminent advent of youth

kapúcchala (Sanskrit) a tuft of hair on the hind part of the head (hanging down like a tail)

pédevádu (Telugu, India) a man upon whose face hair does not grow

Octopus monk

For many men age brings a related and inescapable problem:

katok (Russian) a bald patch (literally, a skating rink)

baakoodo hage (Japanese) said of a man with receding hair who combs what remains at the sides over the top of his head (literally, barcode bald, due to how it looks viewed from above)

hlohlwe (Tsonga, South Africa) a forehead with corners devoid of hair (applied to a person whose hair is receding)

tako-nyudo (Japanese) a baldy (literally, octopus monk)

Oeuf-tête

The French, in particular, have a fine range of expressions for this challenging condition:

> **avoir le melon déplumé** to have a plucked melon
> **avoir une boule de billard** to have a billiard ball
> **ne plus avoir de cresson sur la cafetière** no longer to have watercress on the coffeepot
> **ne plus avoir de gazon sur la platebande** no longer to have a lawn on the flowerbed

> **avoir la casquette en peau de fesses** to have a cap made out of buck skin
> **être chauve comme un genou** to be as bald as a knee
> **avoir un vélodrome à mouches** to have a velodrome for flies

Well-armed

We have upper and lower arms and elbows, but the Swedes have a word for the opposite side of the arm from the elbow – **armveck**. Other useful words stress the practical uses of these appendages:

kwapatira (Chichewa, Malawi) to carry something tucked under the arm
cholat (Malay) to dig with the elbow or the hand
athevotho (Bugotu, Solomon Islands) to swing the arms, wave or clear away smoke

Japanese birthdays

In the West, the birthdays that are particularly celebrated are those of coming of age: 18 and 21. In Japan, the older you get the more solemnly your birthday (**sanga**) is celebrated. The birthdays of especial importance are:

40: **shoro**, the beginning of old age, since Confucius said: 'When I was forty I did not wander.'
61: **kanreki**, the completion of the sixty-year cycle; the celebrant wears a red cap and a red kimono and is congratulated by everybody for having become 'a newborn baby once more'
70: **koki**, rare age, so called because the poet Tu Fu said that it was a privilege for a person to reach the age of seventy
77: **kiju**, long and happy life
88: **beiju**, the rice birthday

These last two birthdays gain their names from the similarity of the Japanese ideograms for 'joy' and 'rice' to those for the numbers 77 and 88 respectively.

Handy

In the Tsonga language of South Africa they have the expressive word **vunyiriri**, the stiffness of hands and feet felt on cold wintry mornings; while the Telugu language of India describes **kamikili**, the hand held with fingers bent and separated. However they're positioned, their uses are manifold:

apphoteti (Pali, India) to clap the hands as a sign of pleasure

aupiupiu (Mailu, Papua New Guinea) to flick an insect off the body

ka-cha-to-re (Car, Nicobar Islands) to hang down by one's hands

duiri (Buli, Ghana) to pass one's hands over skin so that the hairs stand up

pamamaywáng (Tagalog, Philippines) placing the hands on one's hips

geu (Bugotu, Solomon Islands) to thrust one's hand into a bag

And two are even better than one:

raup (Malay) to scoop up with both hands

anjali (Hindi) the cup-shaped hollow formed by joining the two palms together

chal (Car, Nicobar Islands) to lift up something heavy using both hands

kaf faksara (Rotuman, South Pacific) to clap the hands with one finger bent inwards to make a hollow sound

Digital

'Without fingers,' say the Moroccans, 'the hand would be a spoon.'
And where indeed would we be without our essential digits?

gamaza (Arabic) to take with the fingertips
gutól (Tagalog, Philippines) snipping with the fingernails
menonjolkan (Malay) to push one's fingers into someone's face
tstumi-oidagana (Yamana, Chile) to offer one's finger or any
    part of oneself to be bitten
sena (Sinhala, Sri Lanka) the time that elapses while snapping
    the thumb and forefinger ten times

Doigt de seigneur

In French, starting from the one nearest the thumb, you have **index**; **majeur** – biggest finger; **annulaire** – ring finger; and, last
but not least, **auriculaire** – literally, the ear finger, because it's the
only one small enough to stick in your ear. But if your digits don't
stop there, you have to go to the Luvale language of Zambia for the
sambwilo, the sixth finger or toe.

Expansive

In the Malay language, they use the space between the fingers for a
series of useful measurements:

jengkal the span between thumb and finger
jengkul the span between thumb and index finger
telunjok the span between thumb and the joint of the bent
    index finger
ketengkeng the span between thumb and little finger

Classified

Further down the body, one reaches those parts generally described as private. In Southern Africa, they appear to have thought more than most about keeping it that way:

phindzela (Tsonga, South Africa) to cover one's private parts carefully

tswi (Tsonga, South Africa) to expose one's private parts by bending forward

ikokomela (Setswana, Botswana) to look at one's own private parts

Peppers and Parasols

The Japanese have a memorable vocabulary to describe their (male) genitalia:

imo a potato, a penis that is short and fat

tōgarashi a red pepper, a penis that is small and pink

gobō a burdock, a penis that is large and tubular

kenke small, tight testicles (literally pickles)

karakasa a paper parasol, a penis that is unusually top-heavy

Map of the world

French slang uses even more elaborate metaphors. A penis is either **une anguille de calecif**, an underwear eel, or **un cigare à moustache**, a cigar with a moustache. In similarly fanciful fashion, breasts are described as **une mappemonde**, literally, a map of the world (spread across two hemispheres).

Bum deal

Round the back, it seems, we are free to be frank, especially in East Africa and the Philippines:

shuri (Swahili) a person whose buttocks stick out more than those of the average person

tuwad (Maguindanaon, Philippines) to make one's buttocks project

egkisu-kisu (Maguindanaon, Philippines) to move the buttocks little by little

pinginyika (Swahili) to move the buttocks with a circular motion when walking or dancing

Milk bottles

When it comes to the legs, English has no word to describe the back of the knee. Irish Gaelic calls it the **ioscaid**, the Swedes **knäveck**, while the Native American Dakota language calls it **hunyoka-khmin**. Other languages are similarly descriptive about both the appearance and the movement of our lower half:

euischios (Ancient Greek) with beautiful hips

melkflessen (Dutch) bare legs which have not been sun-tanned (literally, milk bottles)

kerchiholl (Albanian) having thin lower legs

anyula (Tsonga, South Africa) to open one's legs indecently

hiza ga warau (Japanese) the wobbly feeling you have in your legs after dashing up several flights of stairs (literally, my knees are laughing)

Thin as a rake

When it comes to the whole package, there are differences of opinion about how substantial you should be. In general, the modern world applauds the skinny, even as our languages hark back to a less prosperous age in their comparisons:

ser magro como um palito (Portuguese) to be as thin as a toothpick

zo mager als een lat zijn (Dutch) to be as thin as a wooden latch

po ru zhu (Mandarin) thin as paper

flaco como un güin (Cuban Spanish) thin as a sugar-cane flower

kostur slab (Macedonian) thin as a skeleton

loksh (Yiddish) a noodle, a tall thin person

Bacon buoy

While fatties come in for all kinds of criticism:

vuthikithiki (Tsonga, South Africa) body fat which shakes at every step

juyaku-bara (Japanese) a paunch (literally, company director's stomach)

tivili (Sinhala, Sri Lanka) a person with three dents in his belly (from fatness)

foca (Spanish) a very fat woman (literally, a seal)

yongzhong (Chinese) too fat and clumsy to move

gordo como una buoya (Cuban Spanish) fat as a buoy

abspecken (German) losing weight (literally, de-baconing)

fai prima a saltargli sopra che girargli intorno (Italian) it's faster to jump over him than go round him (because he's so fat)

Illusory

Not, of course, that you can always judge from appearances:

Sitzriese (German) someone who is actually quite short but
looks tall when they're sitting down (literally, sitting giant)
edtiudan (Maguindanaon, Philippines) to pretend to be lame

IDIOMS OF THE WORLD

You cannot make a silk purse out of a sow's ear

rozhdennyj polzat letat ne mozhet (Russian) if you're born
to crawl you can't fly

on ne peut faire d'une buse un épervier (French) you
can't turn a buzzard into a sparrowhawk

**al draagt een aap een gouden ring, het is en blijft een
lelijk ding** (Dutch) even if the monkey wears a golden ring
it remains ugly

fare le nozze con i fichi secchi (Italian) to celebrate a
wedding with dried figs

10.
Dressed to Kill

siku utakayokwenda uchi ndiyo siku
utakayokutana na mkweo (*Swahili*)
*the day you decide to leave your house naked is
the day you run into your in-laws*

A memorable smile

Whatever Nature has provided you with, you always have the chance to make your own improvements:

sulong (Iban, Sarawak and Brunei) to decorate the front teeth with gold (formerly brass)

nyin-susu (Bambara, West Africa) to blacken someone's gums for cosmetic purposes

pen bilong maus (Tok Pisin, Papua New Guinea) lipstick

False friends

Rock (German) skirt
veste (French) jacket
romp (Afrikaans) skirt
cilinder (Hungarian) top hat
gulp (Dutch) fly (in trousers)

Hairdressed to kill

And hair is one very obvious place for the drastic makeover:

rikuruto-katto (Japanese) a short haircut supposed to
impress prospective employers (literally, recruit cut)

wu-masweeswe (Kalanga, Botswana) shaving the hair in a
sinuous outline across the forehead

emperifollado(a) (Latin American Spanish) dressed to kill,
particularly when it involves a complicated hairdo

Topfschnitt (German) a certain haircut that looks a bit as if
the hairdresser put a saucepan on someone's head and cut
all around it (literally, saucepan cut)

Frigate

Make sure not to overdo it:

cerone (Italian) excessive make-up applied on one's face
(literally, grease paint)
itoyewaton (Dakota, USA) to wear anything that makes one
look frightful
age-otori (Japanese) formally styling one's hair for a coming-
of-age ceremony, but looking worse than before
Verschlimmerung (German) an improvement for the worse
die Fregatte (German) a heavily made-up old woman
(literally, frigate)
yubisakibijin (Japanese) a woman who spends a lot of her
salary tending to her fingernails

On reflection

Ugly beautiful

Though there are hundreds of poetic English words for different beautiful colours, there are very few for those at the less
pleasant end of the spectrum. The Ojibway of North America
say **osawegisan**, which means making something yellow with
smoke, nicotine-stained. The Pali of India have a word for the
bluish-black colour of a corpse – **vinilaka** – which literally
means resembling neither father nor mother. The Amerindian
Mingo words for the basic colours are just as evocative:

uiskwanyë'ta'ê' the colour of rotten wood (brown)
unöwö'ta'ê' the colour of limestone or plaster (white)
uyë'kwææ'ê' the colour of smoke (grey)
tsitkwææ'ê' the colour of bile (yellow)

Berlin backsides

Just because you can't see your own backside doesn't mean that others can't. The Germans certainly notice these things:

> **Arschgeweih** a large symmetrical tattoo on the lower back, just above the bottom, resembling the shape of antlers
> **Liebestoeter** unattractive underwear (literally, love killer)
> **Maurerdekoltee** a bricklayer's cleavage (the part of a man's backside you can see when he stoops deeply and his trouser waistband goes down a little bit)

Sails set

All over the world, people enjoy escaping from their intractable shape in a fine outfit:

> **kambabalegkasan** (Maguindanaon, Philippines) the act of wearing new clothes
> **sich auftakeln** (German) to get all dolled up (literally, with all sails set)
> **housunprässit** (Finnish) trouser creases
> **fifi** (Argentinian Spanish) a fashion-conscious man, dandy
> **kopezya** (Mambwe, Zambia) tipping his hat down over his eyes
> **pagalong** (Maranao, Philippines) to look at oneself in the mirror

Kangaroo teeth

Though what works in one place won't necessarily work in another:

nastā (Hindi) a hole bored in the septum of the nose
wo-kûs'-i-ûk (Maliseet, Canada) a necklace of claws
kechchai (Tamil) little tinkling bells tied to the legs
wowoodteyadla (Kaurna Warra, Australia) two or four kanga-roo teeth bound together with hair and covered with grease and red ochre, worn on the forehead by fully initiated men
okpukpu (Igbo, Nigeria) an ivory bangle worn by women with ten or more children, and sometimes by men to dem-onstrate their proven expertise
borsello (Italian) a man's handbag

Hand-me-downs

'Those who have fine clothes in their chests can wear rags,' say the Italians, but in other parts of the world it's not always true that the higher up you are in society the more likely you are to dress down:

s chuzhovo plecha (Russian) second-hand clothes (literally, from a stranger's shoulder)
kamaeieia (Gilbertese, Oceania) to wear a garment until it is in tatters
xúng xính (Vietnamese) to be dressed in oversized clothes
mabelebele (Setswana, Botswana) the rags and tatters worn by a madman, a pauper or a traditional doctor

Designer knitwear

The two extremes of women's intense relationship with clothes are chronicled by the Japanese. At one end there is **nitto-onna**, a woman so dedicated to her career that she has no time to iron blouses and so resorts to dressing only in knitted tops; and at the other there are **ippaiyoku**, women whose every garment and accessory are made by the same designer.

Fashionista

Most try to keep up with what everyone else is wearing, but there will always be some, thankfully, who remain gloriously independent:

cowichan (British Columbia, Canada) a vividly patterned sweater

buddi (Tamil) someone who wears thick glasses

lambung (Maguindanaon, Philippines) to wear very big clothes

agadagba (Igbo, Nigeria) men's underpants woven from a mix of cotton, grass and tree bark

arse gras (Tok Pisin, Papua New Guinea) a bunch of tanket leaves stuck into a belt to cover a man's backside

So village

For as long as clothes have been around, people have sneered or laughed at what others have chosen to wear:

topeewalla (Hindi) one who wears a hat, generally a European

kampungan (Indonesian) someone who is incredibly out of fashion, outdated (literally, so village)

hemdsärmelig (German) someone who behaves very rustically (literally, shirt-sleeved)

ta-oiny (Car, Nicobar Islands) clothes-wearing foreigners

samopal (Russian) home-made clothing sold under commercial labels (literally, a home-made cap gun)

Clodhoppers

Though hopefully not what they put on their feet:

gállot (Sami, North Scandinavia) a shoe made out of hide
taken from the head of a reindeer
fittocks (Scots) the feet of stockings cut off and worn as shoes
kirza (Russian) imitation leather boots
innesko (Swedish) an indoor shoe
jorg (Scots) the noise of shoes when full of water

Barely there

But then again isn't one of the most enjoyable things about dressing up coming home and stripping off?

huhu (Rapanui, Easter Island) to take off one's clothes in one
go, with a pull
byambula (Tsonga, South Africa) to walk in the open completely naked

Just make sure that when you get dressed again there's no confusion ...

vrenge (Norwegian) the action of putting right clothes which
are inside out
lopodutes (Ancient Greek) one who slips into another's
clothes
terchausser (Gallo, France) to put the right foot into the left
boot and vice versa
embasan (Maguindanaon, Philippines) to wear clothes while
taking a bath

Don't judge a book by its cover

ngam tae rup, jub mai horm (Thai) great looks but bad breath

l'abito non fa il monaco (Italian) clothes do not make the monk

quem vê caras não vê corações (Portuguese) he who sees face doesn't see heart

odijelo ne čini čovjeka (Croatian) a suit doesn't make a man

het zijn niet alleen koks die lange messen dragen (Dutch) it's not only cooks who carry long knives

II.
Stretching Your Legs

zemheride yoğurt isteyen, cebinde
bir inek taşır (*Turkish*)
*he who wants yoghurt in winter must carry a
cow in his pocket*

Travel broadens the mind, they say. But in these days of mass tourism and carbon footprints there's a lot to be said for staying exactly where you are:

> **dlanyaa** (Tsonga, South Africa) to lie on one's back with one's legs apart, gorged with food

> **lezarder** (French) to lie around basking in the sun like a lizard
>
> **bafalala** (Tsonga, South Africa) to lie face down in the sun, to lie asprawl in the open
>
> **naptakhpaya** (Dakota, USA) to lie on one's belly and rest on one's arms
>
> **ngumulo** (Tagalog, Philippines) to put both hands under the head when lying down
>
> **kagwia** (Yamana, Chile) to go upstairs and lie down

Presiding

Not that you have to remain entirely supine to relax:

sumernichat (Russian) to sit outside in the evening doing nothing

seranggong (Malay) to sit with one's elbows on the table

kem-lo-re (Car, Nicobar Islands) to sit on someone's knee

upa-nishád (Sanskrit) sitting down at the feet of another to listen to his words

mâhove'êsee'e (Cheyenne, USA) to have a tired bottom from sitting

babaran-on (Ik, Nilo-Saharan) to sit in a group of people warming up in the early morning sun

---

Go to hell

'See Naples and die' we're all told, but what do you do after you've visited these admirably named places?

Ecce Homo, Switzerland
Egg, Austria
Hell, Norway
No Guts Captain, Pitcairn Island
Saddam Hussein, Sri Lanka
Sexmoan, Philippines
Silly, Belgium
Starbuck Island, Polynesia
Wedding, Germany

Enviable

The Yamana people of Chile have clearly had plenty of time to think about the many permutations of sitting: **utapanus-mutu** is to sit by the side of a person but not close to him; **usata-ponur mutu** is to turn round and sit facing someone; **mumbu-moni** is to sit holding anything between one's lips; while **kupas-aiiua-mutu** is to sit envying a person.

Upright

If you get to your feet it doesn't necessarily mean that you're on the move:

> **pratyutthān** (Hindi) rising from a seat as a mark of respect
>
> **hó'kôhtôheóó'e** (Cheyenne, USA) to stand leaning on a cane
>
> **suka-a.-moni** (Yamana, Chile) to stand dreaming
>
> **hangama** (Tsonga, South Africa) to stand with one's feet wide apart (like a man taking up all the space before a fire)
>
> **távoeóó'e** (Cheyenne, USA) to stand looking goofy

Pedestrian

But once you've put one foot in front of the other there's really no going back:

semeioton (Greek) walking on the spot
diváviharana (Sinhala, Sri Lanka) walking about in the day time
hanyauka (Rukwangali, Namibia) to walk on tiptoe on warm sand
ha shtatin (Albanian) to walk backwards in a bowed position

Tip-tip-toe

Although this simple action comes in many different styles:

vukurukuru (Tsonga, South Africa) the noisy walk of a person in a bad temper
endal (Malay) to walk with the head and shoulders held back and the breast and stomach thrust forward
bikrang (Bikol, Philippines) to walk with the legs apart as if there was some injury to the area of the crotch
onya (Setswana, Botswana) to walk at a slow pace nodding one's head
lonjak (Malay) to walk affectedly on tiptoe
vydelyvat krendelya (Russian) to stagger, to walk crookedly (literally, to do the pretzel)
uluka (Mambwe, Zambia) a person who walks as if he were carried by the wind

The trees are blazed

Be sure you know where you're going...

> **gembelengan** (Indonesian) moving around without any certain direction
>
> **sakgasakgile** (Setswana, Botswana) to wander about like a homeless orphan

... that the way ahead is clear:

> **jimbulwila** (Luvale, Zambia) to walk in an unknown place, where there is no clear path
>
> **tlhotlhomela** (Tsonga, South Africa) to wriggle one's way through thick bush

... that you've decided whether to cover your tracks:

> **kodhola** (Oshindonga, Namibia) to leave marks in the sand when walking
>
> **kikinawadakwaidade** (Ojibway, North America) marks on the trees for the traveller to find the trail through the wood (literally, the trees are blazed)
>
> **tuuna-gamata** (Yamana, Chile) to walk over where others have walked before and thus make the tracks indistinct

... and that the conditions are suitable:

hanmani (Dakota, USA) to walk in the night
tidiwitidiwi (Kerewe, Tanzania) dragging one's steps through sand or mud
pfumbura (Shona, Zimbabwe) to walk raising dust
splerg (Scots) to walk splashing in mud
shatoka (Lozi, Niger-Congo) to jump from one stone or log to another

False friends

lost (Cornish) tail, queue
halt (Swedish) lame, limping
loop (Dutch) walk, gait
murmur (Persian) to creep
silk (Bashgali, India) to be slippery

That sinking feeling

As what could be worse than losing your footing ...

anamni (Dakota, USA) to give way under the foot (as snow does, when there is water under it)
bawela (Tsonga, South Africa) to sink away in deep mud
kawan (Manobo, Philippines) to walk on air above the ground (for example, when walking in the dark and groping for footing, to step and not find footing where you expected it)

... mistaking the ground:

péese'ov (Cheyenne, USA) to step on someone's fingers
trapu psa (Sranan Tongo, Surinam) to step on someone's feet in passing
gobray (Boro, India) to fall into a well unknowingly

... or otherwise getting into difficulties:

dungkal (Bikol, Philippines) to trip and fall head first
gadngád (Tagalog, Philippines) falling on one's nose
kaiyotan (Dakota, USA) to fall in attempting to sit down
ra (Tsonga, South Africa) to fall backwards on something hard
platzen (German) to fall over and burst
af-vegar (Old Icelandic) fallen on one's back and unable to rise
pipilili (Tsonga, South Africa) to fall and roll a few times before stopping

Beard in the postbox

Oh dear, you're back where you started:

nu sitter du med skägget i brevlådan (Swedish) now you are stuck (literally, now you are sitting with your beard in the postbox)

IDIOMS OF THE WORLD

To carry coals to Newcastle

Eulen nach Athen tragen (German) taking owls to Athens

yezdit' b Tulu s svoim samovarom (Russian) he's going to Tula, taking his own samovar

vendere ghiaccio agli eschimesi (Italian) selling ice to the Eskimos

echar agua al mar (Spanish) to throw water into the sea

es como llevar naranjas a Valencia (Spanish) it is like taking oranges to Valencia

vizet hord a Dunába (Hungarian) he is taking water to the Danube

gi bakerbarn brød (Norwegian) to give bread to the child of a baker

vender mel ao colmeeiro (Portuguese) to sell honey to a beemaster

12.
Upping Sticks

suusan tsetsnees yavsan teneg deer
(*Mongolian*)
*a travelling fool is better than a sitting wise
person*

You can't spend your whole life flopping around in one place. Sooner or later, whatever traveller's nerves you may feel, you just have to up sticks and go:

gabkhron (Boro, India) to be afraid of witnessing an adventure

resfeber (Swedish) to be jittery before a journey

andlamuka (Tsonga, South Africa) to pack up and depart, especially with all one's belongings, or to go for good

bishu (Chinese) to be away from a hot place in the summer

campanilismo (Italian) local pride, attachment to the vicinity (literally, bell tower-ism – referring to the fact that people do not want to travel so far as to be out of sight of the bell tower)

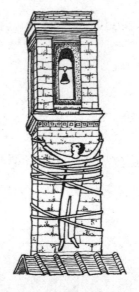

Reindeer's piss

A journey's a journey whether you are going near ...

poronkusema (Finnish) the distance equal to how far a reindeer can travel without a comfort break – about 5 kilometres (literally, reindeer's piss)
tonbogaeri (Japanese) to go somewhere for business and come right back without staying the night (literally, dragonfly's return)

... or far:

donde San Pedro perdió el guarache (Mexican Spanish) to the back of beyond; at the ends of the earth (literally, where St Peter lost his sandal)
tuwatauihaiw-ana (Yamana, Chile) to be absent a very long time and thus cease to remember or care for your country and people (as an emigrant might after a long absence)

False friends

travel (Norwegian) busy
crush (Romani) to get out
bias (Malay) deflected from its course
grind (Dutch) gravel

Wanderlust

Some people just can't wait to get going:

Tapetenwechsel (German) being bored with the place you're
in and wishing to go somewhere else (literally, let's change
the wallpaper)

echarse el pollo (Chilean Spanish) to get out of town (literally, to throw out the chicken)

amenonéhne (Cheyenne, USA) to sing while walking along

henkyoryugaku (Japanese) young women who in their
twenties and thirties rebel against social norms and travel
abroad to devote time to an eccentric art form such as
Balinese dancing (literally, studying abroad in the wild)

Tag-along

But it can get lonely out there, so consider taking a companion:

uatomoceata (Yamana, Chile) to pass your arm within another's and bring him along, as friends do

adi (Swahili) to accompany a person part of their way out of
politeness

Lebensgefahrte (German) one who travels life's road with
you

nochschlepper (Yiddish) a fellow traveller, tag-along, camp
follower, pain in the arse (literally, someone who drags
along after someone else)

ku-sebeya (Ganda, Uganda) to travel with one's husband

Wire donkey

Travel on two wheels is always economical, and can be more or less environmentally sound:

der Drahtesel (German) a bicycle (literally, wire donkey)
washa (Luvale, Zambia) a bicycle (from the sound it makes as it runs along a narrow path brushing against bushes)
stegre (Sranan Tongo, Surinam) to ride a bicycle or a motorized two-wheel vehicle on only the back wheel
bromponie (Afrikaans) a motor scooter (literally, a growling or muttering pony)

Loosely bolted

And though four wheels are faster, there is many a pitfall:

sakapusu (Sranan Tongo, Surinam) an unreliable vehicle, so called because you always need to get out (**saka**) and push (**pusu**)
galungkung (Maguindanaon, Philippines) the rattling sound produced by a loosely bolted car
der Frischfleischwagen (German) an ambulance (literally, fresh meat delivery van)
parte (Chilean Spanish) a traffic ticket; also a baptism or wedding invitation
gagjom (Tibetan) to set up a roadblock and then rob someone

Highway code

Sometimes the greatest danger on the road comes from other users:

faire une queue de poisson (French) to overtake and cut in close in front of a car (literally, to do a fishtail)

Notbremse ziehen (German) to swerve away at the last moment (literally, to pull the handbrake)

shnourkovat' sya (Russian) to change lanes frequently and unreasonably when driving (literally, to lace boots)

autogangsteri (Finnish) a hit-and-run driver

On reflection

Lucky number plates

The Chinese particularly like car number plates with 118, which is pronounced **yat yat fatt** in Cantonese and sounds like 'everyday prospers'; 1128 sounds like 'everyday easily prospers'; and 888 'prosper, prosper, prosper'. A number plate with 1164 is not popular because it sounds like **yat yat look say**, which can mean 'everyday roll over and die'.

A Hong Kong owner (i.e. a Cantonese speaker) would favour a number plate with just 32168, which sounds like **sang yee yat low fatt**, meaning 'a very profitable business all the way'.

Japanese cars can't have the licence plate 4219 because that could be read as **shi ni i ku**, which means something along the lines of 'going to death'.

Jesus's magimix

If all else fails there's always public transport (with all the delights that that entails). As the Germans say, 'We are all equal in the eyes of God and bus drivers':

gondola (Chilean Spanish) a municipal bus

Lumpensammler (German) the last train (literally, rag collector)

Luftkissenboot (German) a hovercraft (literally, air-cushion boat)

Or perhaps it's time to splash out on something special:

magimiks belong Yesus (Tok Pisin, Papua New Guinea) a helicopter

Pushmepullyou

Japanese subways are so crowded that they employ special packers to push people on and others to untangle them and get them off when they get to a station. The pushers-on are addressed as **oshiya-san** (honourable pusher) and the pullers-off as **hagitoriya-san** (honourable puller).

Unknown and uneasy

The truth is that travel is rarely as glamorous as it's portrayed. So whatever happens, keep your nerve:

far-lami (Old Icelandic) unable to go further on a journey
kalangkalang (Manobo, Philippines) to be overtaken by night on a journey with no place to stay and nothing to eat
asusu (Boro, India) to feel unknown and uneasy in a new place
bu fu shultu (Chinese) not accustomed to the climate or food of a new place (said of a stranger)
wewibendam (Ojibway, North America) being in a hurry to return home

Empty trip

And sometimes you will be surprised by unexpected rewards:

inchokkilissa (Alabama, USA) to be alone and experience the quietness of a location
uluphá (Telugu, India) supplies given to any great personage on a journey, and furnished gratis by those who reside on the route

Even if you never actually go:

kara-shutcho (Japanese) to pay or receive travel expenses for a trip not actually taken (literally, empty business trip)

Travellers' tales

Always remember that, as the French say, '**À beau mentir qui vient de loin**', travellers from afar can lie with impunity:

iwaktehda (Dakota, USA) to go home in triumph having taken scalps

IDIOMS OF THE WORLD

To beat about the bush

y aller par quatre chemins (French) to get there by four paths

iddur mal-lewża (Maltese) to go round the almond

å gå som katten rundt den varma grøten (Norwegian) to walk like a cat around hot porridge

menare il can per l'aia (Italian) to lead the dog around the yard

emborrachar la perdiz (Spanish) to get the partridge drunk

13.
Home Sweet Home

Padres, primos e pombos. Os dois primeiros, não servem para casar. Os dois últimos só servem para sujar a casa (*Portuguese*)
Priests, cousins and pigeons. The first two are not good to marry. The last two only make the house dirty

Location, location, location

'Choose the neighbour before the house' goes an old Syrian proverb; and it's as well to check out the people living nearby before you move in:

kwarts-idioot (Dutch) next door to an idiot
espreitadeira (Portuguese) a woman who spies on her neighbours
geitonopoulo/a (Greek) the boy/girl next door
buurvrouw (Dutch) a neighbour's wife
búa-grettur (Old Icelandic) a quarrel between neighbours
keba (Myanmar) a village reserved for outcasts and beggars

Nesting

If you have space and time, and hopefully some good materials, your best bet is probably to build your own:

u'skwææi (Mingo, USA) a brick (literally, cooked stone)
skvorets (Russian) a person transporting building materials to a dacha in a car (literally, a starling – with reference to nest building)
méygirathu (Tamil) to cover a house with grass, leaves, etc.
maaia (Yamana, Chile) to build wigwams here and there, as a large number of people flocking to a place will do rather than crowd into two or three existing wigwams

Pulling together

Things always work out better if you've got people to help you:

akittittuq (Iñupiat, Inuit) a stitch used for sewing a tent made by having one person on the inside while the other is outside (the one on the inside pushes the needle out so that the other person can pull the thread through; the person on the outside then pushes the needle in for the other person to pull); the same stitch is used for sewing a window into place

dugnad (Norwegian) working together in everyone's interest without getting paid (for example, moving into a house, painting, building a cabin, etc.; also applies to parents coming together to paint a kindergarden, or everyone in an apartment building cleaning inside and outside the house together)

imece (Turkish) a social gathering at which everyone pitches in to help a neighbour undertake a large task

False friends

abort (German) lavatory
bang (Korean) room
dig (Gaelic) ditch
sir (Arabic) crack of the door
gate (Norwegian) street
rub (Croatian) edge

Flagging the beam

In Surinam, when the main roof beam of a new house is in place they have a celebration they call **opo-oso**, at which a flower or flag is nailed to the end of the beam, some beer is sprayed on the front of the building and then the builders, owner and others have a drink to celebrate.

Dutch decor

The Dutch have two useful expressions: **kneuterig** describes a particularly bourgeois type of stinginess which someone might display if they spent a fortune buying a new house and then furnished it with the cheapest fittings available, all in the name of saving money; and its opposite **een vlag op een modderschuit**, excessive decoration of a common thing, or trying to make the ugly beautiful (literally, a flag on a mud barge).

Chinese whispers

It is an increasingly common practice to transliterate foreign proper nouns into Chinese characters that sound similar to the original word but give the Western name a highly positive connotation to Chinese ears:

adian	Athens	proper law
zhili	Chile	wisdom benefit
deli	Delhi	virtue hometown
faguo	France	method country
henghe	Ganges	everlasting river
haiya	The Hague	sea tooth
ingguo	England	country of heroes
lundun	London	matching honest
meiguo	America	beautiful country
niuyue	New York	bond agreement
taiguo	Thailand	peaceful country

378   I Never Knew There Was a Word For It

Frog in a well

The Germans have the wonderful word **Gemütlichkeit** for that particular quality of cosiness you can only ever feel at home. In that always-descriptive language, someone who prefers to stay at home is a **Stubenhocker**, literally, a room sitter; and in the end, however splendid the house, it's our intimate individual eyries we actually spend our time in:

pung (Iban, Sarawak and Brunei) to keep to one's room
sucilwa (Mambwe, Zambia) a man who never leaves his hut (literally, all smoked up)
kúpa-mandúka (Sinhala, Sri Lanka) one who never leaves his home, one ignorant of the world (literally, a frog in a well)

The emperor's throne

Different cultures have very different approaches to what we euphemistically call the smallest room in the house. The Spanish have **excusado**, with its polite suggestion of excusing yourself, whereas the German term **wo sogar der Kaiser von China allein hingeht** literally means 'where the emperor of China goes by himself'. Once there, though, we all go through the same motions:

engkilu' (Iban, Sarawak and Brunei) sticks or leaves used as toilet paper
zasedat' (Russian) to sit on the toilet for a long time (literally, to preside)

Toilet museum

Some insist on trying to make us forget why we're there at all:

toirebijutsukan (Japanese) a trend whereby young women moving into an apartment alone for the first time will go to extreme lengths to decorate their lavatory, scent it with perfume and stock it with interesting literature (literally, toilet museum)

Spatially aware

We all know these domestic places and spaces; but not all languages have such precise words for them:

bakatoo (Mandinka, West Africa) the space between the bed and the wall

izungu (Mambwe, Zambia) the space between the bed and the ground

caukā (Hindi) a clean corner in the kitchen for having meals; a rectangular slab of stone

Giftschrank (German) a cupboard where things are kept that may only be lent out to someone with special permission (literally, poison cabinet)

antardvār (Hindi) a private door inside a house

rincón (Spanish) the internal corner (the external corner is **esquina**)

Besucherritze (German) the gap where the middle of three people lies when two single beds are pushed together (literally, a visitor's trench)

Crumb thief

The same is true of the clutter we fill our rooms up with; until, as the Russians say, '**Igolku nygde votknut**', there's nowhere you can throw a needle:

dur dicki mengri (Romani) a telescope (literally, far-seeing-thing)

hap laplap bilong wasim plet (Tok Pisin, Papua New Guinea) a dish cloth

kruimeldief (Dutch) a hoover (literally, a crumb thief)

Staubsauger (German) a vacuum cleaner (literally, dustsucker)

yötwënukwastahkwa' (Mingo, USA) radio (literally, people use it for spreading their voice out)

dinnilos dikkamuktar (Romani) television (literally, fool's looking box)

Flimmerkasten (German) television (literally, flickering box)

Whatever our circumstances, in the end, perhaps, we should just be grateful that we are **á-panna-griha** (Sanskrit), someone whose house has not fallen in.

To make a mountain out of a molehill

tehdä kärpäsestä härkänen (Finnish) to make a bull out of
a fly

se noyer dans un verre d'eau (French) to drown oneself in a
glass of water

til ka taad banaana or **rai ka pahaad banana** (Hindi) to
turn a sesame seed into a large tree or to turn a mustard
seed into a mountain

arcem e cloaca facere (Latin) to make a stronghold out of a
sewer

narediti iz muhe slona (Slovenian) to make an elephant
from a fly

14.
Dinner Time

**kopeklerin duası kabul olsa gökten
kemik yağardı** (*Turkish*)
*if dogs' prayers were accepted it would rain
bones from the sky*

Rushed breakfast

When it comes to eating there is, of course, no such thing as a typical meal:

munkavacsora (Hungarian) a working dinner
kamatuao (Gilbertese, Oceania) a meal for one who wakes during the night
bulunenekinoo (Mandinka, West Africa) the first meal cooked by a bride
ottobrata (Italian) a country outing or picnic in October
hwyaden (Welsh) the small amount of breakfast a newly married man has time to eat when leaving home for work after intimacy with his new wife (literally, a duck)

My tapeworm is talking

And there are still many parts of the world where you can't take any kind of refreshment for granted:

kemarok (Malay) ravenously hungry after an illness
hiukaista (Finnish) to feel hungry for something salty
paragadupu (Telugu, India) the state of the stomach before a person has broken his fast
fulumizya (Mambwe, Zambia) to cook quickly for somebody who is very hungry
étaomêhótsenôhtóvenestse napâhpóneehéhame (Cheyenne, USA) being very hungry (literally, my tapeworm can almost talk by itself)

Sampling

Particular skills are often required to make sure you've got the very best of the ingredients available:

kupit' arbuz navyrez (Russian) to buy a watermelon with the right to sample a section
pale (Scots) to test a cheese by an incision
athukkugirathu (Tamil) to press a fruit softly with the fingers

Stirring it up

And then time must be taken to get things correctly and thoroughly prepared:

jiigi (Buli, Ghana) to stir with much energy, to prepare a hard food that cannot be stirred with one hand
ri-noo-ko che-he-kuo (Car, Nicobar Islands) chopping up with spoons and forks
tikudeni (Maguindanaon, Philippines) to put the correct amount of rice into a pot to be cooked
loyly (Finnish) the wave of heat that engulfs you when you throw water on the hot stove

Surprise water

Now is the moment when a cook's individual skills can make all the difference to the end result. As the Chinese wisely say, 'Never eat in a restaurant where the chef is thin':

tliwat (Tagalog, Philippines) to pour a liquid several times between containers to mix or cool it well

bikkuri mizu (Japanese) a small amount of cold water added to a boiling pot of spaghetti or other noodles just before they are cooked (literally, surprise water: i.e. the cold water surprises the noodles)

ilas-ana (Yamana, Chile) to cut and spread meat open so that it cooks quicker

tuyong (Tagalog, Philippines) water added to make up for water lost (in cooking)

Dead dog

'Hunger is the best cook,' say the Germans, and it's true that when you're starving even the lightest snack will taste as good as anything you've ever eaten:

smörgås (Swedish) a sandwich (literally, butter goose)

ekiben (Japanese) a packed lunch dispensed from station kiosks

dokhlaya sobaka (Russian) a low-quality frankfurter (literally, a dead dog)

Xoox

For the fuller meal, what fine and varied ingredients the world offers:

jordgubbe (Swedish) a strawberry (literally, earth man)
ah (Arabic) egg white
xoox (Eastern Arabic) plums
sneisar-hald (Old Icelandic) the part of a sausage in which the pin is stuck
tsé-péene éškôseeséhotamého'évohkôtse (Cheyenne, USA) a pork sausage

Slug in the hole

Some ingredients might not be to everyone's taste:

lelita' (Iban, Sarawak and Brunei) an edible slug of the swampland
nido (Tagalog, Philippines) an edible bird's nest
brarah (Hebrew) second-rate fruits (specifically oranges)
kavavangaheti (Tsonga, South Africa) a dead animal so large that people cannot finish its meat (for example, hippo, whale or elephant)
cilh-vāns (Hindi) the flesh of a kite (the eating of which is said to produce madness)
mmbwe (Venda, South Africa) a round pebble taken from a crocodile's stomach and swallowed by a chief

Cabbage or cheese

The Italians even approve or disapprove in terms of food:

come i cavoli a merenda totally out of place, inappropriate (literally, like cabbage for a snack)

come il cacio sui maccheroni perfect (literally, like cheese on pasta)

Your legs are long

The actual nosh itself is only part of it. Company is equally important, and in many parts of the world you simply have no idea who's going to show up:

pakiroki (Rapanui, Easter Island) a pauper who comes to someone else's house hoping to be invited to eat

jiao chang (Chinese) your legs are long (said of someone who arrives just as something delicious is being served)

a la suerte de la olla (Chilean Spanish) to arrive at someone's house not knowing what food they will be offering (literally, to the luck of the pot)

bufeťák (Czech) a guy who hangs around cafeterias and eats leftovers

xenodaites (Ancient Greek) a devourer of guests or strangers

Say cheese

When trying to catch a person's attention and have him/her look into the lens, the old Czech photographers' phrase was **pozor, vyleti ptacek**, which literally means 'watch out, a bird will be released/fly out' (from the camera). In Serbia, people are asked to say **ptica**, 'bird'. Danish photographers have a variety of phrases they can use, but their favourite is **sig appelsin**, 'say orange'.

The English word cheese is often used because pronouncing it shapes the mouth into a smile. Other languages have adopted this method, with different words that have a similar sound or effect:

kimchi (Korean) a traditional fermented dish made of seasoned vegetables
qiezi (Mandarin) aubergine
cerise (French) cherry
whisky (Argentinian Spanish)

In Malta, people sometimes jokingly say **ġobon**, their word for cheese, which will obviously result in the exact opposite facial expression.

Gobbling it down

Sometimes your guests are so busy filling their faces that they forget about the politer aspects of sharing a meal:

fresser (Yiddish) someone who eats quickly and noisily

physingoomai (Ancient Greek) to be excited by eating garlic

qarun (Persian) someone who eats two dates or two mouthfuls at once

bwakia (Swahili) to throw into the mouth (for example, pieces of food, nuts, tobacco)

komba (Chewa, South East Africa) to scrape a pot or dish with the forefinger, as children do

pelinti (Buli, Ghana) to move very hot food around inside one's mouth to avoid too close a contact

ikok (Ik, Nilo-Saharan) to knock bones together in order to take out and eat the marrow from inside

waphaka (South African Township) to eat faster than the rest

Miss Manners

Scoffing too fast can be just the start of the problem:

buttare giu tutto come un lavandino (Italian) to eat like a pig (literally, to throw down everything as if one were a sink)

muwel (Manobo, Philippines) to fill the mouth so that one cannot talk

hdaśna (Dakota, USA) to miss when putting food into one's mouth

xom-xoàm (Vietnamese) to speak while one's mouth is full

roic (Gaelic) the sumptuous feasting by boorish people without any of the refined manners of genteel society

---

False friends

sky (Swedish) gravy

tuna (Tuvaluan, Polynesia) prawn or eel

binlíd (Tagalog, Philippines) small broken particles of milled rice

dark (Albanian) evening meal

fig (Caribbean Creole) banana

Slow Food

So, instead, take your time and fully savour the experience:

fyompola (Mambwe, Zambia) to lick honey off the fingers
pisan zapra (Malay) the time needed to eat a banana

Menu envy

For some, the salad next door is always greener:

Futterneid (German) the desire to eat what is on another
person's plate (literally, feeding envy)
lyu mupusulo (Mambwe, Zambia) to eat so as to cheat
another out of his share of food
selongkar (Malay) to steal food off a plate
gagula (Tsonga, South Africa) to take food without permission, showing a lack of good manners

Picky

Others could do with feeling a bit hungry once in a while:

kieskauw (Dutch) a person who trifles with his food
malastigà (Tagalog, Philippines) being bored of eating the same food all the time
Krüsch (northern German) somebody who dislikes a lot of foods (and is therefore difficult to cook for)

My mouth is lonely

And some greedy pigs just don't know when to stop:

amuti (Rapanui, Easter Island) a glutton; someone who will eat anything, such as unripe or out-of-season fruit
akaska (Dakota, USA) to eat after one is full
ngang da (Vietnamese) to lose one's appetite because one has eaten between meals
kuchi ga samishii (Japanese) eating when you don't need to, for the sake of it or out of boredom (literally, my mouth is lonely)
knedlikový (Czech) rather partial to dumplings
hostigar (Chilean Spanish) to gorge on sweets to the point of nausea

Angel cake

In the end, though, it's all in the eye – or rather mouth – of the beholder. For better ...

alsof er een engeltje op je tong piest (Dutch) utterly delicious, heavenly tasting (literally, as if an angel is urinating on your tongue)

kou fu (Chinese) the good luck prerequisite for having opportunities to eat delicious food (literally, mouth fortune)

... or worse:

panshey (Bengali) food that tastes rather flat

ichootakbachi (Alabama, USA) to leave a bad taste in the mouth

tomatoma (Mailu, Papua New Guinea) tasteless food

pikikiwepogosi (Ojibway, North America) having the taste of an animal that was tired out before it was killed

tsitlama (Setswana, Botswana) to make a wry face after eating or drinking something nasty

Restaurant review

Tired of cooking at home, not to mention doing the washing-up and putting-away, we may tell ourselves how nice it is to eat out. But though the fantasy is great, the reality is often less so:

Schlürfbude (German) a fast-food restaurant (literally, slurp dump)
dolorosa (Spanish) a restaurant bill (literally, painful)
Abendteuer (German) an expensive evening (literally, an adventure)

The condemned man is a final meal

Possibly the strangest takeaway of all is described by the Russian word **korova**: this is the unfortunate person that prison camp escapees take with them to eat over their period of flight and in their hideout (it literally means 'a cow').

Too many cooks spoil the broth

sendou ooku shite fune yama ni noboru (Japanese) too
many captains and the boat will go up a mountain

qi shou, ba jiao (Chinese) seven hands, eight feet

idha kathira ar-rababina gharigat as-safina (Arabic) too
many captains sink the ship

zo mangna go lhong mi tshu (Dzongkha, Bhutan) when
there are too many carpenters the door cannot be erected

**seul mui à vugulion a vez, e vez falloc'h gouarnet ar
saout** (Breton, France) the more cowherds there are, the
worse the cows are looked after

puno baba, kilavo dijete (Croatian) with many midwives,
the child will be lazy

veel varkens maken de spoeling dun (Dutch) many pigs
make the slops sparse

zyada jogi math ujaad (Hindi) too many saints can ruin the
monastery

troppi galli a cantar non fa mai giorno (Italian) with too
many cocks singing it is never going to dawn

zuun yamaand jaran uhana (Mongolian) one hundred
goats for sixty billy goats

**u pyati nyanek dyetya byez glaza, u cemyorykh – byez
golovy** (Russian) when there are five nurses the child loses
an eye – with seven nurses the child is finally found to lack
a head

haber más capeadores que toros (Costa Rican Spanish)
there are more bullfighters than bulls

15.
One for the Road

fra børn og fulde folk skal man høre
sandheden (*Danish*)
*from children and drunks you will hear the
truth*

The towel of a hippy

The quenching of thirst is another sensation that brings out evocative descriptions. In Chilean Spanish they say they are **tener mas sed que piojo de muneca**, thirstier than a louse on a doll; or again, in more contemporary usage, **toalla hippy**, than the towel of a hippy:

tarfa (Hausa, Nigeria) to pour out drop by drop
gargalacar (Portuguese) to drink from the bottle
funda (Swahili) to fill the mouth with water until the cheeks are distended
srann (Gaelic) a drink as deep as one's breath will permit
ngalela (Setswana, Botswana) to drink and drain the contents of a container in one go
avoir la dalle en pente (French) to have the throat on a slant (in order to be able to drink constantly)

The milky way

The men of the African Toubari and Massa tribes observe a rite called **gourouna** in which they retire for several months from ordinary pursuits and restraints and drink prodigious amounts of milk.

Social drinking

No one should **boire en Suisse** (French), drink alone in secret (literally, drinking in the Swiss way). It's always healthier to share the experience:

gonets (Russian) one sent to buy alcohol for friends (literally, a herald)

chistra (Breton, France) to go from farm to farm and ask for cider

cayetanas (Mexican Spanish) a code word for apple cider disguised in a beer bottle, ordered by cabaret hostesses who don't want to get drunk

afdrinken (Dutch) let's have a drink and be friends

glaoch (Irish) the act of calling for a round of drinks at a pub

Bob (Dutch) the designated driver, the one who sticks to one beer and drives everybody home from wherever they've been partying (Bob was the name used originally in a famous anti-drink-drive campaign)

Altered states

Soft drinks will satisfy our thirst, but are never as exciting as those which are a bit stronger. It's surely no coincidence that most of the best words about drinks and drinking involve alcohol. As the literal meaning of the Amerindian Mingo word for alcohol, **teka'niköëtényös**, has it, it changes minds from one way to another: whether it's beer you're drinking ...

> **sampa** (Rukwangali, Namibia) to taste beer with one's finger
> **bufferbiertje** (Dutch) the beer that is standing next to the beer you're drinking and serves as a buffer in case you finish drinking your beer before you have a chance to get the barman's attention (literally, buffer beer)
> **der Diesel** (German) a mixture of beer and cola

To your good health?

Around the world the commonest drinking toast is to good health: **Na zdravje** (Slovenian), **Salud** (Spanish), **Saúde** (Brazilian Portuguese), **Kia Ora** (Maori), **Egészségedre** (Hungarian), **Gezondheid** (Flemish). The Ukrainians take this to the next level with **Budmo!**, which means 'let us live forever!'

In contrast, the Scandinavian drinking toast **Skål!** (pronounced 'skoal') has a much more macabre background, as it originally meant 'skull'. The word is alleged to have come down from a custom practised by the warlike Vikings who used the dried-out skulls of their enemies as drinking mugs.

... or something rather more powerful:

Dreimännerwein (German) a wine so disgusting it takes
three men to drink it (two men to make you drink it – you
are the third)

kadamsana (Malawi) a very strong home-made spirit (literally, that which brings darkness during the day – aptly
describing its knock-out effects)

Vodka vocabulary

The Russians, in particular, have a fine set of words for the many styles of tippling:

pogoda shepchet to take time off from work, or a desire to get drunk (literally, the weather is whispering)

bukhat' to drink alone

deryabnut' to drink quickly in order to warm up

gorlo to drink from the bottle

vspryskivat' to drink in celebration of a holiday or a new purchase (literally, to besprinkle)

daganyat' sya to drink in order to get drunk, to try to catch up with the amount of drinking that others have already done

otglyantsevat' to drink beer or wine after vodka (literally, to gloss a photo print)

ostogrammit'sya to drink 100 grams of vodka as a remedy for a hangover

False friends

full (Norwegian) drunk

grogi (Finnish) whisky and soda

pickle (Chilean Spanish) a person who drinks too much

jaw (Zarma, Nigeria) to be thirsty

On a slippery road

And all languages have evocative expressions for being drunk ...

sternhagelvoll (German) full of stars and hail
rangi-changi (Nepalese) slightly too multi-coloured
être rond comme une bille (French) to be as round as a
  marble
redlös (Swedish) ride free
andar cacheteando la banqueta (Mexican Spanish) to go
  along with one's cheek on the pavement

... and for the inevitable results of overdoing it:

khukhurhuteka (Tsonga, South Africa) to walk uncertainly,
  as a drunk man among people seated on the floor
midàbodàboka (Malagasy, Madagascar) to fall over frequently, as drunken men or people on a slippery road
mawibi (Ojibway, North America) drunken weeping
Backhendlfriedhof (Austrian German) a beer belly (literally,
  cemetery for fried chickens)
ne govori ou samoi muzh piatnisa (Russian) a shrug of
  understanding when sharing someone else's problems
  (literally, no need to explain, my husband is a drunk)

Under the monkey

For the French you are as sober as **un chameau** (a camel) but as drunk as **un cochon** (a pig), **une grive** (a thrush), or even **une soupe** (a soup). In Lithuanian you can also be drunk as a pig (**kiaulė**), or then again as a bee (**bitelė**) or a shoemaker (**šiaučius**). Elsewhere you can be **drvo pijan** (Macedonian) drunk as a tree; **jwei ru ni** (Mandarin) drunk as mud; **orracho como una uva** (Cuban Spanish) drunk as a grape; **bull som en kaja** (Swedish) drunk as a jackdaw; **itdek mast** (Uzbek) drunk as a dog; or **einen Affen sitzen haben** (German) to be dead drunk (literally, to have a monkey sit on one).

The morning after

It's only when you get home that you may start to wonder what on earth possessed you:

rhwe (Tsonga, South Africa) to sleep on the floor without a mat and usually drunk and naked

gidravlicheskiy budil'nik (Russian) a full bladder (literally, an hydraulic alarm clock)

sasamudilo (Ndebele, Southern Africa) a drink of beer in the morning after a debauch, a pick-me-up

peregar (Byelorussian) the residual taste of alcohol in the mouth and the heavy stench of low-grade alcohol around a habitual drinker

Vineyard flu

And all drinking cultures have inventive expressions for the horrors of the morning after:

avoir la gueule de bois (French) to have a wooden mouth

babalasi (Venda, South Africa) a trembling hangover

futsukayoi (Japanese) a hangover (literally, second day drunk)

winderdgriep (Afrikaans) a hangover (literally, vineyard flu)

einen Kater haben (German) to have a hangover (literally, to have a tomcat)

scimmia (Italian) to have a hangover (literally, a monkey)

IDIOMS OF THE WORLD

Don't cry over spilt milk

paid â chodi pais ar ôl piso (Welsh) don't lift a petticoat after peeing

kusat sebe lokti (Russian) to bite one's elbows

nasi sudah menjadi bubur (Indonesian) the rice has become porridge

eső után köpönyeg (Hungarian) coat after rain

16.
All in a Day's Work

yesli khochetsya rabotat' lyag pospi
i vsyo proydyot (*Russian*)
*if you feel an urge to work take a nap and it
will pass*

Pounce and decoy

Time was when going out to work meant leaving the cave or hut to forage for food:

mbwandira (Chichewa, Malawi) to catch a small animal like a bird or mouse by pouncing on top of it

puyugaktuq (Iñupiat, Inuit) to approach a sea mammal by crawling

tamigata (Yamana, Chile) to form together in a continuous line in order to drive birds up into a creek and then hemming them round to cut off their retreat to the open water

kanghanzila (Mambwe, Zambia) he who stands behind the game and imitates the lion's roar so as to drive the game into the nets

sendula (Mambwe, Zambia) to find accidentally a dead animal in the forest (and be excited at the thought that a lion or leopard could be still around)

walakatla (Tsonga, South Africa) to fling down in disgust, as a hunter does with his spears when returning empty-handed

Point blank

In our rapidly developing world, this is obviously less and less the case, as age-old skills are replaced by a more up-to-date weapon:

paltik (Kapampangan, Philippines) a home-made gun

otselask (Estonian) a point-blank shot

tsikinika (Oshindonga, Namibia) to shoot something at close range

Dodo

Even if the matching cunning of animals remains much the same:

debideboo (Mandinka, West Africa) a bird which pretends not to be able to fly but slips away any time an attempt is made to catch it

kavraq (Iñupiat, Inuit) a wounded caribou that runs away unobserved

ugutur-kona-ina (Yamana, Chile) to go about on the water evading sight; to hide as ducklings or goslings do to evade the hunter

vulwa-vulwa-vulwa (Tsonga, South Africa) to run a little, stop and look round before proceeding, like a buck anxious not to be seen

Spear hurling

Out on the seas and oceans, however, the traditional tools of hook and net have not been seriously superseded; nor have the associated skills:

zekumuna (Luvale, Zambia) to pull out a fish which flies off the hook and falls onto the ground

alatkaqtuq (Iñupiat, Inuit) to scan the landscape from an elevated point, to look into water for signs of fish

ukomona (Yamana, Chile) to hurl the spear at fish, but at no special one, hoping to spear one among the shoal

wasswa (Ojibway, North America) spearing fish at night by the light of a torch

Eel dribbling

In the countless islands of the Pacific, such techniques have been carefully honed:

kikamu (Hawaiian) the gathering of fish about a hook that they hesitate to bite

atua tapa (Rapanui, Easter Island) the orientation point for fishermen, which is not in front of the boat, but on the side

hakakau (Hawaiian) to stand with precarious footing, as on the edge of a canoe looking for squid

'ea'ea (Hawaiian) to cover the eyebrows, as a fisherman shading the eyes while looking into deep water for fish

ka ro'iro'i i te koreha (Rapanui, Easter Island) to dribble on the eel, to drop your spittle, mixed with chewed bait, into the water to attract the eel

Sea women

In Japan, abalone fishing is often done in husband and wife teams. The women, who are thought to be better at holding their breath and withstanding the cold for long periods, do the pearl diving, while the husbands take charge of the boat and the lifeline. The wives are known as **ama** – 'sea women'.

Bamboo cutters

Once the world moved on from hunting and gathering, a degree of occupational specialization was bound to creep in:

baradi'l (Arabic) a maker of donkey saddles

murd-shuy (Persian) a washer of dead bodies

ngmoruk-yaaroaba (Buli, Ghana) a ritual rain-maker

médara (Telugu, India) belonging to the caste that cut bamboos and live by selling them

gardziiba (Tibetan) an astrologist or a person in charge of the cups and dishes during parties

bakamyi (Rwanda and Burundi dialect) a person credited with supernatural powers who milked the royal cows

Mekametz (Talmudic Hebrew) a man who gathers dog faeces so that he may hand them over to the **Burskai**, men who process animal skins

Angel makers

As societies became more developed, so jobs became more rarified ...

netty (Scots) a woman who traverses the country in search of wool

sunba (Tibetan) someone who looks after irrigation canals

bagaceiro (Portuguese) a workman who feeds sugar-cane husks into a furnace

poppendokter (Dutch) a mender of dolls (literally, a doll doctor)

catadeira (Portuguese) a woman who culls coffee beans by hand

faiseur d'anges (French) an illegal abortionist (literally, an angel maker)

paçaci (Turkish) a man who sells sheep's trotters

khãndika (Sanskrit) a seller of sugar plums

bengaleiro (Portuguese) an umbrella maker or salesman

False friends

trafik (Hungarian) tobacconist

agenda (French) notebook, diary

basin (Turkish) the press

fabric (Russian) factory

pasta (Portuguese) briefcase, folder

Soul plumbers

... until we end up with occupations that are entirely sophisticated and modern:

amanuensis (Dutch) a laboratory attendant

arquitonto (Central American Spanish) a stupid architect

basura (Spanish) rubbish inspectors

dal'noboishitsa (Russian) a prostitute who specializes in a clientele of truckers

değnekçi (Turkish) an unofficial/self-appointed parking attendant

Seelenklempner (German) a psychiatrist (literally, a soul plumber)

culero (Spanish) a drug smuggler who hides the drugs in his rectum

jasusa (Arabic) a woman spy

profesores taximetros (Columbian Spanish) part-time professors who hold a number of teaching positions at various institutions from and to which they rush by taxi (literally, taxicab professors)

Hippopotomonstrosesquipedalianism (the practice of using long words)

The Germans are renowned for their love of long words where several words are compounded to form an extremely specific word, often to do with the world of work, such as:

Donaudampfschifffahrtsgesellschaftskapitänsjacken-knopfloch the buttonhole in the jacket of a captain of the Danube steam boat company

or **Reichseisenbahnhinundherschiebershäuschen** the little house of the state railway track shunter

But other languages also have their own lengthy words:

megszentségtelenithetetlenségeskedéseltekért (Hungarian) for your unprofaneable actions

kindercarnavalsoptochtvoorbereidingswerkzaamheden (Dutch) preparation activities for a children's carnival procession

inconstitucionalissimamente (Portuguese) very unconstitutionally

prijestolonaslijednikovica (Croatian) wife of an heir to the throne

Low profile

Of course, to do a job properly, certain key skills are useful:

aprovechar (Spanish) to get the best out of or make the most
of an opportunity

diam ubi (Malay) to work quietly or with a low profile until
successful

kamgar (Persian) one who accomplishes whatever he wishes

dub-skelper (Scots) one who goes his way regardless of mud
and puddles (used light-heartedly of a young bank clerk
whose duty it is to run about giving notice that bills are
due)

coyote (Mexican Spanish) a person who handles certain trou-
blesome legal procedures at government agencies on behalf
of third parties and for a fee, by means of kick-backs and/or
bribes (literally, coyote, a wolflike wild dog)

Horn diggers

However, we should never underestimate the virtue of good, old-fashioned graft:

> **greadan** (Gaelic) spending a considerable time and giving all one's might to anything
>
> **balebosteven** (Yiddish) to bustle like a meticulous housewife
>
> **ryt' rogom zemlyu** (Russian) to make great efforts (literally, to dig up the ground with one's horn)
>
> **echar la casa por la ventana** (Latin American Spanish) to go all out (literally, to throw the house out of the window)

> **sisu** (Finnish) obstinate determination, heroic guts, stubborn persistence
>
> **dumog** (Tagalog, Philippines) to be absorbed in the fulfilment of one's task

Mice milkers

Even so, diligence isn't everything. There are some poor workers who bust a gut but fail to please simply because they can't see the bigger picture. The French describe this as **chercher midi à quatorze**, literally, to look for midday at two o'clock in the afternoon. To the Dutch, a person who pays excessive attention to detail is a **mierenneuker** – literally, an ant fucker; or, more charitably, a **muggenzifter** (mosquito sifter) or a **punaisepoetser** (pin polisher). But all cultures are colourful in their criticism:

Erbsenzaehler (German) someone concerned with small things (literally, counter of peas)

pilkunnussija (Finnish) an extreme pedant (literally, comma fucker)

taburaka (Gilbertese, Oceania) one who exaggerates rules and regulations, a stickler for the letter of the law

Mäusemelker (German) someone who eagerly concentrates on the nitty-gritty rather than the wider overview (literally, someone who milks mice)

gladit' shnurki (Russian) to be over-solicitous, to do too much (literally, to iron someone's shoelaces)

Jobsworth

Other colleagues bring other problems:

Schnarchnase (German) someone who is slow in acting (literally, snoring nose)

pezezengdeng (Manobo, Philippines) to be spoken to but sit motionless and ignore their request

reke (Yoruba, Nigeria, Benin and Togo) to wait in expectation of another's mistake

kyag-kyag (Tibetan) throwing obstacles in the way of another's work, out of spite

švejkování (Czech) deviously undermining your boss or circumventing your supervisor's wishes while appearing angelically innocent and even rather simple (in the manner of the *Good Soldier Svejk*, the novel by Jaroslav Hasek)

suthi vuttiya (Tamil) the method used by call centre employees to avoid taking people's calls by changing their place on the list

Promises, promises

At least you can rely on the hopeless, spiteful and devious to be counterproductive. Worse are those who promise to help but never deliver, or who rush around frantically but never get anywhere:

kaengeng (Gilbertese, Oceania) to say 'yes yes' and do nothing about it

llamarada de petate (Central American Spanish) an undertaking started with great enthusiasm and suddenly dropped (**petate** is a woven reed mat used for sleeping)

hubyahubyeka (Tsonga, South Africa) to hurry here and there achieving nothing

ningas-kugon (Tagalog, Philippines) the sudden spurt of enthusiasm followed by a slowing down and an eventual slipping back into old habits

robota ne vovk, v lis ne vtiče (Ukrainian proverb) I can get back to doing that later (literally, work is not a wolf, it doesn't run into the woods)

nakinaki (Mandinka, West Africa) to go here and there pretending to be busy in order to avoid work

mikka bouzu (Japanese) a quitter (literally, three-day monk: a person who leaves the monkhood only three days after taking his vows)

Pedalling in yoghurt

The French, in particular, have a fine range of metaphors for not getting things done for one reason or another. **Brasser de l'air** is to give the impression of being busy (literally, to shuffle the air); **peigner la girafe** is to waste time in idle pursuits (literally, to comb the giraffe); **pedaler dans le yaourt** means to be getting nowhere fast (literally, to be pedalling in yoghurt); while **un coup d'épée dans l'eau** is a wasted effort (literally, a sword blow into water).

Counting the stars

One would almost prefer to work alongside those who model their lives on the Mexican Spanish expression **el trabajo embrutece**, work brutalizes ...

poltrone (Italian) lazybones (literally, easy chairs)
shitat zvyozdy (Russian) to twiddle one's thumbs (literally, to count the stars)
jeta (Swahili) a lazy person who does not stir himself to get the things he wants, but asks others to fetch them, even though the things may be quite near to him
bulat (Maguindanaon, Philippines) to have a phobia of certain jobs
imilila (Mambwe, Zambia) to work half-heartedly, all the time thinking about leaving

The company tribe

... or are perhaps waiting in hope for those sought-after positions that will surely, eventually, come up:

enchufe (Spanish) a cushy job (literally, a plug or socket)
anichado (Portuguese) hidden away, as in a niche; well-placed
in a good job
der Tintenpisser (German) a bureaucrat (literally, ink pisser)
tagapagpaganáp (Tagalog, Philippines) an executive
ntlhelavasati (Tsonga, South Africa) a place where one works
that is not too distant from home
shayo-zoku (Japanese) employees living extravagantly on
company money (literally, the company tribe)

Sell out

Although it's wise to remember that blind loyalty to the organization is much overrated:

ser líder charro (Mexican Spanish) to be a union leader who
sells out to company management
wegloben (German) to laud away (i.e. if a superior wants to
get rid of a co-worker he draws up an exaggerated testimonial to ensure that the unloved staffer leaves the company)
extraknäck (Swedish) a job on the side
kutu-loncat (Indonesian) someone who constantly moves
from job to job for better prospects or wages (literally,
jumping bug)

Lilies of the field

Perhaps the luckiest are those who don't have to do anything at all:

> **goyang kaki** (Malay) to shake one's leg; to live comfortably without having to work hard; to live off one's land or fortune or legacy
> **caer en blandito** (Latin American Spanish) to have a situation turn out extremely well without much effort (literally, to fall on a soft surface)
> **péter dans la soie** (French) to live the life of Riley (literally, to fart in silk)

IDIOMS OF THE WORLD

Bad workman blames his tools

el mal escribano le echa la culpa a la pluma/el cojo le echa la culpa al empedrado (Spanish) the poor writer blames the pen/the limping man blames the pavement
złej baletnicy przeszkadza rąbek u spódnicy (Polish) a poor dancer will be disturbed even by the hem of her skirt
'araj al jamal min shiffatu (Arabic) the camel limped from its split lip
plokhomu tantsory (i) yaytsa meshayut (Russian) a poor dancer is impeded (even) by his own balls

17.
Game Theory

kush nuk di ç'është lodhja, ai nuk di ç'është çlodhja (*Albanian*)
who does not know tiredness, does not know how to relax

Celebrating Monday

However hard we work, it's important to take time off, even if we have to be clever about how we arrange it:

hacer San Lunes (Mexican Spanish) to take Monday off because the weekend was too exhausting (literally, to celebrate St Monday)

puente (Spanish) bridge; the Spanish have their bank holidays on a Tuesday so that Monday will, on most occasions, be treated as a bridge day (an extra day of holiday), ensuring a four-day weekend; there is also a **viaducto**, which is when holidays fall on a Tuesday and a Thursday, thus enabling someone to take the whole week off

Slow start

How wonderful to let slip the usual routines, take your time, take it easy:

faire la grasse matinée (French) to sleep in (literally, to make a fat morning)

pegar(sele) las sábanas a (alguien) (Latin American Spanish) to oversleep (literally, to have the sheets stick to you)

guzu guzu suru (Japanese) being slow when you have something you should be doing; a half-wakeful sleep, especially in the morning when you have sort of woken up but are still playing with your dreams

faire le tour du cadran (French) to sleep the day away (literally, to do the tour of the clock's face)

Idle time

Even when one has fully woken up there's no pressure to do anything:

cangkul angin (Malay) hoeing the air; putting one's feet up in the air or doing useless things

Although sometimes the lack of pressure can be pressurizing in itself:

Zeit totschlagen (German) somebody who has free time but doesn't know what to do, so does something senseless (literally, to beat time to death)

egkila-kila (Maguindanaon, Philippines) to act foolishly as a means to combat boredom

tsurumun (Japanese) a single woman who dreads being alone on national holidays and invents reasons to visit friends

False friends

black (Swedish) ink
brief (German) letter
fart (French) ski wax
gong (Balinese) orchestra
war-side (Somali) newspaper
urinator (Latin) diver
rust (Dutch) rest or tranquillity

Cucumber troop

There are all kinds of things one can do with time off. What about watching some football? Fans would surely agree that few players can be a **peleon** (Puerto Rican Spanish), one who plays like Pele, but the Germans have gathered an evocative vocabulary for the highs (and lows) of watching a match:

> **der Schlachtenbummler** a football fan who travels to support his team at home and away (literally, battle stroller)
>
> **der Hexenkessel** a football stadium of the opposing team, with the fans creating a heated atmosphere (literally, witch's cauldron)
>
> **kleinklein** passing the ball from player to player without a plan (literally, small small)
>
> **Blutgratsche** a nasty tackle
>
> **die Gurkentruppe** a team that plays badly and unprofessionally, a disaster area, incompetent bunch of players (literally, cucumber troop)

Aggro

Or one could take up a heavier or more demanding sport:

bariga (Tagalog, Philippines) being thrown down in wrestling (literally, the bigger end of an egg)

atuila (Yamana, Chile) to press down on someone and make his legs give way so that he can be held down

munasat (Persian) taking hold of one another's forelocks when fighting

binti (Manobo, Philippines) a test of strength in which one man stands with his legs apart and his opponent runs from behind and kicks him in the calf of the leg with his shin in an attempt to knock him over; they then change places and continue until one is clearly defeated or gives up because of the pain

Ski-lane terror

Up in the mountains, it's fast, dangerous, but always fun:

Pistenschreck (German) a skier you have to watch out for
(literally, ski-lane terrorist)

tulee! (Finnish) look out! I'm skiing/sledging down towards
you at high speed! (literally, it's coming!)

ahterijarrut (Finnish) falling off your skis and using your tail-
end to stop (literally, arse-brakes)

Fackelabfahrt (German) a flaming-torchlight ski-run down
the side of a steep snowy mountain, undertaken at night by
around fifty skiers

The sound of your heart racing

Every language has onomatopoeic words, whose sound and rhythm vividly describe the sound or action they describe:

hara hara doki doki (Japanese) the feeling of your heart racing when you're scared or nervous

nyurrugu (Yidiny, Australia) the noise of talking heard a long way off when the words cannot be made out

vuhubya-hubya (Tsonga, South Africa) the flapping of pendulous breasts of a woman hurrying

krog-krog (Tibetan) a sound produced by grinding hard brittle objects together

empap (Malay) the sound of a flat object falling on a soft surface

mswatswa (Chichewa, Malawi) the sound of footsteps on dry grass

ndlangandzandlangandza (Tsonga, South Africa) the sound of drums during an exorcism ritual, beaten to cure a possessed person

geeuw (Dutch) a yawn

guntak (Malay) the rattle of pips in a dry fruit

gwarlingo (Welsh) the rushing sound a grandfather clock makes before striking the hour

phut (Vietnamese) the noise of string or rope that snaps

zhaghzhagh (Persian) the noise made by almonds or by other nuts shaken together in a bag

schwupp (German) quick as a flash (short for **schwuppdiwupp**)

szelescic (Polish) the sound when someone folds paper (pronounced scheleshchich)

Taking a dip

Down by the sea, river or lakeside, the activity on our day off is altogether gentler:

nchala-nchala-nchala (Tsonga, South Africa) to swim noise-lessly and swiftly

zaplyvats (Byelorussian) to swim far out

maulep (Maguindanaon, Philippines) a diver who can stay underwater for a long time, holding his breath

kataobairi (Gilbertese, Oceania) to go under the surface of the water with only one's nostrils above

terkapai-kapai (Malay) nervously moving the arms about (said of a bad swimmer)

tankah (Hawaiian Pidgin) a surfboard that seats six

limilimi (Hawaiian) to be turned over and over in the surf

Dizzy dancing

In many parts of the world, though, resources dictate that they have to make their own fun:

akkharikā (Pali, India) a game recognizing syllables written in the air or on one's back

antyākshrī (Hindi) a poetic competition in which a contestant recites a couplet beginning with the last letter recited by the previous contestant and which is then carried on by rival teams

kapana (Setswana, Botswana) to catch each other with both hands when taking turns to fall from a height

sikki (Ilokano, Philippines) a game played by tossing pebbles aloft and catching as many of them as possible on the back of the hand

pitz/pokolpok (Mayan, Central America) a game in which the object is to put a rubber ball through a stone ring using only hips, knees and elbows

mmamadikwadikwane (Setswana, Botswana) a game in which a child spins round until dizzy; it's also the term for ballroom dancing

Taking part

The Tagalog language of the Philippines has some great words to describe how – literally speaking – to play the game:

salimpusà asking someone to participate in a game to appease him, although he is not necessarily wanted

perdegana an agreement in certain games whereby the loser wins

haplít the final burst of energy when trying to win a race

Suits and tricks

If you're **grebleyi na kon'kakh** (Russian) incompetent at sports (literally, to row on skates), perhaps it's wiser to seek alternative thrills:

aéstomêhasené (Cheyenne, USA) to play cards for nothing; that is, to play without betting anything

hila' (Manobo, Philippines) to take a trick with a winning card

orobairi (Gilbertese, Oceania) to hit the nose of the loser in cards

Kiebitz (German) an onlooker at a card game who interferes with unwanted advice

kofu kofu (Sranan Tongo, Surinam) a bet where the winner gets to hit the loser

Live entertainment

'Those who have free tickets to the theatre have the most criticism to make,' say the Chinese, but live entertainment can often be surprisingly enjoyable (for those taking part, that is):

recevoir son morceau de sucre (French) to be applauded the moment one first appears on stage (literally, to receive one's piece of sugar)

Sitzfleisch (German) the ability to sit through long and boring events without losing concentration (literally, seat meat)

One is fun

For the Japanese, gentler pleasures suffice:

sabi a feeling of quiet grandeur enjoyed in solitude (normally involving the beauty that comes from the natural ageing of things)

shibui a transcendently beautiful and balanced image, such as an autumn garden (literally, sour, astringent)

Stories with bears

Or one could indulge one's creative urges:

brat s potolka (Russian) to make something up (literally, to take something from the ceiling)

hohátôhta'hàne (Cheyenne, USA) to laugh while storytelling

istories gia arkudes (Greek) narrated events that are so wild and crazy it seems that they can't possibly be true (literally, stories with bears)

Bookmark

Or just kick back and enjoy the efforts of others:

kioskvältare (Swedish) a bestselling film/book (literally, something that tips over the booth)

hinmekuru (Japanese) to turn a page over violently

ádi (Telugu, India) a mark left in a book to show the place where the reader left off

Drooping tongue

However hard you try to prevent it, our day of recreation draws to its inevitable end:

bantil (Bikol, Philippines) to pinch the back of the neck to relieve weariness

traer la lengua de corbata (Latin American Spanish) to be worn out; to be exhausted (literally, to have your tongue hanging out like a man's tie)

Nodding off

And in different postures and places we drift into blessed oblivion:

corra-chodal (Gaelic) sleeping on one's elbow
clavar el pico (Latin American Spanish) to fall asleep in a sitting position
kakkawornendi (Kaurna Warra, Australia) to nod when sleeping
itanochi (Alabama, USA) to go to sleep on the floor or by a fire
yum (Car, Nicobar Islands) to sleep with someone in one's arms

Staying up

Among the Cheyenne people of the USA, sleep may be the last thing they get up to at night:

vóonâhá'ené to cook all night
vóonâhtóohe to howl all night
vóona'haso'he to ride a horse all night
vóonâše'še to drink all night
vóonêhasené to play cards all night
vóoneméohe to run all night
vóoneóó'e to stand all night
vóonévánéne to fart all night
vóonóé'ó to float all night
vóonôhtóvá to sell all night
vóono'eétahe to have sex all night
vóonó'eohtsé to travel by wagon all night
vóonotse'ohe to work all night

IDIOMS OF THE WORLD

To take a sledgehammer to crack a nut

mogi jabeeryuda chogasamgan da taewonda (Korean) burning your whole house trying to catch a mosquito

tuo kuzi fang pi (Mandarin) to take your trousers off to fart

pire için yorgan yakmak (Turkish) to burn the duvet because of one flea

kee chang jahb thak-a-thaen (Thai) ride an elephant to catch a grasshopper

met een kanon op een mug schieten (Dutch) to shoot a mosquito with a cannon

gubbi mEle bramhAstravE? (Kannada, India) a nuclear weapon on a sparrow?

18.
Animal Magic

hilm il-'utaat kullu firaan (*Arabic*)
the dream of cats is all about mice

When humans looked around them and saw the animals that inhabited their world they often came up with names that described what each animal looked or sounded like, or how it behaved. Among the Amerindian tribes the Navaho word for squirrel is the phrase 'it has a bushy tail' and the word from the Arapaho for elephant is 'it has a bent nose'. The Mingo language was particularly expressive in this regard:

uæhkwëönyö' a peacock (literally, it puts suns all over it)
teyunö'kêôt a sheep (literally, it's got two horns attached)
këötanëhkwi a horse (literally, it hauls logs)
teka'nyakáíte' a mole (literally, both of its hands are slanted)
tewathsistúkwas a firefly (literally, it scatters sparks)
tsyúwë'staka' a seagull (literally, it is known for being around sea-foam)
uthëhtæǽhtáne' a caterpillar (literally, its fuzz itches)
teyu'skwæǽt a bull (literally, two standing stones – referring to the bull's testicles)

The great rat with a pocket

Likewise, when Chinese voyagers first saw the kangaroo they described the way it looked to them: **dai shu**, pocket rat, or great rat with a pocket. The Yoruba of West Africa, unused to zebras, called them 'striped horses'. The Indian nations of the Americas were astounded at the sight of the horse when it appeared, brought by the early Spanish conquerors. The Aztecs thought it was a hornless deer. The Sioux named it **shuñka wakãn**, supernatural dog, and the Cheyenne referred to it as **mo-eheno'ha**, domesticated elk. Another animal new to the Cheyenne, the pig, joined their language as **eshkoseesehotame**, dog with sharp nose.

False friends

snog (Danish) grass snake
asp (Pahlavi, Iran) horse
dud (Arabic) caterpillar, worm
formica (Latin) ant
hunt (Estonian) wolf
hunt (Yiddish) dog
lamb (Amharic, Ethiopia) cow

long (Chinese) dragon
moron (Munduruku, Brazil) toad

Fluttering and kicking

Those peoples living closely with animals developed vocabulary to describe all sorts of precisely observed behaviour on land ...

vweluka (Mambwe, Zambia) to jump from branch to branch (said of a monkey)

gigigigigi (Tsonga, South Africa) to stand about dispersed and all looking intently at something in the distance, as cattle seeing a lion

telki (Swahili) the quick ambling gait of a donkey, half walk, half run

thakgantse (Setswana, Botswana) to kick in all directions (as an ox when one leg is held by a thong)

glamarsaich (Gaelic) the noisy lapping (as of a hungry dog)

shebwoso (Potawatomi, USA) a rabbit running fast

... of fish and other creatures at sea:

tekab (Maguindanaon, Philippines) a fish opening its mouth and producing bubbles

siponaina (Yamana, Chile) to go along on the surface of the water and cause a ripple, as fish do

aiagata (Yamana, Chile) to rise up on end and take a deep dive, as the whale when it raises up its flukes

itupi (Mambwe, Zambia) dead fish found floating

hu-q-a (Nuuchahnulth, Canada) a salmon going along with its dorsal fin out of the water

... and of birds and insects on the ground and in the air:

abhinibbijjhati (Pali, India) to break quite through (said of
the chick coming through the shell of the egg)

magaatu (Yamana, Chile) to tuck the head under the wing, as
birds do when composed for sleep

ava-sam-dīna (Sanskrit) the united downward flight of birds

khpa (Dakota, USA) to be wet or clogged, as mosquitos' wings
with dew

tikutamoamo (Gilbertese, Oceania) to alight everywhere (of
a dragonfly)

Scratch, chew, tear, beat

Some actions are common to many creatures:

kwe-swanta (Ganda, Uganda) to lick one's chops when one
has not had enough to eat

kengerhele (Tsonga, South Africa) to stop suddenly in
surprise, be on the alert, as animals hearing a noise

kukuta (Swahili) to shake off water after getting wet, in the
way a bird or dog does

zeula (Kalanga, Botswana) the chewing of animals late at
night

hachistitabatli (Alabama, USA) to beat the tail on the ground

imba (Mambwe, Zambia) to tear away the prey from one
another, as animals fighting over food

Wriggle, wriggle

There are words for sounds too, even those surely heard only by those who live cheek by jowl with the fauna of the world:

pasáw (Tagalog, Philippines) the noise of fish wriggling in the water

rerejat (Iban, Sarawak and Brunei) the noise made by a cricket on landing

kíchchu (Tamil) the chirping of birds; the whining of infants

ekkaranam (Tamil) a noise which a bull makes when about to attack another

saratata (Buli, Ghana) the sound and behaviour of running animals (leaving a trail of dust in the air)

tyaka-tyaka (Tsonga, South Africa) the noise of cattle crashing through dry bush

gungurhu-gungurhu-gungurhu (Tsonga, South Africa) to clatter like a rat trapped in a box

andala (Arabic) the song of the nightingale

atit (Arabic) the moaning bray of a camel

inchasàaya (Alabama, USA) a rattlesnake's rattle

Sunday roast

There are words to describe the most detailed aspects of an animal's appearance ...

scory (Scots) the wrinkled texture of a hedgehog's cheeks
gansuthi (Boro, India) the first-grown feather of a bird's wing
kapy-āsa (Sanskrit) the buttocks of an ape
sondi (Pali, India) the neck of a tortoise
sprochaille (Irish) the loose fold of skin between the legs of a turkey
mokadi (Setswana, Botswana) the fat of a bullfrog
kuris (Manobo, Philippines) the fortune of a chicken written in the scales of its feet

Tucked away

... how they store their food:

bráða-hola (Old Icelandic) a hole where the wild beasts carry their prey
wakhedan (Dakota, USA) the places from which squirrels dig up food
achnátus (Karuk, North America) a place where a rat stores its food
tsembetuta (Chichewa, Malawi) a type of mouse known for saving food for the future
indagitagan (Ojibway, North America) the place where a wild animal goes to eat in the woods

Crocodile skid

... even how they behave in specific and group ways:

kekerikaki (Gilbertese, Oceania) a fish which sometimes swims backwards

teosammul (Estonian) the speed of a snail

atiqtuq (Iñupiat, Inuit) bears going down to the sea

wosdohedan (Dakota, USA) paths made by squirrels in the grass

pe'mkowe't (Potawatomi, USA) bear tracks in the snow

lantar (Iban, Sarawak and Brunei) the skidmark left on a riverbank by a boat or crocodile sliding into the water

Wa!

Originally, humans began by treating animals as hostile, to be hunted, chased away or killed:

phongoloxa (Tsonga, South Africa) to throw stones or sticks at an animal to frighten it away

p'isqeyay (Quechuan, Andes) to scare off birds

khapela (Tsonga, South Africa) to drive animals into another's land so that they may do damage there

bohnaskinyan (Dakota, USA) to make an animal crazy or furious by shooting

phitsisitse (Setswana, Botswana) to kill an insect by crushing it between the finger and thumb

Down on the farm

But then came the thought of using certain breeds to their advantage:

nanagi (Rapanui, Easter Island) to mark a chicken as one's property by biting one of its toes

piya (Kalanga, Botswana) to hold a goat's leg under one's knee while milking it

verotouaire (Gallo, France) a woman who helps a boar (**vero**) to copulate with the sow (**tree**)

féauðnu-maðr (Old Icelandic) a man lucky with his sheep

Commanding

With this came a new range of calls and cries:

ouk (British Columbian dialect, Canada) a command to a sledge-dog to turn right

koosi (Buli, Ghana) to call chickens by smacking one's tongue

cethreinwr (Welsh) someone who walks backwards, in front of an ox, prompting it with a combination of a song and a sharp stick

To the hand

The Scots, in particular, have a fine collection of animal instructions:

irrnowt a shepherd's call to his dog to pursue cattle
who-yauds a call to dogs to pursue horses
iss a call to a dog to attack
hut a call to a careless horse
re a call to a horse to turn to the right
shug a call to a horse to come to the hand

On reflection

Animals online

In these days of intense email use, it seems amazing that there is still no official name for @. It is generally called the 'at' symbol. Other languages have come up with all kinds of mostly animal nicknames. Polish calls it **malpa**, monkey; in Afrikaans it is **aapstert**, monkey's tail; in German it is **Klammeraffe**, clinging monkey. The Finns and Swedes see it as a cat curled up

Aw, aw!

As does the Pashto language of Afghanistan and Pakistan:

drhey	when addressing sheep
eekh eekh	when addressing camels
asha asha	when addressing donkeys
aw aw	when addressing oxen
tsh tsh	when addressing horses
kutsh kutsh	when addressing dogs

---

with its tail. Swedish has **kattsvans**, and Finnish has at least three names for this idea: **kissanhäntä**, cat tail, **miaumerkki**, meow sign, and **miukumauku**, which means something like meow-meow. In French, Korean, Indonesian, Hebrew and Italian it's a snail. In Turkish (**kulak**) and Arabic (**uthun**) it's an ear, in Spanish it's an elephant's ear (**elefantora**), in Danish it's an elephant's trunk (**snabel**), and elsewhere:

zavinac (Czech) pickled herring

xiao lao-shu (Taiwanese) little mouse

kukac (Hungarian) worm or maggot

sobachka (Russian) little dog

papaki (Greek) duckling

grisehale (Norwegian) curly pig's tail

kanelbulle (Swedish) cinnamon roll

gül (Turkish) rose

How to count on your chickens

In the Gallo dialect in France there is some very specific vocabulary about ensuring that there are always enough eggs:

un anijouet an egg left in a hen's nest to encourage it to lay more in the same place
chaponner to stick a finger up a chicken's bottom to see if it is laying an egg

Man's best friend

It's hardly surprising that that species thought of as closest to humans is described in the most loving detail:

agkew (Manobo, Philippines) to try to snatch food which is hung up out of reach (said of a dog)
manàntsona (Malagasy, Madagascar) to smell or sniff before entering a house, as a dog does
ihdaśna (Dakota, USA) to miss in biting oneself, as a dog trying to bite its own tail
kwiiua-iella (Yamana, Chile) to bite and leave, as a dog does with a strong animal it cannot kill
amulaw (Bikol, Philippines) the barking of dogs in pursuit of game

Roof-gutter rabbit

Our second favourite animal is less loyal and more selfish, but brings us luck if it crosses our path:

lapin de gouttière (French) a cat (literally, roof-gutter rabbit)
echafoureré (Gallo, France) a tickled cat hiding under a table or chair
bilāra-nissakkana (Pali, India) large enough for a cat to creep through
amotóm (Cheyenne, USA) to carry something in the mouth (said especially of a mother cat)
bvoko (Tsonga, South Africa) to spring unsuccessfully at or after, as a cat springs at a mouse which just saves itself

Gee gee

Next up has to be the one that has always helped us get around, and has also let us experience speed, excitement and other less welcome sensations:

asvatthāma (Sanskrit) having the strength of a horse
lekgetla (Setswana, Botswana) the droop of the ears of a tired horse
dzádintsu (Telugu, India) to flap about as a horse does his tail, to reprove by speech
cagailt (Gaelic) a roll of chewed grass in a horse's mouth
ibiihokcho (Alabama, USA) to pass gas in someone's face (as a horse will)

Moo

Fourth on our list is free to roam in India, enjoying its sacred status, while elsewhere it offers sustenance of more than one kind:

kárámpasu (Tamil) a cow whose udder is black, held in great esteem by the Hindus

nyakula (Lozi, Niger-Congo) to try to untie itself by kicking (as a cow tied up by its legs)

silehile (Lozi, Niger-Congo) to besmirch with dung the teats of a cow which refuses to be milked, in order to keep its calf away

deothas (Gaelic) the longing or eagerness of a calf for its mother

clardingo (Welsh) to flee in panic from a warble-fly (said of a herd of cows)

gokuradiya (Sinhala, Sri Lanka) the water in a hole made by a cow's hoof

Drinking twice

We rarely see our fifth and last away from a zoo or safari park, but in the wild this creature certainly lives up to the poet's description as 'Nature's great masterpiece':

dvi-pa (Sanskrit) an elephant (literally, drinking twice – with his trunk and his mouth)

gagau (Malay) an elephant picking up with its trunk

polak (Hindi) straw tied to the end of a bamboo stick which is used to frighten and restrain a furious elephant

isīkā (Sanskrit) an elephant's eyeball

tun-mada (Sinhala, Sri Lanka) an elephant in rut, alluding to the three liquids which exude from him in the rutting season, namely from his temples, his eyes and his penis

Flying low

And then there are those others that we admire, but generally only from a distance:

arspag (Gaelic) the largest seagull

tihunyi (Tsonga, South Africa) a crested cuckoo which sings before the rains and reminds people to collect firewood

jimbi (Luvale, Zambia) a bird which does not yet sing

sarad (Manobo, Philippines) to fly low, at about the height of a coconut palm

Don't count your chickens before they're hatched

Swahili advises us not to curse the crocodile before we've crossed the river and there are all kinds of similar warnings from around the world about not being too hasty:

mithl ilh yibi' samak fi al bahar (Arabic) it's like selling fish still in the sea

man skal ikke sælge skindet, før bjørnen er skudt (Danish) one should not sell the fur before the bear has been shot

älä nuolaise ennen kuin pöydällä tipahtaa (Finnish) don't start licking it up before it drops onto the table

guthimba ti kuura (Kikuyu, Kenya) having rain clouds is not the same as having rain

na neroden Petko kapa mu skroile (Macedonian) they sewed a hat to Peter who is not born yet

tsiplyat po oseni schitayut (Russian) one should count chicks in autumn

ne govori gop, poka ne pereskochish (Russian) don't say hop until you jumped over

ino manga ondjupa ongombe inaayi vala (Ndonga, Namibia) don't hang the churning calabash before the cow has calved

non dire gatto se non l'hai nel sacco (Italian) never say 'cat' if you have not got it in your sack

dereyi görmeden paçaları sıvama (Turkish) do not roll up your trouser legs before you see the stream

19.
Climate Change

gode ord skal du hogge i berg, de
dårligere i snø (*Norwegian*)
carve your good words in stone, the bad in snow

Tiwilight

The world goes round, and at innumerable different times, the day begins. Down in the Antipodes, the Tiwi people of northern Australia describe the sequence before the sun finally appears:

arawunga early morning before dawn
tokwampari early morning when birds sing
yartijumurra darkness before daylight
wujakari first light before sunrise

The dawn chorus

The Hungarians have a specific word – **hajnalpir** – for the first blush of dawn; the Japanese distinguish **ariake**, dawn when the moon is still showing; while the German word **Morgengrauen** (literally, morning greying) describes both the horror of the morning and its grey and sunless colour.

Sun's up

In the Dakota language of the USA, the moon is **hangyetuwi**, the night-sun. Come dawn it can no longer compete with **anpetuwi**, the day-sun:

glukocharazo (Greek) to glow in the dawn light
tavanam (Tamil) the heat of the sun
amaśtenaptapta (Dakota, USA) the glimmering of vapour in the sun's heat
greigh (Gaelic) the uncommon heat of the sun after bursting out from behind a cloud

Weather report

Ah, that famous topic, food for hundreds of thousands of conversations every day. And we are not alone in observing and describing its many moods:

pestpokkenweer (Dutch) dirty rotten weather

dul'avā (Virdainas, Baltics) fog with drizzle

cilala (Bemba, Zambia) the dry spell in a rainy season

boule (Scots) a gap, break; an opening in the clouds betokening fine weather

Postkartenwetter (German) the kind of weather that is too wonderful to be real (literally, postcard weather)

Heat haze

The secondary meanings of weather terms are often very evocative of the climate they describe. For instance, the Scots description of heat haze – **summer-flaws** – is also used for a swarm of gnats dancing in the air; while the Yamana of Chile **unda-tu** also describes the wavy appearance of the air seen over a fire.

The wind of change

Beautifully still conditions never last for long, certainly not in this country:

> **pew** (Scots) the least breath of wind or smoke; the least ripple on the sea
> **sivisivivi** (Mailu, Papua New Guinea) marks on water of a coming wind
> **kacee** (Tsonga, South Africa) to feel a breeze or smell coming towards one
> **fuaradh-froik** (Gaelic) the breeze preceding a shower

False friends

dim (Bosnian) smoke
estate (Italian) summer
lung (Sherpa, Nepal) air
santa (Bosnian) iceberg
tall (Arabic) hill, elevation

Storm warning

We can always sense that moment when things are on the turn:

oi (Vietnamese) to be sultry, muggy, hot and sticky
tvankas (Virdainas, Baltics) stuffy air
bingo (Chewa, South East Africa) the distant roll of thunder
gwangalakwahla (Tsonga, South Africa) a thunderclap is
very near
kixansiksuya (Dakota, USA) to know by one's feelings that
unpleasant weather is due

Sunshine shower

After the storm, the rain is lighter, subtler; indeed, it may not be clear quite what's going on:

tmoq yungay (Aboriginal Tayal, Taiwan) a light rain (literally,
monkey piss)
fa-fa-fa (Tsonga, South Africa) to fall in a shower of drops
mvula-tshikole (Venda, South Africa) rain with sunshine
ördög veri a feleségét (Hungarian) the devil is hitting his
wife (usually said when the sun is shining but rain is falling
at the same time)
bijregenboog (Dutch) a secondary rainbow

In a flood

Down on the ground, everything changes:

douh (Somali) a dry watercourse which turns into a fast-
moving stream after every downpour

calalalala (Tsonga, South Africa) to come down, as a river in a
flood; a glitter (of a large expanse of water or an army with
polished weapons)

túvánam (Tamil) rain driven by the wind through the doors
or windows

zolilinga (Luvale, Zambia) the watermark made by rain (as on
a wooden door)

Soaking up the weather

And all kinds of fun can be had:

edtimbulan (Maguindanaon, Philippines) to walk in the rain

wadlopen (Dutch) to walk sloshing through seamud

chokok (Malay) to splash water in fun

dynke (Norwegian) the act of dunking somebody's face in
snow

kram snø (Norwegian) snow which is sticky (excellent for
making snowballs and snowmen)

You fish on your side...

Several places in Norway and Sweden are simply called Å. It means river in various Scandanavian languages, but that's all the name tells us about them. But if you go for something rather longer, an awful lot of information can be contained in a name. For instance, Webster Lake in Massachussetts, USA, is also known as

Chargoggagoggmanchauggauggagoggchaubunagunga-maugg

which was a native word for a neutral fishing place near a boundary, a meeting and fishing spot shared by several tribes. A popular interpretation is: 'You fish on your side, I fish on my side, nobody fishes in the middle.' The longest placename still in regular use is for a hill in New Zealand. The ninety-letter Maori name

Taumatawhakatangihangakoauaotamateaurehaeaturi-pukapihimaungahoronukupokaiwhenuaakitana-rahu

means 'The brow of the hill where Tamatea, the man with the big knees, who slid, climbed and ate mountains, the great traveller, sat and played on the flute to his beloved.'

Compass comparisons

The sun features strongly in how other cultures have described the compass points. The Mingo of the USA describe north as **te'kææhkwææhkö**, the sun isn't there; and west as **hekææhkwë's**, the sun habitually drops down over there. The Bambara people of Mali have more complicated associations:

EAST is the colour white; the land of the dead and of wild and domestic animals.

WEST is the land of the 'sunset people' and of birds; the source of custom and of all goodness and loveliness.

NORTH is identified with the seventh heaven, a far distant country, the dwelling of the great god Faro, who created the world in all its present form; the north is the home of all water creatures – fish, crocodiles and frogs.

SOUTH is peopled by plants and the evil beings whom Faro was forced to destroy at the beginning of time, because they had stolen speech from him; the home of pollution.

Coucher de soleil

Rain or shine, windy or still, the sun sinks down towards the horizon, and the day winds towards its close:

tainunu (Gilbertese, Oceania) the time when shadows lengthen in the late afternoon

pakupaku (Rapanui, Easter Island) to come down in a straight line like the rays of the sun

sig (Sumerian, Mesopotamia) the colour of the low setting sun (reddish-yellow or gold)

iltarusko (Finnish) sunset glow

ahiahi-ata (Rapanui, Easter Island) the last moments of light before nightfall

Silver goddess

Darkness falls, and the night-sun reappears, bringing with it mystery and magic:

jyótsnā (Sanskrit) a moonlight night

yakmoez (Turkish) the effect of moonlight sparkling on water

kuunsilta (Finnish) the long reflection of the moon when it is low in the sky and shining on the calm surface of a lake (literally, moon bridge)

hasi istitta-ammi (Alabama, USA) to bathe one's face in the moon, wash the face four times in moonlight

It's raining cats and dogs

ou vrouens met knopkieries reen (Afrikaans) it's raining
old women with clubs

padají trakaře (Czech) it's raining wheelbarrows

det regner skomagerdrenge (Danish) it's raining shoemak-
ers' apprentices

het regent pijpenstelen (Dutch) it's raining pipestems

baron mesleh dobeh asb mirized (Persian) it's raining like
the tail of the horse

brékhei kareklopódara (Greek) it's raining chair legs

il pleut comme vache qui pisse (French) it's raining like a
pissing cow

es regnet Schusterbuben (German) it's raining young
cobblers

estan lloviendo hasta maridos (Spanish) it's even raining
husbands

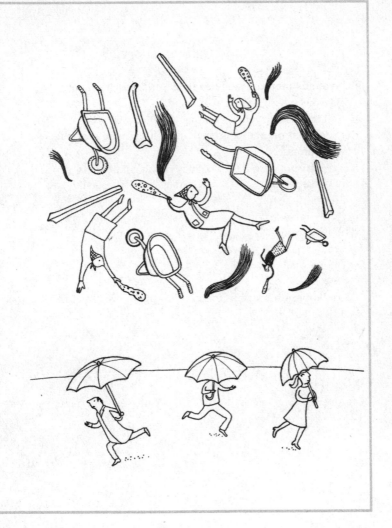

20.
The Root of All Evil

ahjar habib fis-suq minn mitt
skud fis-senduq (*Maltese*)
*a friend in the market is better than one
hundred gold coins in the chest*

A frog's armpit

'Don't offer me advice, give me money,' say the Spanish – and who would disagree, certainly if they're in a tight spot financially:

mas limpio que sobaco de rana (Venezuelan Spanish)
   broke (literally, cleaner than a frog's armpit)

auf den Hund kommen (German) to be broke (literally, to
   get to the dog; in medieval times, a dog was painted on the
   bottom of money chests – if you could see the dog, you had
   run out of money)
n'avoir plus un radis (French) to be stone broke (literally, to
   be without a single radish)
kukla (Russian) a roll of bills in which the inner bills have
   been replaced by worthless paper (literally, a doll)

Cutting gold

Most of us would be more than happy with an easy escape from such an unfortunate predicament:

gaji buta (Malay) getting paid without having to work
att skära guld med täljkniv (Swedish) to make money with
  very little effort (literally, to cut gold with a pocket knife)
dawo (Yoruba, Nigeria, Benin and Togo) to produce money by
  magic

Gifted

While others find different ways to stay afloat:

pakimkím (Tagalog, Philippines) money given by a godparent
hustrulon (Swedish) a wife's salary
namidakin (Japanese) a small amount of consolation money
  (literally, tear money)
pujo (Korean) a congratulatory gift or condolence money

Up against it

It's certainly true that the folding stuff can be elusive; and the occasion when you really need it may be the one time you are unable to find it:

ipatapata (Lozi, Niger-Congo) to try hard to find money with
  which to make an urgent purchase
lukupu (Mambwe, Zambia) to miss gaining riches by a
  narrow margin

On the floor

When you do finally get some, for heaven's sake be careful with it:

pagar el piso (Chilean Spanish) to take out all your friends and pay with the first pay packet from your new job (literally, to pay for the floor)

madyelakhwirhini (Tsonga, South Africa) a man who immediately spends all he earns and sends nothing home; a spendthrift

peaglatata (Dakota, USA) to exhaust one's own supply by giving to others

It's the thought that counts

To demonstrate their wealth, the Kwakiutl Indians of Vancouver Island destroyed it. Their chiefs publicly burned food, blankets, canoes and ornaments in the ceremony of **potlatch**, a word that means 'giving'. A **potlatch** might be held for a variety of reasons, which varied from group to group, but included puberty rites and death commemorations. It involved a great feast at which the host lavishly distributed valuable property to all the assembled guests. The hitch was that the guests had to reciprocate at some future date – with interest of up to 100 per cent.

An umbrella at midnight

Two proverbs from the Kannada language of Southern India speak eloquently of the paradoxes of getting rich. **HalliddAga kaDle illa; kaDle iddAga hallilla** – there are no nuts when one has teeth and there are no teeth when there are nuts; in other words, when you are young you have no money, and when you have money the chance of enjoying it is often gone. But perhaps this is all as it should be. For the second proverb points up the absurdity of some people's behaviour when they are in a fit state to enjoy their money: **Aishwarya bandre ardha rAthrili koDe hiDkonDa** – when a poor fellow gets rich, he has an umbrella over his head at midnight; which is to say that a newly wealthy man will flaunt the symbol of the well-off, a parasol to shield him from the sun, even in the dark.

False friends

Reformhaus (German) health food store

top (Dutch) done! agreed! it's a bargain!

stershit (Albanian) to sell everything that one has

Detail (German) retail

hamstring (Swedish) hoarding (derives from hamster)

male (Italian) bad, wicked

Cowherd's cake

Sometimes the destitute may just have to make do with a payment in kind:

legopelo (Setswana, Botswana) a piece of meat that is given to someone who has helped skin a cow

angauriyā (Hindi) a ploughman making use of a farmer's plough instead of receiving wages in money or kind

bonnach-iomanach (Gaelic) a cowherd's cake (a special reward for good herding at calving time)

matao ni bwe (Gilbertese, Oceania) the price paid in fish for the loan of a canoe or fishing net

To see thirty-six candles

The French refer to many things in terms of the number thirty-six:

j'ai trente-six choses à faire I have many things to do

tous les trente-six du mois once in a blue moon (literally, each thirty-sixth of the month)

faire les trente-six volontés de quelqu'un to be at someone's beck and call (literally, to do the thirty-six wills of someone)

voir trente-six chandelles to see stars after getting hit on the head (literally, to see thirty-six candles)

Stall

'**Gol' na vydumku khitra**,' say the Russians – poverty is crafty; and it's surely true that having no money can become the spur for entrepreneurial activity, even of the most basic kind:

bahu (Bugotu, Solomon Islands) to barter food for money
ditan (Chinese) a street vendor's stand (with the goods spread out on the ground)
higgler (Jamaican creole) a person selling fruit and vegetables by the roadside
gujrī (Hindi) a roadside market set up in the late afternoons
sitoa (Gilbertese, Oceania) a small trading ship whose decks are set up as stores
chelnoki (Russian) shuttle traders (who buy goods from the back of lorries)
limpiaparabrisas (Mexican Spanish) street kids who gather at intersections with traffic lights and rush to wash the windscreen of cars waiting for the lights to change and then demand to be paid

Red shells out, white shells back

The Kiriwina of the Trobriand Islands in the Pacific have an elaborate gift exchange system called the **kula**. The islanders set off round the islands in large, ocean-going canoes and trade red shell necklaces (**veigun**) in a clockwise direction, and white shell bracelets (**mwali**) in an anti-clockwise direction. The round trip is several hundred miles.

The art of selling

There's a lot of skill (even magic) in encouraging people to part with their hard-earned dosh:

spruik (Australian slang) to talk to attract customers; to hold forth like a showman

verlierlen (Yiddish) to lose a customer to a fellow salesman

vparivat' (Russian) to palm off defective goods

fare orecchie da mercante (Italian) pretending not to understand (literally, to have a merchant's ears)

palulud (Maguindanaon, Philippines) a charm that is supposed to have the power to attract customers

Smoke and mirrors

Although the further up the scale you go, the less need you have for actual goods:

muhaqala (Arabic) the sale of grain while still in growth, dealing in grain futures

dymoprodukt (Russian) an advertised product that is not yet being produced (literally, smoke product)

wheeler (Scots) one who bids at an auction simply to raise the price

One-armed bandit

There are, of course, other ways of making money, if you're prepared to take a chance:

agi (Maranao, Philippines) to win continually in gambling
airi (Maranao, Philippines) to bet again on a card which has just won
an non (Vietnamese) to quit gambling as soon as one has won
balato (Tagalog, Philippines) money given away by a winning gambler as a sign of goodwill

Losers

However, even the most hardened practitioners know that in the long run the betting tables don't pay. As the Germans say, 'Young gamblers, old beggars':

borona (Malagasy, Madagascar) having nothing with which to pay money lost in betting
biho (Maranao, Philippines) a bet, money asked for from winners by losers
pelasada (Maranao, Philippines) the percentage taken from bets by the owner of a gambling place

Tokyo tricks

The Japanese have two words to describe what happens as the temptation to cheat gets stronger:

dakko the flicking movement of the palm that will send goods up into the sleeve

dosa a player with an exceptionally bad hand who will flick a compromising card up his sleeve and quickly substitute a more favourable one

Retail therapy

So what to do with it when you finally have it? Why, hit the streets, of course; and this is an occupation, if not an art, in itself:

faire du lèche-vitrines (French) to go window-shopping (literally, to lick windows)

chokuegambo (Japanese) the wish that there were more designer-brand shops on a given street; the desire to buy things at luxury brand shops

arimuhunán (Tagalog, Philippines) something worth taking although not needed

emax (Latin) fond of buying

You're safer with prison

What a fine array of products the world has in its shop window:

Atum Bom Portuguese tinned tuna
Bimbo Mexican biscuits
Kevin French aftershave
Polio Czech detergent
Vaccine Dutch aftershave
Flirt Austrian cigarettes
Meltykiss Japanese chocolate
Climax Kenyan disinfectant
Hot Piss Japanese antifreeze spray
Naked New Zealand fruit and nut bar
Noisy French butter
Last Climax Japanese tissues
Happy Swedish chocolate
Prison Ugandan body spray

As easy as falling off a log

så let som at klø sig i nakken (Danish) as easy as scratching the back of your neck

semudah membalikkan telapak tangan (Indonesian) as easy as turning your palm around

facile come bere un bicchier d'acqua (Italian) as easy as drinking a glass of water

asameshi mae (Japanese) before breakfast (something that's so easy, you could finish it before breakfast)

nuwoseo tdeokmeokki (Korean) lying on one's back and eating rice cakes

tereyağýndan kýl çeker gibi (Turkish) as if pulling a strand of hair from butter

ežiku ponjatno (Russian) understandable to a hedgehog

21.
The Criminal Life

le diable chie toujours au même
endroit (*French*)
the devil always shits in the same place

Tea leaf

Why work, or even gamble for that matter, when there are far easier ways of enriching yourself?

lipoushka (Russian) a stick with a gluey end for stealing money from a counter (literally, flypaper)

butron (Spanish) a type of jacket with inner pockets worn by shoplifters

levare le scarpe (Italian) to steal the tyres from a car (literally, to take someone else's shoes off)

rounstow (Scots) to cut off the ears of a sheep, and so obliterate its distinctive marks of ownership

False friends

bait (Arabic) incentive or motive

egg (Norwegian, Swedish) knife edge

gulp (Afrikaans) to slit, gush, spout

guru (Japanese) a partner in crime

plaster (Hebrew) deceitful or fraudulent

roof (Dutch) robbery

Gangland

Although once you step over that line, who knows what company you may be forced to keep:

ladenlichter (Dutch) a till-robber

pisau cukur (Malay) a female hustler who cons men into giving her money

harza-duzd (Persian) someone who steals something of no use to him or anyone else

adukalipewo (Mandinka, West Africa) a highway robber (literally, give me the purse)

belochnik (Russian) a thief specializing in stealing linen off clothes lines (this was very lucrative in the early 1980s)

Scissorhand

Considerable skill, experience and bravado may be required for success:

> **forbice** (Italian) pickpocketing by putting the index and middle fingers into the victim's pocket (literally, scissors)
>
> **cepat tangan** (Malay) quick with the hands (in pickpocketing or shoplifting or hitting someone)
>
> **poniwata** (Korean) a victim who at first glance looks provincial and not worth robbing, but on closer scrutiny shows definite signs of hidden wealth
>
> **komissar** (Russian) a robber who impersonates a police officer

And sometimes even magic:

> **walala** (Luvale, Zambia) a thieves' fetish which is supposed to keep people asleep while the thief steals
>
> **za-koosirik** (Buli, Ghana) a person who transfers the plants of a neighbour's field to his own by magic

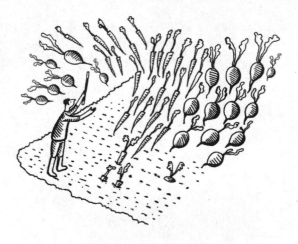

Lost in translation

In their eagerness to move into and conquer new markets, many huge Western companies forgot to do their homework. When the name Microsoft was first translated into Chinese, they went for a literal translation of the two parts of the name which, unfortunately, meant 'small and flaccid'.

Pepsi's famous slogan 'Come Alive with Pepsi' was dropped in China after it was translated as 'Pepsi brings your ancestors back from the grave'.

When American Airlines wanted to advertise its new leather first-class seats in the Mexican market, it translated its 'Fly in Leather' campaign literally, but **vuela en cuero** meant 'Fly Naked' in Spanish.

Colgate introduced in France a toothpaste called **Cue**, the name of a notorious pornographic magazine.

Coca-Cola was horrified to discover that its name was first read by the Chinese as **kekoukela**, meaning either 'bite the wax tadpole' or 'female horse stuffed with wax', depending on the dialect. Coke then researched 40,000 characters to find a phonetic equivalent – **kokou kole** – which translates as 'happiness in the mouth'

Kindling

Their trains and tubes are punctual to the nearest second; equal efficiency seems to characterize those Japanese who take criminal advantage of such crowded environments:

nakanuku, inside pull-out: to carefully slip one's hand into a victim's trouser pocket, draw out the wallet, flick it open, whip out cash and credit cards, close it and slip it back into the victim's trouser pocket

oitore, walking next to a well-dressed victim, plunging a razor-sharp instrument into his attaché case and cutting the side open

okinagashi, put and flow: those who climb on a local train at one station, grab bags and coats, cameras and camcorders, and then jump off at the following station

takudasu, kindle and pull out: to drop, as if by mistake, a lit cigarette into a victim's jacket or open shirt, and then, while the victim is frantically trying to locate the burning butt, come to his aid, helping him unbutton and frisk through jacket, shirt and undershirt, taking the opportunity to lift wallets and other valuables out of pockets and bags

Descending spiders

Nor does this fine vocabulary dry up when describing the activity of Japanese burglars: **maemakuri**, lifting the skirt from the front, means they enter through the front gates; while **shirimakuri**, lifting the skirt from behind, describes entry through a gate or fence at the rear of the house. One obvious hazard is the **gabinta**, the dog, that starts barking or snarling at the intruders (the word literally means 'this animal has no respect for its superiors'). There is only one way to deal with such an obstacle: **inukoro o abuseru**, the deadly pork chop, otherwise known as **shūtome o kudoku**, silencing one's mother-in-law. Once at the door you confront the **mimochi musume**, the lock (literally, the pregnant daughter), who must be handled with the softest of touches, unless of course you are in possession of the **nezumi**, the mice (or master keys).

As for the crooks themselves, they come in all varieties. There is the **sagarigumo**, or descending spider, the man or woman who braves the slippery tiles of the roof to reach their target; the **denshinkasegi**, the telegram breadwinners, who get there by shinning up telephone poles; the **shinobikomi**, thieves who enter crawling; the **odorikomi**, who enter 'dancing', i.e. brash criminals with guns; the **mae**, or fronts, debonair thieves who simply walk up to the main door; or the super-sly **ninkātā**, who leaves no trace: the master thief.

There is the **ichimaimono**, the thief who works alone; and the **hikiai**, those who pull together, i.e. partners in crime. There are **nitchūshi**, broad-daylight specialists, and **yonashi**, night specialists; even **miyashi**, shrine specialists. There are **akisunerai**, empty-nest targeters, those who specialize in targeting unattended houses; **neshi**, sleep specialists, the men who target bedrooms after the loot has been assembled and packed; and even evil **tsukeme**, literally, touching eyes: thieves who barge into bedrooms to rape sleeping victims.

Radish with glasses

Not content with colourful descriptions of robbers, the Japanese have an extensive vocabulary for cops too: there are the **gokiburi**, the cockroaches, policemen on motorcycles, who can follow burglars over pavements and through parks; the **kazaguruma**, the windmill, an officer who circles the streets and alleys, getting closer and closer to the area where the criminals are working; the **daikon megane**, the radish with glasses, the naive young officer who's not going to be a problem for the experienced crook; or the more problematic **oji**, the uncle, the dangerous middle-aged patrolman who knows all the members of the gang by name and is liable to blow the whistle first and ask questions later.

As if that wasn't enough, policemen on those overcrowded islands can also be described as **aobuta** (blue pigs), **en** (monkeys), **etekō** (apes), **karasu** (crows), **aokarasu** (blue crows), **itachi** (weasels), **ahiru** (ducks), **hayabusa** (falcons), **ahōdori** (idiotic birds, or albatrosses), **kē** (dogs), **barori** (Korean for pig), and **koyani** (cat, from the Korean **koyangi**). Officers even turn into insects such as **hachi** (bees), **dani** (ticks), **kumo** (spiders), **mushi** (bugs) and **kejirami** (pubic lice).

When crimes go wrong

'Punishment,' say the Spanish, 'is a cripple, but it arrives.' Criminals may get away with it for a while, but in the end justice of some kind generally catches up with them:

chacha (Korean) the disastrous act of each gang member dashing down a different alley
afersata (Amharic, Ethiopia) the custom, when a crime is committed, of rounding up all local inhabitants in an enclosure until the guilty person is revealed
andare a picco (Italian) to sink (to be wanted by the police)
cizyatiko (Mambwe, Zambia) to make a man believe that he is safe so as to make time for others to arrest him
panier à salade (French) a salad shaker (a police van)
annussāveti (Pali, India) to proclaim aloud the guilt of a criminal

Pig box

All except the perpetrator are happy to see that anyone taking the immoral shortcut to personal enrichment ends up in a very bad place:

obez' yannik (Russian) a detention ward in a police station (literally, monkey house)
butabako (Japanese) the cooler, clink (literally, pig box)
bufala (Italian) a meat ration distributed in jail (literally, she-buffalo – so called because of its toughness)

Into the pit

And society may exact its just deserts:

gbaa ose (Igbo, Nigeria) to rub in pepper by way of punishment or torture

kitti (Tamil) a kind of torture in which the hands, ears or noses of culprits are pressed between two sticks

dhautī (Sanskrit) a kind of penance (consisting of washing a strip of white cloth, swallowing it and then drawing it out of the mouth)

ráhu-mukhaya (Sinhala, Sri Lanka) a punishment inflicted on criminals in which the tongue is forced out and wrapped in cloth soaked in oil and set on fire

barathrum (Ancient Greek) a deep pit into which condemned criminals were thrown to die

tu-tù (Vietnamese) a prisoner ready for the electric chair

As thick as thieves

aralarindan su sizmaz (Turkish) not even water can pass between them

entendre comme cul et chemise (French) to get along like one's buttocks and shirt

uni comme les doigts de la main (French) tied like the fingers of a hand

una y carne ser como (Spanish)/**como una y mugre** (Mexican Spanish) to be fingernail and flesh/like a fingernail and its dirt

sange paye ghazwin (Persian) as thick as volcanic stone

22.
Realpolitik

em rio que tem piranha, jacaré nada
de costas (*Brazilian Portuguese*)
in a piranha-infested river, alligators do
backstroke

Pipe and sunshade

Once upon a time life was straightforward: the chief ran the show and everyone fell in behind:

pfhatla-pfhatla (Tsonga, South Africa) to make a present to the chief to abate his anger

tarriqu-zan (Persian) an officer who clears the road for a prince

chātra (Pali, India) one who carries his master's sunshade

vwatika (Mambwe, Zambia) to place the pipe in the mouth of the chief

kapita mwene (Mambwe, Zambia) the time of the stroll taken by the chief (between 9 and 10 p.m., when everyone had retired, the chief would go about quietly, eavesdropping to find out those talking about him)

magani (Mindanao, Philippines) the custom of obtaining leadership and the right to wear red clothes through killing a certain number of people

tirai (Tamil) a tribute paid by one king to another more powerful

ramanga (Betsileo, Madagascar) a group of men whose business is to eat all the nail-parings and to lick up all the spilt blood of the nobles (literally, blue blood)

mangkat (Indonesian) to die for one's king or queen

A gift

Things weren't so great for those at the bottom of the pile, however interesting their duties:

ravey (Manobo, Philippines) to enslave someone because he
  didn't obey a command
dapa (Malay) a slave-messenger sent as a gift with a proposal
  of marriage
dayo (Bikol, Philippines) a slave who stands guard over the
  grave of a leading member of the community so that the
  body will not be disinterred by sorcerers
pachal (Malay) a slave of a slave
golamkhana (Bengali) a factory for imbuing people with a
  slave mentality

False friends

tank (Tocharic, Turkey) to interfere
tilts (Latvian) bridge
Transparent (German) banner, placard
bingo (Kapampangan, Philippines) chip in a blade
doshman (Romani) enemy
exito (Spanish) success
Parole (German) motto, slogan

Changing shirts

Democracy freed us from the old hierarchies and gave us the power to choose our own destinies ...

valboskap (Swedish) ignorant voters (who vote as they are told)

qualunquismo (Italian) an attitude of indifference to political and social issues

apocheirotonesis (Ancient Greek) a rejection by a show of hands

chaquetero (Central American Spanish) someone who changes political ideas as easily as changing shirts

porros (Mexican Spanish) thugs who stand around polling stations and intimidate voters

Full poodle

... with leaders directly answerable to us and our interests:

phak kanmuang (Thai) political parties that become active only during or prior to elections

Politpopper (German) politically correct and correctly dressed (literally, a square politician)

göra en hel Pudel (Swedish) a politician, or some other well-known person who has done something bad, publicly admitting being bad but promising not to do it again and humbly asking for forgiveness (literally, do a full poodle)

Muffled

Perhaps we just have to accept that the political mindset is never going to change that radically:

aincātānī (Hindi) the manipulation and manoeuvring, tugging and pulling, a struggle inspired by selfish motives

ficcarsi (Italian) to get access to a group to gain advantages from them

başına çorap örmek (Turkish) to plot against someone (literally, to knit a sock for the head)

akal bulus (Indonesian) a cunning ploy (literally, a turtle's trick)

akarnok (Hungarian) someone with unscrupulous ambition

Power corrupts

It's commonly accepted that there are all kinds of unofficial extra benefits to being in power. The phrase in the Sinhala language of Sri Lanka for a local member of parliament, **dheshapaalana adhikaari**, also means crook and someone born out of wedlock:

sglaim (Gaelic) a great deal of the good things of life acquired in a questionable way

dedocratico (Spanish) an undemocratic appointment to a governmental position

zalatwic (Polish) using acquaintances to accomplish things unofficially

bal tutan parmağını yalar (Turkish proverb) a person who holds the honey licks his finger (a person given a job involving valuables will gain some benefit for himself)

kazyonnovo kozla za khvost poderzhat – mozhno shubu sshit' (Russian proverb) just even from having once held a state goat's tail one can make a fur coat (i.e. an official can make money by bribes)

Tail between legs

Many everyday English words are derived from other languages. Finding out more about their roots often casts a fascinating new light on the word itself:

accolade derives from the French **accoler** (to embrace) because knighthoods were initially conferred with an embrace

agony comes from the Ancient Greek **agonia** (contest): the athletes in training for the Olympic Games put their bodies through intense discipline to reach the peak of fitness, denying themselves normal pleasures and enduring punishing physical tests

coward comes from the Old French **couard** (tail) and thus we have the image of a dog retreating with its tail between its legs

jargon comes from the Old French word **jargoun** (twittering), the sound made by birds, incomprehensible to others

muscle is descended from the Latin word **musculus** (little mouse), a rather apt description of the moving and changing form under the skin, especially of the arms and legs

Talk box

The language of politics is famous for both **rollo** (Spanish), the long boring speech (literally, a paper roll), and for double speak. All round the world it's very important to listen extremely closely to what politicans say – and to what they don't:

borutela (Tsonga, South Africa) to praise another in his presence but malign him behind his back

feleka (Setswana, Botswana) to speak so as to conceal one's meaning; to be intentionally ambiguous

chíndugirathu (Tamil) to give a sign by pressing with the finger, unobserved by any third party

tok bokkis (Tok Pisin, Papua New Guinea) a way of giving words hidden meanings (literally, talk box)

achakiy (Quechuan, Andes) to say one thing and do something else

Problem solving

The Bambuti people of Congo have no chiefs or formal system of government; problems and disputes are solved by general discussion often involving the use of humour. Elsewhere, people have other ways of achieving agreement:

taraadin (Arabic) a compromise; a way of solving a problem
without anyone losing face

mochi (Chinese) the rapport or teamwork that enables people
to cooperate smoothly (literally, silent contract)

remettre les pendules à l'heure (French) to re-align something, for example, in establishing who is the boss, or how
we work (literally, to set the clocks at the right time again)

biritululo (Kiriwani, Papua New Guinea) comparing yams to
settle a dispute

War elephants

What a shame that such delightful methods can't be universally employed. But from the start of time dispute-resolution has often been alarmingly violent:

gazi (Mauritanian dialect) a plundering raid in which at least forty camels are employed

falurombolás (Hungarian) the destruction of villages

Schrecklichkeit (German) a deliberate policy of terrorizing non-combatants

edsabil (Maguindanaon, Philippines) to fight until death for the cause of Allah

nuulone (Anywa, Nilo-Saharan) a victory dance with rifles after a war

Cancer forces

All that's changed over the years is the deadliness of the weapons used:

dagadaga (Sranan Tongo, Surinam) a machine gun

plofstof (Afrikaans) explosive (literally, puff/bang stuff)

springstof (Dutch) an explosive (literally, jump matter)

rakovye voiska (Russian) strategic missile forces (literally, cancer forces – referring to the numerous cancerous diseases caused by radiation)

Heroes

On the battlefield itself individuals make extraordinary sacrifices ...

lwa manyanga (Mambwe, Zambia) to fight one another crawling along on all fours

mamakakaua (Hawaiian) the leading man in battle who bears the brunt of the fighting

ohiampunut (Finnish) one who has survived in battle (literally, shot/fired past)

abhí-vīra (Sanskrit) surrounded by heroes

Yellow-bellies

... or not, as the case may be:

ngivhe (Venda, South Africa) to hit with the butt-end of a spear (a blow given as a warning to escape)

rafizat (Persian) a body of soldiers who deserted their commander and retreated

imboscarsi (Italian) to lie in ambush, to evade military service, to avoid working, or to retreat to a secluded place to make love (literally, to take to the woods)

palias (Maranao, Philippines) the power or magic which protects its possessor from a bullet in battle

Handschuhschneeballwerfer (German) somebody who wears gloves to throw snowballs – used in general for all cowards

War trophies

There are no limits to cruelty, savagery and treachery:

liput (Manobo, Philippines) to throw someone off guard, through an appearance of goodwill, in order to kill him

usauara (Yamana, Chile) to shout, as a group of men, when ready to make an assault on someone they intend to kill

áhaneoha'ov (Cheyenne, USA) to kill someone by stepping on him

tsantsa (Jivaro, Ecuador) a human head shrunken and dried as a war trophy

tzompantli (Aztec) a rack of skulls

Legacy

But when it's all over, what are we left with?

aidos (Ancient Greek) the understanding of the need for humility at the point of victory

Gleichgültigkeit (German) the feeling of dreadful moral insensibility and detachment which is a peculiar legacy of wars

Cucumbers and shaving brushes

And, all too often, a large standing army. Who better than the Russians to tell us all about the realities of that sort of organization?

ogourets a soldier in his first six months of service (literally, a cucumber – referring to the colour green, which signifies inexperience)

pomazok a soldier who has served more than one year and is therefore released from certain menial tasks (literally, a shaving brush)

chelovek-amfibiya a soldier on dishwashing duty (literally, an amphibian man)

khoronit' okourok a punishment for soldiers who drop their cigarette butts on the ground; when even one such butt is found all soldiers are woken up in the middle of the night and forced to spend hours digging deep holes to bury individual butts

lekarstvo ot lyubvi two years of army service (literally, a cure for love, meaning that girlfriends rarely wait for soldiers to come home)

Something is rotten in the state of Denmark

hay un gato encerrado (Spanish) there's a cat shut up

les dés sont pipés (French) the dice are cheated

il y a anguille sous roche (French) there is an eel under the rock

iskat' igolku v stoge sena (Russian) there is a needle in the haystack

hayya min taht tibn (Arabic) a snake under the hay

23.
From Better to Hearse

Dios es el que sana, y el medico lleva
la plata (*Spanish*)
*God cures the patient and the doctor pockets
the fee*

Fagged out

We have all kinds of habits that aren't exactly good for us. As the Italian proverb cheerily goes: '**Bacco, tabacco e Venere, riducon l'uomo in cenere**', Bacchus, tobacco and Venus make men into ashes:

Glimmstengel (German) a cigarette (literally, a glowing stick)
pitillo (Spanish) a cigarette (literally, a small whistle)
bychkovat' (Russian) to smoke only part of a cigarette so as to save the butt
sassakisibingweiabas (Ojibway, North America) feeling a burning pain in my eyes from too much smoke

Peaky

The simplest symptoms can announce forthcoming suffering:

hí (Rapanui, Easter Island) to have a headache or to blow one's nose
kirukiruppu (Tamil) dizziness
cloch (Scots) to cough frequently and feebly
koodho (Anywa, Nilo-Saharan) to fart repeatedly
ku-susuukirira (Ganda, Uganda) to feel the first shivers of a fever
svimfardig (Swedish) ready to faint
motami-ella (Yamana, Chile) to go home or to a place eastwards and throw up

Hypo

Some people are more likely to succumb to illness than others:

niba n aoraki (Gilbertese, Oceania) a person very susceptible to catching every disease

mabuk darah (Malay) one who becomes sick upon seeing blood

wakakhtakeća (Dakota, USA) one who is made sick by a little matter, one who is nervous

aráttam (Tamil) the anxiety of a sick person

STD

Love is often described using the terminology of disease, as with **dongai** (Fijian) love sickness; while sex is seen both as a cause of sickness and as a cure:

pham-phòng (Vietnamese) to become sick after having intercourse

una cachiaspirina (Chilean Spanish) refers to how one will sweat heavily during sex and thus kill a cold

Sweating carrots

All too soon things become more serious:

zweet peentjes (Dutch) sweating like a pig (literally, sweating carrots)

fare i gattini (Italian) to vomit (literally, to make the kittens)

ca-ca-ca (Tsonga, South Africa) to have diarrhoea; to rain heavily

sarar burer (Chorti, Guatemala) a fever accompanied by an itch

útsu (Telugu, India) the falling out of the hair from sickness

oka/shete (Ndonga, Namibia) urination difficulties caused by eating frogs before the rain has duly fallen

kinudegan (Maguindanaon, Philippines) a disease in men that causes the penis to retract inside the body

Quack remedies

Routine must be interrupted and steps must be taken:

krankfeiern (German) to call in sick (literally, to celebrate illness)

tombola (Kalanga, Botswana) to extract a thorn from flesh using a safety pin

tervismuda (Estonian) curative mud

verkwakzalveren (Dutch) to spend money on quack remedies

kudóripannugirathu (Tamil) to slit or cut the top of the head in order to put in medicine to cure dangerous diseases

Docteur, docteur

Few enjoy handing themselves over to doctors, but sometimes it's unavoidable; or, as they say in France, **inévitable**:

trente-trois say ah! (literally, thirty-three – said by a doctor to the patient)

artilleur de la pièce humide a male nurse (literally, artilleryman of the wet gun)

passer sur le billard to undergo surgery (literally, to go onto the billiard table)

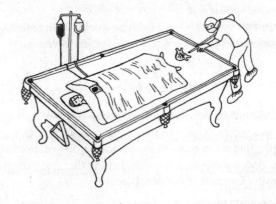

Surgical spirit

In some societies recommended cures may not be primarily medical:

> **millu** (Quechuan, Andes) a rock of aluminium sulphate used by witch doctors, who diagnose illnesses by analysing its colour change when it is thrown into a fire
>
> **ti-luoiny** (Car, Nicobar Islands) to call on the spirit of a sick man to return
>
> **tawák** (Tagalog, Philippines) a quack doctor with magic saliva
>
> **anavinakárayá** (Sinhala, Sri Lanka) a juggler, one who practises incantations upon persons who have been poisoned or bitten by a serpent
>
> **i^{n}dahli** (Alabama, USA) to cut stripe marks on, in order to suck out blood (applied to a hexed or sick person)

Hex

A Chilote Indian, who has gathered up the spittle of an enemy, will put it in a potato, hang it in the smoke, and utter certain spells in the belief that his enemy will waste away as the potato dries in the smoke. And many others, likewise, believe that one person can be responsible for another's physical decline:

> **khmungha** (Dakota, USA) to cause sickness or death in a supernatural way

The devil's in the detail

If it's an evil spirit to blame, it will need to be expelled. Methods differ:

tin-fu-ko (Car, Nicobar Islands) the driving out of the devil from a man by beating the ground with the thick stubs of a coconut leaf

sosela (Tsonga, South Africa) to cure a person by exorcism through the beating of drums

phurbu (Tibetan) ceremonial nails with which evil demons are symbolically nailed fast and banished

Corpse in the middle

The Koreans, Japanese and Chinese (both in Cantonese and Mandarin) avoid the number 4 since in all these languages it has a very similar pronunciation to the word for death. Chinese and Korean buildings often do not have a fourth floor, replacing the number 4 (**sa**) with the letter F. This is not the only number that the Chinese are wary of: the number 1414 is especially avoided because when spoken it sounds just like the words 'definite death, definite death'. Many traditional Chinese people believe that having an uneven number of people in a photograph brings bad luck. To have three people is of greater consequence as the person in the middle will die.

Recuperation

With luck, however outlandish it is, the cure will work and time will do the rest:

   mimai (Japanese) to visit a sick person in the hospital
   hletela (Tsonga, South Africa) to help a sick person to walk; to lead, as a hen does her chickens
   samaya (Maguindanaon, Philippines) a party held to celebrate the promised cure for someone who is sick
   i^{n}sobáayli (Alabama, USA) to have the feeling come back to a body part
   amūlha-vinaya (Pali, India) an acquittal on the grounds of restored sanity

Curtains

But nothing can ever be taken for granted:

   doi (Vietnamese) to make one's last recommendations before death
   urdhwaswása (Sinhala, Sri Lanka) the rattling in the throat which precedes death
   agonia (Spanish) the dying breath
   sa-soa (Bakweri, Cameroon) a comb; to make deathbed statements as to the disposition of property

Clogs and slippers

We kick the bucket or turn up our toes. The Russians play the snake, throw their hooves outwards, glue up their slippers, or throw out their best skates. The theme of no longer being shod and upright on your feet is widespread ...

estirar la pata (Latin American Spanish) to stretch out your leg
colgar los tenis (Mexican Spanish) to hang up or hand in your tennis shoes
at stille træskoene (Danish) to put aside the clogs
zaklepat bačkorama (Czech) to bang together a pair of slippers
oikaista koipensa (Finnish) to straighten one's shanks
nalları havaya dikmek (Turkish) to raise horse shoes to the sky

... but not exclusive:

gaan bokveld toe (Afrikaans) to go to the goat field
cerrar el paraguas (Costa Rican Spanish) to close the umbrella
liar el petate (Spanish) to roll up the sleeping mat
passer l'arme a gauche (French) to pass the firearm to the left
ins Gras beißen (German) to bite into the grass
a da colțul (Romanian) to turn around the corner
hälsa hem (Swedish) to send home one's regards
irse al patio de los callados (Chilean Spanish) to go to the courtyard of the hushed
ya kwanta dama (Hausa, Nigeria) he is lying on his right arm (Muslims are buried not lying on their backs but on the right arm facing the Kaabah)

A thousand cuts

To die of an illness is not ideal, but in comfortable surroundings, with loved ones around us, perhaps better than some of the alternatives:

lepur (Malay) to die through suffocation in mud
asa (Korean) death from starvation
áhano'xéohtsé (Cheyenne, USA) to die from carrying a load
skeelah (Hebrew) stoning to death
lang-trì (Vietnamese) death by a thousand cuts (an ancient punishment)
prayopaveshī (Hindi) one who undertakes a fast unto death
chŏngsa (Korean) love suicide, double suicide
fwa imfwa leza (Mambwe, Zambia) to die abandoned and alone (without having anyone to fold one's arms and legs for the burial)
lavu (Manobo, Philippines) to drown someone by overturning their canoe

Another way to go

The Fore tribe of New Guinea suffer from a terrible disease called **kuru**, which means shaking death. It is also known as the laughing sickness from the disease's second stage in which the sufferers laugh uncontrollably. It has a 100 per cent fatality rate.

Stiff

There's no saving us now; the best we can hope for is a little dignity:

tlanyi (Tsonga, South Africa) to find a person lying dead when one thought him alive

bahk' e chamen (Chorti, Guatemala) the fright caused by looking at a corpse

kreng (Dutch) a dead body which is bloated from being submerged in water for a substantial period of time (also a bitch)

gruz 200 (Russian) corpses transported by air (literally, load 200)

False friends

arm (Estonian) scar
cocoa (Nahuatl, Mexico) to suffer pain
halal (Hungarian) death
kill (Amharic, Ethiopia) skull
kiss (Swedish) pee
men (Thai) a bad smell
rib (Somali) contraction
rat (Romani) blood
safari (Zarma, Nigeria) medicine
wish (Bashgali, India) poison; medicine

Feet first

Every culture attaches importance to a respectful disposal of the dead; but *how* exactly they do it is different all over:

vynosit' (Russian) to bury someone (literally, to carry someone out feet first)

monoklautos (Ancient Greek) with one mourner

tomboka (Luvale, Zambia) to dance (said of an executioner)

sahagamanamu (Telugu, India) the burning alive of a widow, with her dead husband

Leichenschmaus (German) the meal after the funeral (literally, corpse banquet)

xuxo (Tsonga, South Africa) the spot where an important man died; when rites are observed for his spirit, people go first to that place, then to his grave

Funeral crashers

'A beautiful funeral does not necessarily lead to paradise,' runs a Creole proverb and, were we still able to care, such a thought might be reassuring:

tumeakana (Yamana, Chile) to not show the grief for a friend who has died that is expected from relatives, to act when a mourner as though one was not a mourner

pesamenteiro (Portuguese) one who habitually joins groups of mourners at the home of a deceased person, ostensibly to offer condolences but in reality to partake of the refreshments which he expects will be served

In loving memory

Now all that's left is for those who remain to remember and express their feelings:

di-huong (Vietnamese) the memory of a dead lover

keriah (Hebrew) a tear in clothes to signify a broken heart

miàti-drànomàso (Malagasy, Madagascar) to go up to the palace to weep on the decease of the sovereign

nyekar (Indonesian) to visit and lay flowers on the grave of a dead relative or friend

prātahsmaranīya (Hindi) worthy of being remembered every morning; revered

yortsayt (Yiddish) the anniversary of someone's death

Hex revenge

While some love and remember, there are others who believe that if someone is ill and dies there must be someone to blame; and appropriate action may have to be taken:

> **rihehlo** (Tsonga, South Africa) a spell cast upon a person by putting medicines on the grave of one killed by his witchcraft

Radish tips

Once under the ground we say we are 'pushing up daisies'. For the French, though, to be dead and buried is either **engraisser les asticots**, fattening the maggots, or **manger les pissenlits par la racine**, eating dandelions by the roots. Even more imaginatively the Germans have **sich die Radieschen von unten angucken**, he's looking at the radishes from below.

Out of the frying pan and into the fire

min taht al dalf lataht al mizrab (Arabic) from under the drip to under the spout

dostat se z bláta do louıe (Czech) out of the mud into the puddle

aasmaan se gire khajoor mein atke (Hindi) down from the skies into the date tree

takut akan lumpur lari ke duri (Indonesian) afraid of mud, escape to thorns

sudah jatuh tertimpa tangga pula (Indonesian) already fallen and hit by the stairs as well

lepas dari mulut harimau masuk ke mulut buaya (Indonesian) freed from the tiger's mouth to enter the crocodile's mouth

iz ognya da v polymya (Russian) from fire to flame

yağmurdan kaçarken doluya yakalanmak (Turkish) caught by the hail while running away from the rain

24.
The Great Beyond

człowiek strzela, Pan Bóg kule nosi
(*Polish*)
man shoots, God carries the bullets

So where do we go once the body has been burned, buried or, as with the Zoroastrian Parsees of India, pecked off the skeleton by vultures? It's hard for us to believe that the particular vitality that once animated the face of a loved one hasn't gone somewhere:

hanmdohdaka (Dakota, USA) to tell of one's intercourse with the spiritual world, to speak unintelligibly

dagok (Malay) clouds on the horizon of weird and changing form (believed to be ghosts of murdered men)

beina-fœrsla (Old Icelandic) the removal of bones (from one churchyard to another)

Fancy meeting you again

For Hindus, Buddhists and Native Americans, among others, the afterlife is not necessarily another place:

gatâgati (Sanskrit) going and coming, dying and being born again

púsápalan panninavan (Tamil) one who in the present life receives the reward of merit acquired in a former state

apagabbha (Pali, India) not entering another womb (i.e. not destined for another rebirth)

tihanmdeya (Dakota, USA) to have been acquainted in a former state of existence

Just a jealous guy

For others, the spirits of the dead may well stick around and remain animate enough to be called on in times of need:

hanmde (Dakota, USA) to have intercourse with the spirit world

zangu (Luvale, Zambia) a dance to immunize an adulterous woman to the spirit of her dead husband

ngar (Kaurna Warra, Australia) the call of a dead person

kuinyo (Kaurna Warra, Australia) the voice of the dead

andoa (Bakweri, Cameroon) to invoke spirits by spitting out the juice of leaves

havu (Bugotu, Solomon Islands) to make an offering to a ghost

False friends

sad (Sanskrit) being
pop (Bosnian) priest
bigot (French) sanctimonious
eleven (Hungarian) the living
fun (Lao) dream
hell (Norwegian) luck

Holy cockerel

Sometimes mere spirits aren't enough and stronger supernatural agents have to be called on. Many and varied are the prayers and rituals offered to the world's deities:

kahók (Tagalog, Philippines) the act of dipping fingers in holy water

a-cāmati (Sanskrit) to sip water from the palm of one's hand for purification

hacer (se) cruces (Latin American Spanish) to cross yourself in the hope that God will help you to understand.

thì thup (Vietnamese) to go down on one's knees then get up again, to make repeated obeisances

kiam (Malay) to stand during prayer

anda (Latin American Spanish) a wooden frame for carrying images of saints in processions

miau (Iban, Sarawak and Brunei) to wave a cockerel over a person while uttering a prayer

Broken sewing needles

Many and varied too are the building of their shrines and how they are decorated:

abhi-gamana (Sanskrit) the act of cleansing and smearing with cowdung the way leading to the image of the deity

laplap bilong alta (Tok Pisin, Papua New Guinea) an altar cloth

hari kuyo (Japanese) a shrine for broken sewing needles (out of respect for the tools of the sewing trade)

tintueta-wen (Buli, Ghana) the personal god of a living or dead person whose shrine has not yet been transferred to the front of the house

bìt torng lăng prá (Thai) doing a good deed in secret (literally, pasting gold leaf onto the back of the Buddha image)

One who understands

In most cultures, one spirit stands pre-eminent above all others and is always the One to be both consulted and worshipped:

Hawëníyu' (Mingo, USA) God (literally, he is the one whose word/voice is good)

olumonron (Yoruba, Nigeria, Benin and Togo) one who understands people's problems, God

Candle cormorant

'He who is near the church is often far from God,' say the French; and there is always a risk of substituting religiosity for virtue:

hywl (Welsh) religious or emotional fervour, as experienced with preaching, poetry reading, sporting events, etc.

une grenouille de bénitier (French) an extremely devout churchwoman (literally, a frog of the holy-water basin)

Kerzlschlucker (Austrian German) an insufferably pious person who never misses a mass (literally, a candle cormorant)

On a hedgehog's back

The English language is full of relics of our former, more religious days. The expression 'crikey' is a truncation of the oath 'by Christ's key' and 'bloody' of 'by our Lady'. Socrates swore **ni ton kuna**, by the dog; and Pythagoras is said to have sworn **ma tin tetrakton**, by the number four. Even atheistic Baudelaire swore by the sacred St Onion. The following expressions of astonished disbelief are just as outlandish:

Kors i taket! (Swedish) Cross in the ceiling! (used when something rare happens)

Toushite svet, vynosite chemodany! (Russian) Switch off the light and take out your suitcases! (used when something is a great surprise)

Holla die Waldfee! (German) Ooh, the forest's fairy! (exclamation of surprise, often with an ironic connotation)

In groppa al riccio! (Italian) On a hedgehog's back! (the response to which is **Con le mutande di ghisa!**, Wearing underpants made of cast iron!)

Sounds better

Japanese monks invented pious euphemisms so as not to taint the inner sanctum with jarring worldly words. Whipping came to be called **nazu** (caressing), tears **shiotaru** (dropping salt), money **moku** (eyes), testicles **ryōgyaku** (spiritual globes), and toilets **kishisho** (a place of truth).

Charismatic

However much some would prefer it if none of us believed in anything, it seems that holy men (and women) are here to stay:

vusitavant (Pali, India) one who has reached perfection (in chaste living)

mana (Polynesian dialect) the spiritual charisma attributed to holy people

samádhi (Tamil) the abstract contemplation of an ascetic, in which the soul is considered to be independent of the senses; a sepulchre, grave

nésajjika-dhutanga (Sinhala, Sri Lanka) a religious observance which restrains a man from sleeping or lying down

an-avakānkshamāna (Sanskrit) not wishing impatiently (said of ascetics who, having renounced all food, expect death without impatience)

anupabbajjā (Pali, India) giving up worldly life in imitation of another

Magic numbers

Certain groupings have particular significance, particularly in Southern Asia.

3 **tam-cuong** (Vietnamese) the three fundamental bonds – prince and minister, father and son, husband and wife

4 **tu-linh** (Vietnamese) the four supernatural creatures – dragon, unicorn, tortoise, phoenix

5 **bani khoms** (Yemeni) practitioners of the five despised trades (barber, butcher, bloodletter, bath attendant and tanner)

6 **luc-nghe** (Vietnamese) the six arts – propriety, music, archery, charioteering, writing and mathematics

7 **saptavidha-ratnaya** (Sinhala, Sri Lanka) the seven gems or treasures of a Chakrawarti king – chariot wheel, wife, jewel, elephant, horse, son, prime minister

8 **ashtāng** (Hindi) prostration in salutation or adoration, so as to touch the ground with the eight principal parts of the body, i.e. with the knees, hands, feet, breasts, eyes, head, mouth and mind

9 **nasāya-ratna** (Sanskrit) the nine precious gems (pearl, ruby, topaz, diamond, emerald, lapis lazuli, coral, sapphire and garnet) which are supposed to be related to the nine planets

10 **dasa-mūtraka** (Sanskrit) the urine of ten (elephant, buffalo, camel, cow, goat, sheep, horse, donkey, man and woman)

Whistling in the wind

If your god isn't interested you may just have to fall back on other means:

itinatalagá (Tagalog, Philippines) to place oneself at the mercy of fate

uhranout (Czech) to cast the evil eye on somebody, to bewitch someone

bino (Gilbertese, Oceania) an incantation to get a woman back by turning a gourd very rapidly and allowing the wind to whistle into the opening

naffata (Arabic) a woman who spits on the knots (in exercising a form of Arabian witchcraft in which women tie knots in a cord and spit upon them with an imprecation)

The crystal ball

You might think that the advice of spirits and gods would be enough to comfort and direct humankind, but not a bit of it. We are so desperate to know what the future holds for us that almost anything will do:

fakane (Bugotu, Solomon Islands) to divine, using a broken coconut shell

koffiedik kijken (Dutch) reading tea leaves, predicting the future (literally, coffee-grounds-looking)

ber-dreymr (Old Icelandic) having clear dreams as to the future

lowa (Setswana, Botswana) a particular pattern in which a diviner's bones have fallen

onnevalamine (Estonian) telling one's fortune by pouring molten lead into cold water (on New Year's Eve)

chichiri-wiirik (Buli, Ghana) a man who can call on fairies to reveal things to him; a type of diviner

vayasa mutírtsu (Telugu, India) a crow crossing from the left side to the right (which Hindus consider a good omen)

Fringed with noodles

We all hope things will turn out well but there are all kinds of superstitions that wishing each other good luck might bring its reverse. When someone in Norway goes fishing, he is wished **skitt fiske**, lousy fishing.

German has two expressions for being lucky: **Schwein haben**, to have a pig – as a pig symbolizes good luck and lots of sausages; and **Sott haben**, to have soot – because, according to folklore, touching a chimney sweep brings luck. The French describe someone who is incredibly lucky as **il a le cul bordé de nouilles**, literally, his arse is fringed with noodles.

IDIOMS OF THE WORLD

When pigs fly

na kukovo ljato (Bulgarian) in a cuckoo summer

kad na vrbi rodi grožđe (Croatian) when willows bear grapes

når der er to torsdage i en uge (Danish) when a week has two Thursdays

quand les poules auront des dents (French) when hens have teeth

am Sankt Nimmerleinstag (German) on St Never-ever-day

majd ha piros hó esik (Hungarian) when it's snowing red snowflakes

quando Pasqua viene a maggio (Italian) when Easter falls in May

tuyaning dumi yerga tekkanda (Uzbek) when the camel's tail reaches the ground

când o fi bunica fată mare (Romanian) when my grandma will be a virgin again

kag-da rak svist-nyet (Russian) when the crayfish whistles

balık ağaca / kavağa çıkınca (Turkish) when fish climb
   trees/poplar trees
cuando las ranas críen pelos (Spanish) when frogs grow
   hair

The Wonder of Whiffling

CLATTERFARTS AND JAISIES

Getting acquainted

Great talkers should be crop'd,
for they have no need of ears

(Franklin: *Poor Richard's Almanack* 1738)

Once upon a time, your first contact with someone was likely to be face to face. These days you're as likely to get together via the computer:

floodgaters people who send you email inquiries and, after receiving any kind of response, begin swamping you with multiple messages of little or no interest

digerati those who have, or claim to have, expertise in computers or the Internet

disemvowel to remove the vowels from a word in an email, text message, etc, to abbreviate it

bitslag all the useless rubble one must plough through on the Net to get to the rich information ore

ham legitimate email messages (as opposed to spam)

DOG AND BONE

Possibly the most used English word of greeting – **hello** – only came into common usage with the arrival of the telephone. Its inventor, Alexander Graham Bell, felt that the usual Victorian greeting of **'How do you do?'** was too long and old-fashioned for his new device. He suggested the sailor's cry **ahoy!** as the best way to answer his machine and operators at the first exchange did just that. But ahoy! didn't prove popular because it felt too abrupt. Compromise was soon reached with **hello!**, a word that came straight from the hunting-field. But could Bell ever have foreseen some of the ways in which his device would come to be used?

Hollywood no (US slang 1992) a lack of response (to a proposal, phone call, message etc.)

scotchie (South African slang) a 'missed call' which communicates some pre-arranged message or requires the receiver to call back at their expense, thereby saving the first caller the cost of the call

fox hole (UK slang 2007) the area beneath one's desk (in these days of open-plan offices) where telephone calls can take place peacefully

SNAIL MAIL

Of course, the old-fashioned letter still has its uses, as these Service slang words indicate: the key one being, in these days of retentive hard drives, that once you've destroyed your message, it leaves no trace:

yam yum a love letter

giz to read a pal's letter to his girlfriend; to offer advice

gander a look through the mail, a glance over another's shoulder at a letter or paper

flimsies the rice paper on which important messages are written and which can be eaten without discomfort in case of capture

VISITING HOURS

Or you can do that wonderfully traditional thing and pay a call in person:

pasteboard (1864) to leave one's visiting card at someone's residence

cohonestation (17C) honouring with one's company

gin pennant (Royal Navy slang) a green and white triangular pennant flown to indicate an invitation on board for drinks

GR8

The arrival of mobile phones on the scene led immediately to some interesting usages. In the first wave of texting came shortened versions of much-used phrases:

F2T	free to talk
AFAIK	as far as I know
T+	think positive
BCNU	be seeing you
HAND	have a nice day
KIT	keep in touch
CUL8R	see you later
ZZZ	tired, bored

When people switched to predictive text, they discovered the phenomenon of the phone's software coming up with the wrong word; most famously **book** for **cool** (so teenagers started describing their hipper friends as 'book'). Other **textonyms** include:

lips for **kiss**
shag for **rich**
carnage for **barmaid**
poisoned for **Smirnoff**

A LITTLE SOMETHING

A gift, however small, will always go down well:

toecover (1948) an inexpensive and useless present
xenium (Latin 1706) a gift given to a guest
exennium (Old English law) a gift given at New Year
groundbait (Royal Navy slang) a box of chocolates or something
    similar given to a lady friend in pursuit of a greater prize

DIGNITY AND PRIDE

In the US, the knuckles touched together are called, variously, **closed-fist high fives**, **knuckle buckles** or **fist jabs**. Done horizontally, the gesture is called a **pound**; vertically it's the **dap** (which some say is an acronym of 'dignity and pride'). Other greetings, of course, involve words, but hopefully not misunderstandings:

dymsassenach (Cheshire) a mangled Welsh phrase meaning 'I don't understand English'

shaggledick (Australian slang) an affectionate greeting for someone who is familiar but whose name doesn't come to mind

take me with you (Tudor–Stuart) let me understand you clearly

thuten (Middle English 1100–1500) to say 'thou' to a person, to become a close friend

ALL RIGHT, MATE?

You never get a second chance to make a first impression, so be aware of how you're coming across:

corduroy voice (US 1950s) a voice that continually fluctuates between high and low (from the up-and-down ridges in corduroy)

yomp (Cheshire) to shout with the mouth wide open

snoach (1387) to speak through the nose

psellism (1799) an indistinct pronunciation, such as produced by a lisp or by stammering

RABBIT, RABBIT

Though there are always those who just can't help themselves:

macrology (1586) much talk with little to say
clatterfart (1552) a babbler, chatterer
chelp (Northern and Midlands 19C) to chatter or speak out of turn
blatteroon (1645) a person who will not stop talking
clitherer (Galway) a woman with too much to say
air one's vocabulary (*c.*1820) to talk for the sake of talking

SMOOTH CUSTOMER

Chit-chat apart, good manners always go down well (however bogus they may be):

garbist (1640) one who is adept at engaging in polite behaviour
jaisy (Midlands) a polite, effeminate man
sahlifahly (Nottinghamshire) to make flattering speeches
court holy water (1519) to say fair words without sincere intention; to flatter
deipnosophist (1656) a skilful dinner conversationalist

PETER PIPER: TONGUE TWISTERS

There are tongue twisters in every language. These phrases are designed to be difficult to say and to get harder and harder as you say them faster. They're not just for fun. Therapists and elocution teachers use them to tame speech impediments and iron out strong accents.

Repeat after me (being particularly careful with the last one) ...

Sister Sue sells sea shells. She sells sea shells on shore. The shells she sells. Are sea shells she sees. Sure she sees shells she sells

You've known me to light a night light on a light night like tonight. There's no need to light a night light on a light night like tonight, for a night light's a slight light on tonight's light night

I'm not the pheasant plucker. I'm the pheasant plucker's son. I'm only plucking pheasants till the pheasant plucker comes

Some short words or phrases 'become' tongue-twisters when repeated, a number of times fast:

Thin Thing
French Friend
Red Leather, Yellow Leather
Unique New York
Sometimes Sunshine
Irish Wristwatch
Big Whip

CLEVER CLOGS

*B*ut let's not go too far. Nothing, surely is worse than those people who put on airs and graces …

nosism (1829) the use of the royal 'we' in speaking of oneself
peel eggs (*c.*1860) to stand on ceremony
gedge (Scotland 1733) to talk idly with stupid gravity
godwottery (1939) the affected use of archaic language

… or claim to know more than they do:

ultracrepidarian (1819) one who makes pronouncements on topics beyond his knowledge
raw-gabbit (Scotland 1911) speaking confidently on a subject of which one is ignorant
to talk like the back of a cigarette card (UK slang 1930s) to pretend to greater knowledge than one has (the cards carried a picture on the front and a description or potted biography on the back)

MANNER OF SPEAKING

All's fair in love and war, but a good classical education provides a conversational armoury that is hard to match:

diasyrm (1678) a rhetorical device of damning with faint praise
sermocination (1753) a speaker who quickly answers his own question
paraleipsis (Ancient Greek 1586) mentioning something by saying you won't mention it
eutrapely (1596) pleasantness in conversation (one of the seven virtues enumerated by Aristotle)

IRONY IN THE SOUL

Other tricks can leave the Average Joe standing ...

charientism (1589) an insult so gracefully veiled as to seem unintended
asteism (1589) polite and ingenuous mockery
to talk packthread (b.1811) to use indecent language well hidden, as a tinker carefully folds and tucks thread back away into his pack of goods
vilipend (1529) verbally to belittle someone

... and make the rest of us look like idiots:

onomatomania (1895) vexation in having difficulty in finding the right word
palilalia (1908) a speech disorder characterized by the repetition of words, phrases or sentences
verbigeration (1886) the repetition of the same word or phrase in a meaningless fashion (as a symptom of mental disease)

WORD JOURNEYS

Originally these common words and phrases meant something very different:

constipate (16C from Latin) to crowd together into a narrow room
anthology (17C from Ancient Greek) a collection of flowers
round robin (17C) a petition of protest whose signatures were originally arranged in a circle so that no name headed the list and no one person seemed to be the author (the robin does not refer to the bird but to the French *rond* for round and *ruban* for ribbon)
costume (18C) manners and customs belonging to a particular time and place

STICKYBEAK

Character

Let him that would be happy for a day,
go to the barber; for a week, marry a wife;
for a month, buy him a new horse; for a
year, build him a new house; for all his
life time, be an honest man

(1662)

According to legal statute an **idiot** is an individual with an IQ of less than 20, an **imbecile** between 21 and 49 and a **moron** between 50 and 70. As you cast around for insults it may be worth remembering these categories. But then again, the English language has never been short of slurs for the stupid. Historically, you could have been a **clumperton** (mid 16C), a **dull-pickle** or a **fopdoodle** (both 17C); and more recently, **two ants short of a picnic, two wafers short of a communion** or even **a few vouchers short of a pop-up toaster**.

Over the centuries, some other fine reproaches have included:

doddypoll (1401) a hornless cow, hence a fool
jobbernowl (1599) a blockhead
slubberdegullion (1616) a dirty, wretched slob
goostrumnoodle (Cornwall 1871) a stupid person, a fool

LOOSE KANGAROOS

Australians, in particular, specialize in scorn for the intellectually challenged. In the 1950s you could have been as **mad** (or **silly**) as a **cut snake**, a **hatful of worms** or a **Woolworth's watch**. More recently, in the 1980s, you might have been a **couple of tinnies short of a slab** or a **few snags short of a barbie** (where a **tinnie** is a beer can, a **slab** is a stack of cans and a **snag** is a sausage). Then again, a real idiot or **drongo** couldn't **blow the froth off a glass of beer, knock the skin off a rice-pudding, pick a seat at the pictures, find a grand piano in a one-roomed house,** or **tell the time if the town-hall clock fell on them**. Other memorable expressions of Antipodean scorn include **there's a kangaroo loose in the top paddock** and **the wheel is turning, but the hamster is dead**.

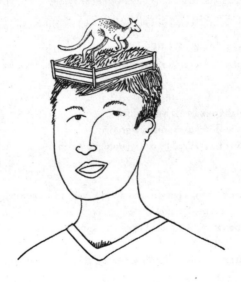

MEN OF STRAW

Fools can often be enthusiastic in their idiocy. Arguably more irritating are those whose marbles are all present, but who somehow just lack the drive:

dardledumdue (Norfolk 1893) a person without energy
maulifuff (Scotland) a young woman who makes a lot of fuss but accomplishes very little
gongoozler (1904) an idle person who stands staring for prolonged periods at anything unusual
mulligrubs (1599) a state of depression of spirits
accidie (Old French *c*.1230) spiritual torpor, world weariness

WHAT NOW?

Other types it's as well to steer clear of include the mean ...

chinchin (Middle English 1100–1500) to be stingy
stiff (hotel trade jargon) any customer that fails to leave a tip

the moaning ...

crusty-gripes (1887) a grumbler
choowow (Fife) to grumble, a grudge
forplaint (1423) tired by complaining so much

the nosey ...

quidnunc (1709) a person who always wants to know what is going on (from Latin: 'what now')
stickybeak (New Zealand 1937) an inquisitive person; also the nose of a nosy-parker
pysmatic (1652) interrogatory, always asking questions or inquiring

the elusive . . .

didapper (1612) someone who disappears and then pops up again
whiffler (1659) one who uses shifts and evasions in argument
kinshens (Scotland 1870) an evasive answer: 'I don't know, I cannot tell'
salt one up (US slang) to tell a different lie when covering up something
salvo (1659) a false excuse; an expedient to save a reputation or soothe
hurt feelings

the unattractive . . .

farouche (Horace Walpole 1765) sullen, shy and repellent in manner
yahoo (Swift: *Gulliver's Travels* 1726) a crude or brutish person
ramstamphish (Scotland 1821) rough, blunt, unceremonious; forward
and noisy

the tedious . . .

meh (US slang popularized by *The Simpsons*) boring, apathetic or
unimpressive
whennie (UK current slang) a person who bores listeners with tales of
past exploits

and the just plain impossible . . .

quisquous (Scotland 1720) hard to handle, ticklish
utzy (LA slang 1989) uncomfortable, bothered, uneasy
argol-bargolous (1822) quarrelsome, contentious about trifles
camstroudgeous (Fife) wild, unmanageable, obstinate, perverse
whiffling (1613) trifling, pettifogging, fiddling

TWO GENTLEMEN

In the early nineteenth century two gentlemen in particular were to be avoided. Though both types persist, social developments may mean we see more of the second than the first these days. **A gentleman of three ins** was 'in gaol, indicted, and in danger of being hanged in chains'. While **a gentleman of three outs** was 'without money, without wit, and without manners'.

HIGH HAT

Foppish, conceited behaviour – once known as **coxcombical** (1716) – seems too to be a persistently male trait:

jackanapes (Northern 1839) a conceited, affected, puppyish young man
princock (1540) a pert, forward, saucy boy; a conceited young man
flapadosha (Yorkshire) an eccentric, showy person with superficial manners

WITCH'S BROOM

Women, by contrast, have come in for all kinds of criticism:

mackabroin (1546) a hideous old woman
Xanthippe (1596) an ill-tempered woman, a shrew (after Socrates's wife)
cantlax (Westmoreland) a silly, giddy woman
termagant (1659) a violent, brawling, quarrelsome woman
bungo-bessy (Jamaican 1940) a woman whose busybody qualities are considered highly undesirable
criss-miss (West Indian 1950s) a pretentious woman who overestimates her abilities, charms and allure

YUPPIES

Everyone's so used to the word yuppie now that they forget that only twenty-five years ago it was a brand new acronym for Young Urban Professional. Here are some other acronyms coined subsequently to that famous first:

SPURMO a Straight, Proud, Unmarried Man Over 30
SADFAB Single And Desperate For A Baby
CORGI a Couple Of Really Ghastly Individuals
SITCOM Single Income, Two Children, Oppressive Mortgage
KIPPERS Kids In Parental Property Eroding Retirement Savings
SKIERS Spending their Kids Inheritance (on travel, health and leisure activities)

SLYBOOTS

Better, perhaps, those who assume airs than those who seem straightforward but aren't:

janjansy (Cornwall 1888) a two-faced person
accismus (Medieval Latin 1753) feigning a lack of interest in something while actually desiring it
mouth-honour (G. B. Shaw: *Major Barbara* 1907) civility without sincerity
mawworm (1850) a hypocrite with delusions of sanctity
Podsnap (from the character in Dickens' *Our Mutual Friend* 1864) a complacent, self-satisfied person who refuses to face unpleasant facts
skilamalink (East London slang late 19C) secret, shady

REGULAR GUY

Such characters make one long for that remarkable thing: the straightforward, decent, or just thoroughly good person . . .

rumblegumption (Burns: letter 1787) common sense
pancreatic (1660) fully disciplined or exercised in mind, having a
    universal mastery of accomplishments
towardliness (1569) a good disposition towards something, willingness,
    promise, aptness to learn
Rhadamanthine (Thackeray: *Paris Sketchbook* 1840) strictly honest and
    just (Rhadamanthus, Zeus's half-human son, was made a judge of the
    souls of the dead due to his inflexible integrity)

. . . this is someone we all want to spend time with, and stay loyal to . . .

wine (Old English) a friend
bully (Geordie) a brother, comrade
bread-and-cheese friend (Sussex) a true friend as distinguished
    from a **cupboard-lover** (a personal attachment that appears to be
    motivated by love but stems from the hope of gain)

WORD JOURNEYS

amnesty (16C from Ancient Greek) forgetfulness, oblivion

nice (13C from Latin nescire: to be ignorant) foolish; then (14C) coy, shy; then (16C) fastidious, precise; then (18C) agreeable, delightful

obnoxious (16C from Latin) exposed to harm

generous (16C from Latin via Old French) nobly born

GOING POSTAL
Emotions

Be not too sad of thy sorrow,
of thy joy be not too glad

(c.1450)

Throughout the world the British were once famed for their stiff upper lip; but is this sort of imperturbability really no more than a paper-thin façade for some extremely strong feelings beneath?

ugsomeness (1440) loathing

jump salty (US slang 1996) to become angry

brain (Middle English 1100–1500) furious

throw sarcasm (Jamaican English 1835) to relieve one's emotions by speaking out about one's dislike for or sense of grievance against another

unbosom (1628) to disclose one's personal thoughts or feelings

HOPPING MAD

It's now generally agreed that it's better to let it all out than keep it in:

dudgeon (1597) a resentful anger (dudgeon was a wood used to make dagger hilts)

mumpish (1721) sullenly angry; depressed in spirits

wooden swearing (US slang b.1935) showing anger by acts of violence or roughness, as in knocking furniture about

go postal (US slang 1986) to lose your temper, behave with irrational violence, especially as a result of workplace stress (from a postal worker who killed fourteen fellow employees and wounded six before shooting himself)

JESUS WEPT

Tears, too, are regarded as a good thing these days. But it doesn't stop them sometimes making for a **kankedort** (Chaucer: *Troylus* 1374) an awkward situation:

gowl (*c.*1300) to weep bitterly or threateningly
skirllie-weeack (Banffshire) to cry with a shrill voice
grizzle (1842) to fret, sulk; to cry in a whining or whimpering fashion
sinsorg (Anglo-Saxon) perpetual grief
bubble (Geordie) to weep

BRING ME SUNSHINE

Luckily sunshine eventually follows rain. Words describing happiness offer fascinating barometers into history. For instance, the Old English word for joy, **dream,** also describes music and ecstasy – an intriguing view into the mind-frame of our ancestors ...

froligozene (Tudor–Stuart) rejoice! be happy!

fleshment (Shakespeare: *King Lear* 1605) excitement from a first success

felicificability (1865) capacity for happiness

macarism (mid 19C) taking pleasure in another's joy

maffick (1900) to rejoice with an extravagant and boisterous public celebration

kef (1808) a state of voluptuous dreaminess, full of languid contentment (originally used to describe the effects of opium)

MAKE 'EM LAUGH

We can't all be a **grinagog** (1565), one who is always grinning. But the contrast is all the better when we do finally get to see the funny side:

cachinnate (1824) to laugh loudly and immoderately
winnick (Lincolnshire) to giggle and laugh alternatively
snirtle (1785) to laugh in a quiet or restrained manner
popjoy (1853) to amuse oneself
goistering (Sussex) loud feminine laughter

HA HA BONK

Humour is often cruel. At the heart of slapstick is a series of jokes that amuse only those who set them up:

press ham (US college slang 1950s) to press a bare buttock against a window and shock passers-by

squelch-belch (Winchester College 1920) a paper bag of water dropped from an upper window onto people below

to catch the owl (late 18C) to play a trick on an innocent countryman, who is decoyed into a barn under the pretext of catching an owl: when he enters, a bucket of water is poured on his head

tiddley-bumpin' (Lincolnshire) tapping on a window pane with a button on a length of cotton secured to the frame by a pin (a device used by boys to annoy neighbours)

pigeon's milk (1777) an imaginary article for which children are sent on a fool's errand (traditionally on April 1st)

squashed tomatoes (1950s) a game that involves knocking on a door and then rushing away as the homeowner answers it (also known as **knock down ginger** (England and Canada), **ding-dong ditch** (US), **chappy** (Scotland), **dolly knock** (Ireland))

WORD JOURNEYS

jest (13C from Latin and French) a deed or exploit; then (15C) idle talk

engine (13C from Latin via Old French) contrivance, artifice; then (14C) genius

frantic (14C) insane

negotiate (16C from Latin) ill at ease; not at leisure

to have a chip on one's shoulder (US 19C) of a custom in which a boy who wanted to give vent to his feelings placed a chip of wood on his shoulder in order to challenge any boy who dared to knock it off

TWIDDLE-DIDDLES
Body language

Keep the head and feet warm,
and the rest will take nae harm

(1832)

In the developed world these days, one of the greatest concerns is being overweight, whether you are an adult or a child. But the evidence of language is that not being thin is hardly a new thing. Nor are people's reactions:

fubsy (1780) being chubby and somewhat squat
flodge (Banffshire) a big, fat, awkward person
ploffy (Cornwall 1846) plump; also soft and spongy
pursy (Scotland) short-breathed and fat
fustilug (1607) a fat sloppy woman
five by five (North American black 1930s) a short fat man (i.e. his girth is the same as his height)

CHUBBY CHOPS

It's not just the whole but the parts that get labelled. In the UK people talk about **bingo wings** for flabby upper arms, a **muffin top** to describe that unsightly roll of flesh above tight jeans, a **buffalo hump** for an area of fat in the upper back and **cankles** for ankles so thick that they have no distinction from the calf. Over the pond recent slang is just as critical:

bat wings flabby undersides of the upper arms
banana fold fat below the buttocks
chubb fat around the kneecaps
hail damage cellulite (from its pitted similarity to the effects of hail)

MODEL FIGURES

So it must be reassuring to some that being skinny can also attract unfavourable notice (especially when combined with height):

windlestraw (1818) a thin, lanky person

straight up six o'clock girl (US black 1940s) a thin woman

slindgy (Yorkshire 1897) tall, gaunt and sinewy

gammerstang (1570) a tall, awkward woman

stridewallops (Yorkshire) a tall, long-legged girl

flacket (Suffolk) a girl, tall and slender, who flounces about in loose hanging clothes

NAPOLEON COMPLEX

The awful truth is that from the playground onwards, people who don't meet the average have always had to put up with mockery. Luckily, vertically challenged role models from Alexander the Great to Napoleon have often had the last laugh:

youfat (Ayrshire 1821) diminutive, puny

gudget (Donegal) a short thick-set man

dobbet (Cornwall) a short, stumpy little person

pyknic (1925) short and squat in build, with small hands and feet, short limbs and neck, a round face and a domed abdomen

endomorphic (1888) being short but powerful

NIP AND TUCK

So in the short term what can you do to change things? Wear platform shoes. Go on a diet. Or consider having some 'work' done:

pumping party (Miami slang 2003) illegal gatherings where plastic surgeons give back street injections of silicone, botox, etc.

rhytidectomy (1931) the surgical removal of facial wrinkles

roider (US slang 2005) someone who injects illegal steroids to enhance his body

reveal party (US current slang) a party held to celebrate successful cosmetic treatment, especially cosmetic surgery or dentistry

MAKEOVER

Then again, you could just pop down to the salon and have a less final and painful sort of revamp:

whiffle cut a very short haircut worn by US soldiers in the Second World War
farmer's haircut (US slang 1984) a short haircut that leaves a white strip of skin showing between the bottom of the hair and the tanned portion of the neck
follow-me-lads (mid 19C) curls that hang over a woman's shoulder
krobylos (Ancient Greek 1850) a tuft of hair on top of one's head
acersecomic (1612) one whose hair has never been cut

FACE FUNGUS

Ever since William the Conqueror passed a law against beards, facial hair has gone in and out of fashion. After the return of the heroic soldiers from the Crimea in the 1850s, the hirsute look became wildly popular:

dundrearies (1858) a pair of whiskers that, cut sideways from the chin, are grown as long as possible (named after the comic character Lord Dundreary in the popular Victorian play *Our American Cousin*; these excessive sidechops, popular with gentlemen perambulating the centre of the capital, were also known as **Piccadilly Weepers**)
burke (*c.*1870) to dye one's moustache
bostruchizer (Oxford University *c.*1870) a small comb for curling the whiskers

THREADBARE

From **five o'clock stubble** to the **pudding ring** (Florida slang), a facial decoration made up of a moustache and a goatee, many men cherish their beards because it's the only kind of hair they have left:

pilgarlic (1529) a bald man (referring to a peeled head of garlic)
skating rink (US current slang) a bald head
egg-shell blonde (New Zealand 1949) a bald man

Better such terms as these than being fingered for having a **brillo** (UK playground slang), a merciless expression for the style of a middle-aged male who is attempting to fluff up every hair to disguise his ever-expanding pate.

SNIFFER

air can do only so much to frame a face. You can't escape the features you've been given, especially that one in the middle:

simous (1634) having a very flat nose or with the end turned up
proboscidiform (1837) having a nose like an elephant's trunk
macrosmatic (1890) having a supersensitive nose
meldrop (c.1480) a drop of mucus at the end of the nose

A WORD IN YOUR SHELL-LIKE

Even the highest in the land have to learn to live with the particular shape of their auditory nerves:

FA Cup (UK playground slang 1990s) a person with protruding ears
leav-lug't (Cumberland) having ears which hang down instead of standing erect
sowl (Tudor–Stuart 1607) to pull by the ears

PEEPERS

Eyes are more than mere features, they are extraordinary organs we should do our very best to look after:

saccade (French 1953) the rapid jump made by the eye as it shifts from one object to another
canthus (Latin 1646) the angle between the eyelids at the corner of the eye
eyes in two watches (Royal Navy slang) of someone whose eyes appear to be moving independently of each other as a result of drunkenness or tiredness or both

especially if there's only one of them ...

half-a-surprise (UK slang late 19C) a single black eye
seven-sided animal (18C riddle) a person with only one eye (they have a right side and a left side, a foreside and a backside, an outside, an inside and a blind side)

CAKE HOLE

The **glabella** (Latin 1598) is the gap between the eyebrows, and the **philtrum** (Latin 17C) the groove below the nose. But though the mouth below attracts such crude names as **gob, gash** and **kisser**, its features and actions are more delicately described:

wikins (Lincolnshire) the corners of the mouth
fipple (Scottish and Northern) the lower lip
fissilingual (b.1913) having a forked tongue
bivver (Gloucestershire) to quiver one's lips
mimp (1786) to speak in a prissy manner usually with pursed lips

GNASHERS

An evocative Australian expression describes **teeth like a row of condemned houses**. In this state, the only cure is to have them out and replaced with **graveyard chompers**, a Down Under phrase for false teeth, intriguingly similar to the Service slang **dead man's effects**. But dental problems persist from the earliest night-time cries onwards:

neg (Cornwall 1854) a baby's tooth
shoul (Shropshire) to shed the first teeth
laser lips; metal mouth; tin grin (US campus slang 1970s) a wearer of braces
gubbertushed (1621) having projecting teeth
snag (Gloucestershire) a tooth standing alone

CHEEK BY JOWL

What face would be complete without all those interesting bits in between?

joblocks (Shropshire) fleshy, hanging cheeks
bucculent (1656) fat-cheeked and wide-mouthed
pogonion (1897) the most projecting part of the midline of the chin
prognathous (1836) having a jaw which extends past the rest of one's
  face

... not to mention other decorative
surface additions:

push (Tudor–Stuart) a pimple
turkey eggs (Lincolnshire) freckles
christened by the baker (late
  18C) freckle-faced

BOTTLING IT

Having broad shoulders has generally been seen to be a good thing, both literally and metaphorically. Other shapes are for some reason considered less reliable:

bible-backed (1857) round-shouldered, like one who is always poring over a book

champagne shoulders (*c.*1860) sloping shoulders (from the likeness to the bottle's shape)

Coke-bottle shoulders (Royal Navy slang) shoulders possessed by those individuals who are unwilling to take responsibility in any matter (after its rounded shape)

SINISTER

Most of us are right-handed. Once again, it's the odd ones out who get noticed, and not kindly. Left-handed people have been variously described as **molly-dukered**, **corrie-fisted** and **skerry-handit** (Scotland); **car-handed**, **cack-handed** and **cowie-handed** (North East); **kay-fist-ed**, **kibbo**, **key-pawed** and **caggy-ont** (Lancashire); **cuddy-wifter** (Northumbria); **kay-neeaved** or **dolly-posh** (Yorkshire); **keggy** (East Midlands) and **Marlborough-handed** (Wiltshire); while **awk** (1440) is an old English word which means 'with or from the left hand' and thus the wrong way, backhanded, perverse or clumsy (hence awkward).

PAWS

But all hands are carefully observed, both for how they are and for what they're doing:

pugil (1576) what is carried between the thumb and two first fingers
yepsen (14C) as much as the cupped hands will hold
gowpins (Yorkshire) the two hands full when held together
quobbled (Wiltshire) of a woman's hands: shrivelled and wrinkled from being too long in the washtub
clumpst (1388) of hands stiff with cold (hence clumsy)
rope-hooky (UK nautical jargon late 19C) with fingers curled in (from years of handling ropes)

... right down to the detail of specific digits:

lik-pot (Middle English 1100–1500) the forefinger of the right hand
mercurial finger (Tudor–Stuart) the little finger (as in palmistry it was assigned to Mercury)
flesh-spades (Fielding: *Tom Jones* 1749) fingernails
gifts (UK slang b.1811) small white specks under the fingernails, said to portend gifts or presents
lirp (1548) to snap one's fingers
fillip (1543) a jerk of the finger let go from the thumb
vig (Somerset) to rub a finger quickly and gently forwards and backwards

JOHN THOMAS

Further down are those parts often described as 'private', but subject also to any number of other euphemisms and nicknames:

twiddle-diddles (b.1811) testicles

melvin (US slang 1991) to grab by the testicles

be docked smack smooth (mid 18C) to have had one's penis amputated

merkin (1617) counterfeit hair for women's private parts

hinchinarfer (late 19C) a grumpy woman (i.e. 'inch-and-a-halfer' referring to the length of the disgruntled woman's husband's penis)

BUNS

The Ancient Greek-derived word **callipygian** (1646) has long been used to describe shapely buttocks, while in US slang **badonkadonk** indicates a bottom of exceptional quality and bounce. Unfortunately, rather more ubiquitous are displays of a less appealing kind:

working man's smile (US slang) a builders' bottom

LEGS ELEVEN

Below that, it's good to have shapely **stumps** and elegant **plates of meat**, whatever the individual components look like:

prayerbones (1900s) the knees

baker's knee (1784) a knee bent inwards (from carrying a heavy bread-basket on the right arm)

Sciapodous (1798) having feet large enough to be used as a sunshade to shelter the whole body

hallux (1831) a big toe

NOISES OFF

Cock-throppled (1617) describes one of those people whose Adam's apple is largely developed; **noop** (1818) is Scottish dialect for the sharp point of the elbow; and both **axilla** (1616) and **oxter** (1597) are names for the armpit. But perhaps the oddest words of all are those describing the noises that bodies can make:

yask (Shropshire) the sound made by a violent effort to get rid of something in the throat

plapper (Banffshire) to make a soft noise with the lips

borborygmus (1719) the rumbling, gurgling, growling sounds made by the stomach

WORD JOURNEYS

handsome (1435) easy to handle; then (1577) convenient; then (Samuel Johnson 1755) beautiful, with dignity

fathom (Old English) the span of one's outstretched arms

shampoo (18C from Hindi) to massage the limbs

complexion (from Latin) woven together; then (14C) the bodily constitution, the combination of the four humours

cold shoulder (from Medieval French) relating to a chateau guest who was served a cold shoulder of beef or mutton instead of hot meat, as a not-so gentle hint that he had overstayed his welcome

PRICK-ME-DAINTY
Clothes

Under greasie clothes,
are oft found rare virtues

(1666)

Even if you're not, as the Australians say, **as flash as a rat with a gold tooth,** you can still make time to be well turned out:

prick-me-dainty (1529) one that is finicky about dress; a dandy (of either sex)

pavisand (Kipling: *Simple Simon* 1910) to flaunt opulent or expensive clothing or jewels in a peacock-like fashion

flamfew (1580) a gaudily dressed female, whose chief pleasure consists of dress

sashmaree (Yorkshire) an elderly female conspicuous for the quaintness of her finery

UNMENTIONABLES

Not that all clothes are inherently smart:

cover-slut (1639) a clean apron over a dirty
    dress
orphan collar (US b.1902) a collar unsuitable
    to the shirt with which it is worn
stilt (Lincolnshire) to pull down and re-knit the
    feet of worn stockings or socks if the legs are
    still good
coax (UK slang mid 18C) to hide a dirty or torn
    part of one's stocking in one's shoes
apple-catchers (Herefordshire) outsized
    knickers (as one could use them for harvest-
    ing apples)

SKIMPIES

Garments that leave less to the imagination often attract greater interest:

banana hammock (US slang) a very brief
    men's swimsuit
pasties (strip club jargon 1961) coverings
    worn over the nipples
    of a showgirl's or topless dancer's breasts
    (to comply with legal
    requirements for entertainers)
budgie smugglers (Australian slang)
    tight-fitting swimming trunks

TREWS

But even slinging on a pair of trousers may not stop the ogling:

like Edgware Road (UK slang 20C) a phrase describing tight trousers (because it's got no ballroom either)

continuations (1825) trousers (since they continued a Victorian male's waistcoat in a direction too delicate to mention)

galligaskins (1577) loose breeches

spatterdashes (1687) coverings for the legs by which the wet is kept off (especially in riding)

gravity-bags (Westmorland) the seat of the trousers

yorks (Wales) the practice of tying colliers' and other workmen's trousers above the ankles to prevent dirt and dust from reaching the upper parts of the body

GYM SHOES

Here at home we mainly call them trainers these days. But around the country and the English-speaking world the slang varies widely. In Newcastle they're known as **sandshoes**; in Liverpool **gollies**; in Bristol and into Wales **daps**; in Nottingham **pumps**; in London **plimsolls**; in Dublin **whiteslippers**; and in Belfast **gutties**. Other types of footwear vary widely:

ferryboat (US 20C) a large, clumsy shoe

cod-heads (Glasgow 1930s) shoes that have worn out at the toe

done-promote (Jamaican English 1943) sandals made from worn out car tyres (i.e. one has been promoted from bare feet)

excruciators (19C) very tight, pointed shoes (forerunners of the 20C winklepickers)

KITTED OUT

Some occupations leave little choice as to what you wear:

lightning conductors (Royal Navy jargon) gold stripes running down
the trouser seams of a Captain's or Flag Officer's Mess Dress uniform
devil's claw (*c*.1850) the broad arrow on convicts' uniform
fruit salad (Service slang) a large collection of medal ribbons which
runs to three or more rows

SUITS YOU

There are all kinds of useful names for specific parts of clothing. Imagine
how much easier life could be if you could define which pocket your keys
are kept in or why exactly you have to turn down that fourth helping of
turkey . . .

gerve (US late 19C) the breast-pocket in a jacket
britch (US late 19C) the inside jacket pocket
coppish (Glamorgan) the part of the trousers that have buttons in front
slave (US military slang) the part of a garment covering an arm only
yule-hole (Scots b.1911) the last hole to which a man could stretch his
belt at a Christmas feast

REBELS IN BOATERS

Boys at Winchester College developed a rich lingo to describe how they wore their uniform. You could **sport** . . .

a fringe (1920) to allow the bottom of one's gown to become tattered
an advertisement (1892) to turn down the collar of a College gown to
    show the velvet
an angle (1920) to wear your straw hat crooked

Or more precisely:

a halo (1920) to have your hat tilted like a halo so that the hair was
    showing in front

PERUKE

Looking round at all the shaven heads and brillos of today, perhaps men should consider a return to something that was once an essential accessory, even if the language used to describe it was somewhat less than heroic:

cauliflower (1753) a large white wig, such as is worn by the dignified
    clergy and formerly by physicians
dildo (1688) a cylindrical or 'sausage' curl on a wig
caxon (1756) a worn-out wig
Nazarene foretop (1785) the foretop of a wig made in imitation of
    Christ's head of hair, as represented by the painters and sculptors

TOPPING

Or else, fly in the face of contemporary fashion and sport some other headgear:

liripipe (1737) the long tail of a graduate's hood

cow's breakfast (Canadian slang) a large straw hat

gibus (1848) an opera or crush hat

havelock (1861) a cloth hanging from the back of a soldier's cap to protect his neck from the sun

biggin (1530) a tight-fitting cap tied under the chin, usually worn by children or as a nightcap by men

goodgodster (Winchester College 1920) a brown bowler hat (from the exclamation necessarily uttered by anyone seeing so strange a thing)

WORD JOURNEYS

corset (14C from Latin and Old French) a little body
mitten (14C from Old French) divided in the middle
garter (14C from Old French) the bend in the knee
tuxedo (from Amerindian) a wolf; then the name of a lake near New
    York whose residents in 1886 became so socially important that its
    name was given to a new style of dinner coats

GOING WEST

Illness, death and spiritual matters

Sicknesse doth wound or afflict the flesh,
but it cures the soule

(1624)

The idealized body is all very well to look at, in a painting or beautiful photograph. But in life, of course, bodies are constantly working organisms, managing repetitive functions that we often try and pretend are not actually happening to us. Just look at the string of euphemisms for our regular trips to the loo or restroom. We **go and check the price of wheat in Chicago** (Fife), **see the vicar and book a seat for evensong** (Isle of Wight), **shake the dew from one's orchid** (Cumbria) or **wring out one's socks** (Kent).

WIND AND WATER

Related functions can cause us huge embarrassment, as we attempt to ignore the fact that air needs to be released or that sometimes the body will reject what we try and put into it:

fluff (Yorkshire) to break wind silently

dumb insolence (1916) breaking wind on parade

thorough cough (b.1811) coughing and breaking wind backwards at the same time

bespawl (Tudor–Stuart) to bespatter with saliva

vurp (UK teen talk) a belching action that's somewhere between vomiting and burping

bake it (late 19C) to refrain from visiting the loo when one should go there

ELF WARNING

Nor, sadly, can we rely on the body always to be in tip-top condition:

phthisickin (Essex) a slight, tickling cough

waff (1808) just the slightest touch of illness (especially of a cold)

aelfsogooa (Anglo-Saxon) a hiccough, thought to have been caused by elves

blepharospasm (1872) uncontrollable winking

galea (1854) a headache which covers the entire head like a helmet

mubble-fubbles (1589) a fit of depression

sirkenton (Ayrshire) one who is very careful to avoid pain or cold and keeps near the fire

MENS SANA

Though sometimes malfunction of the body has more to do with the mind that controls it . . .

formication (1707) the sensation of bugs crawling over one's body
trichotillomania (1889) the compulsive desire to pull out one's hair
boanthropy (1864) the belief that one is an ox
uranomania (1890) the delusion that one is of Heavenly descent
calenture (1593) a distemper peculiar to sailors in hot climates, where
    they imagine the sea to be green fields, and will throw themselves
    into it

DOCTOR IN THE HOUSE

Calling in professional assistance is sure to be a good plan, even if the treatment prescribed may sometimes seem a bit unusual:

urtication (1837) the act of whipping a palsied or benumbed limb with nettles to restore its feeling
bezoar (1580) a stone from a goat's stomach considered a universal antidote to poisons
organ recital (medical jargon) a detailing of one's medical history (especially of a hypochondriac's)
emporiatrics (medical terminology) the science of travellers' health (jet lag, exotic infections, overexposure to hot or cold, altitude sickness etc.)

GOD KNOWS

Irreverent medical acronyms are used by some doctors on patients' charts:

UBI Unexplained Beer Injury
PAFO Pissed And Fell Over
GORK God Only Really Knows (a hospital patient who is, and may well remain, comatose)
TEETH Tried Everything Else, Try Homeopathy
GPO Good for Parts Only

It has been known that certain medics use the letters **O** and **Q** to describe their very oldest patients, with respectively, their mouths open, and their tongues out.

PULLING THROUGH

The sad fact remains that in the lottery of illness, some are fortunate ...

umbersorrow (Scotland) hardy, resisting disease or the effects of severe
   weather
lysis (1877) the gradual reduction of the symptoms of a disease
to cheat the worms (b.1887) to recover from a serious illness
creaking gate (1854) an invalid who outlives an apparently healthier
   person (as a creaking gate hangs longest on the hinges)

... while others are less so (whatever their visitors think):

goodly-badly (Cumberland) of a sick person whose looks belie their
   illness
floccillation (1842) the action of a feverish patient in picking at the
   bedclothes during delirium
churchyard cough (1693) a cough that is likely to terminate in death
circling the drain (hospital jargon) a patient near death who refuses to
   give up the ghost
wag-at-the-wall (Jamaican English) a ghost that haunts the kitchen
   and moves backwards and forwards before the death of one of the
   family

LAST WORDS

Your time has come, and this is a journey with no return ticket:

thanatopsis (1816) the contemplation of death
viaticum (Latin 1562) Holy Communion given to a dying person
thratch (Scotland 1806) to gasp convulsively in the death-agony
dormition (1483) a peaceful and painless death

THE GOLDEN STAIRCASE

This final action of the body is also something that people prefer not to refer to directly, as the following euphemisms for dying attest:

buy the farm (US slang early 1900s)
climb the golden staircase (US slang late 1800s)
coil up one's ropes (British naval slang)
stick one's spoon in the wall (British slang 1800s)
meet one's Waterloo (Australian slang)
go trumpet-cleaning (late 19C: the trumpeter being the angel Gabriel)
chuck seven (late 19C: as a dice-cube has no 7)
drop one's leaf (*c.*1820)
take the everlasting knock (1889)
pass in one's cheeks (b.1872)

DEATH BY HONEY

Not of course that illness is the only way to go:

buddle (Somerset) to suffocate in mud
burke (1829) to smother people in order to sell their bodies for dissection (after the notorious Edinburgh body-snatchers Burke and Hare)
scaphism (b.1913) an old Persian method of executing criminals by covering them with honey and letting the sun and the insects finish the job

A HEARTY JOKE

When hanging was the ultimate penalty in this country, as it was for many centuries, a particular kind of gloating black humour went along with the licensed murder of wicked people:

hemp cravat (late 18C) a hangman's noose

to cry cockles (b.1811) to be hanged (from the noise made whilst being strangled)

artichoke (underworld slang 1834) a hanging (a 'hearty choke')

horse's nightcap (late 18C) the cap drawn over a criminal's eyes at his hanging (also known as **Paddington spectacles** (early 19C) from the execution of malefactors at Tyburn in the above parish)

keep an ironmonger's shop by the side of a common (1780) to be hanged in chains

sheriff's picture frame (UK slang b.1811) the gallows

dismal ditty (c.1690) a psalm sung by a criminal just before his death at the gallows

DUST TO DUST

However you meet your end, it's off to church for one last time:

ecopod (UK 1994) a coffin specially designed to be environmentally friendly

shillibeer (1835) a hearse with seats for mourners

wheelicruise (Orkney Isles) a churchyard

boot hill (American West 19C) a graveyard (where the occupants died 'with their boots on' i.e. violently)

parentate (1620) to celebrate one's parents' funerals

KNOCKING-ON

Not that death is necessarily the end of your consequence on earth:

dustsceawung (Anglo-Saxon) a visit to a grave ('a viewing of dust')

carrion-crow man (Guyanese English) a man who canvasses business for an undertaker following a death

umest (1400) the coverlet of a bed, often claimed by a priest at the death of a parishioner

to add a stone to someone's cairn (18C) to honour a person as much as possible after their death

memorial diamond (US slang 2001) a diamond created from carbon extracted from the remains of a cremated body

deodand (1523) an object that has been the direct cause of death of a human being (such as a boat from which a person has fallen and drowned) which was forfeited to the crown to be used as an offering to God

ELYSIAN FIELDS

The spirit has most definitely left the body, but to travel who knows where? Over the centuries there have been many different answers to this fascinating question:

fiddlers' green (1825) the place where sailors expect to go when they die: a place of fiddling, dancing, rum and tobacco

psychopannychy (1545) the sleep of the soul between death and the day of judgment

Lubberland (1598) a mythical paradise reserved for those who are lazy

GOD'S IN HIS HEAVEN

Back on earth, those left behind try and make sense of this alarming flight. Many find a visit to a church helpful in all kinds of ways ...

scaldabanco (1670) a preacher who delivers a fiery sermon
utraquist (1894) one who partakes of the wine as well as the bread at communion
officers of the 52nd (b.1909) young men rigidly going to church on the 52 Sundays in a year

... though some motives are more suspect than others:

thorough churchman (b.1811) a person who goes in at one door of a church, and out at the other without stopping
autem-diver (17C) a pickpocket specializing in the robbery of church congregations

SPEAK OF THE DEVIL

God is known by few names: God, Allah, Jehovah. But his old adversary has any number of monikers: **author of evil, black gentleman, fallen angel, old scratch, old split-foot** and **the noseless one**. Just in the north-east of England he's been **Clootie, Awd Horney, Auld Nick** and the **Bad Man**, while Yorkshire has had him as **Dicky Devlin**; Gloucestershire as **Miffy** and Suffolk as **Jack-a-Dells**.

THE UNCERTAIN FUTURE

Religion asks us to accept our fate, whatever that may be. For many that's not good enough. They need more concrete assurance of the good or bad things to come:

onychomancy (1652) fortune-telling using reflected light on oiled fingernails

pessomancy (1727) divination by throwing pebbles

belomancy (1646) divination using arrows marked with symbols or questions, guidance being sought by firing the arrows or drawing them at random from a bag or quiver

planchette (French 1920s) a small, heart-shaped board on casters with a pencil attached; when participants in a séance touched it lightly the planchette allegedly wrote messages from the dead

>O

WORD JOURNEYS

juggernaut (17C) from Hindi jagannath: a title of the god Vishnu 'lord of the world'. It was believed that devotees of Vishnu threw themselves beneath the wheels of a cart bearing his image in procession

mortgage (14C from Old French) a death pledge, a promise to pay upon a person's death

bask (14C) to bathe in blood

bless (Old English) to redden with blood; then to consecrate

SLAPSAUCE
Food

An apple pie without the cheese is like
the kiss without the squeeze

(1929)

British food is often unfavourably compared with the cuisines of other nations. But why on earth should this be?

dribble-beards (Scotland 1829) long strips of cabbage in broth
dog and maggot (UK military forces) biscuits and cheese
chussha-wagga (Worcestershire) inferior cheese
druschoch (Ayrshire) any liquid food of a nauseating appearance

HORSE FODDER

Dr Johnson famously described oats as 'a grain which is in England given to horses, but in Scotland supports the people'. Turnips on the other hand have long sustained people on both sides of the border. In the dialect of north-east England they have been known as **bagies, naggies, narkies, nashers, snadgers, snaggers, snannies, snarters, tungies** and **yammies**. In Scotland they're called **neeps**, as in **bashed neeps** (mashed turnips) the traditional accompaniment to haggis.

KITCHEN CONFIDENTIAL

Pig-months (19C) are those months in the year which have an 'r' in their name: that is, all except the summer months of May, June, July or August, when it was traditionally considered unwise to eat pork (or shellfish). But however safe your ingredients, correct preparation is essential:

spitchcock (1675) to prepare an eel for the table

bonx (Essex) to beat up batter for pudding

engastration (1814) the act of stuffing one bird into another (the result is called a **turducken**)

sclench (Shropshire) to check water at its boiling point, by dashing cold water into it

swinge (Newfoundland 1896) to burn the down off sea-birds after plucking the feathers

CAT'S PRAYERS

Fancy names abound for different types of food, whether they be barely edible, plain or thought of as a delicacy:

Boston strawberries (US late 19C) baked beans

call-dog (Jamaican English 1943) a fish too small for human consumption (so one calls the dog to eat it)

first lady (US drugstore jargon 1930s) spare ribs (Eve was made from Adam's rib)

scuttle-mouth (1848) a small oyster in a very large shell

pishpash (Anglo-Indian) a slop of rice-soup with small pieces of meat in it

bobby-jub (Yorkshire) strawberries and cream

dandyfunk (nautical jargon 1883) a ship's biscuit, soaked in water, mixed with fat and molasses, and baked in a pan

spadger (Tudor–Stuart) a sparrow; something small and tasty (sparrows were an Elizabethan delicacy)

armored cow (US army slang 1940s) canned milk

honeymoon salad (US diner jargon) lettuce alone (i.e. 'let us alone')

Adam and Eve on a raft (US diner jargon) two fried eggs on a piece of toast

GIVE AND TAKE AND EAT IT –
RHYMING SLANG

Some rhyming slang simply rhymes but the best stuff takes it further, with the meaning carried across:

borrow and beg (late 19C) an egg (the term enjoyed a fresh lease of life during the Second World War food-rationing period)

give and take (20C) cake (no cake can be eaten that has not been given)

satin and silk (American Pacific Coast 20C) milk (suggestive of this liquid food's smoothness)

army and navy (early 20C) gravy (which was plentiful at meal times in both services)

didn't ought (late 19C) port (based on the replies of ladies who, when asked to 'have another', said that they 'didn't ought')

PLUS ONE

Whatever you put on your table, you can be fairly sure that there'll be someone around to hoover it up:

smell-feast (1519) one who haunts good tables, a greedy sponger

cosherer (1634) someone who feasts or lives upon the industry of others

slapsauce (1573) a person who enjoys eating fine food, a glutton

hodger (US slang) a guest who eats all of the host's food and drinks all of the host's drinks

STOP PINGLING

Perhaps the best you can hope for is reasonable table manners:

dooadge (Yorkshire) to handle food in a messy way (often said of children)

mimp (1861) to play with one's food

pingle (Suffolk) to move food about on the plate for want of an appetite

sword swallower (Australian slang) someone eating from his knife, especially among shearers

yaffle (1788) to eat or drink especially noisily or greedily

... or at least guests who aren't fussy eaters:

pica (1563) a strong and unnatural craving for unsuitable food (such as chalk), which occurs during pregnancy

omophagist (1884) a person who eats raw flesh

pozzy-wallah (Tommies' slang 1914–18) a man inordinately fond of jam

POST-PRANDIAL

And then, hunger sated, you have the opportunity to sit back, digest and relax. Just keep an eye on all your guests ...

rizzle (1890) to enjoy a short period of absolute idleness after a meal
nooningscaup (Yorkshire 18C) the labourer's resting time after dinner
dando (19C) one who frequents hotels, eating-houses and other such
    places, satisfies his appetite and decamps without payment

---

➤○ WORD JOURNEYS

omelette (17C from French via Latin) a thin flat blade
pittance (13C from Latin via Old French) originally a pious request;
    then (14C) donations to monastic orders on a person's death to be
    spent on food and wine to be served on the anniversary of the
    donor's death; then (16C) these diminished to the extent of mean-
    ing a sparing allowance
bulb (17C from Ancient Greek via Latin) an onion
companion (18C from Latin) someone who eats bread with you

CRAMBAZZLED
Drink

It's all right to drink like a fish
– if you drink what a fish drinks

(1938)

After your meal, what could be better than a cup of tea. Just make sure you've remembered to warm the pot and observe all the other niceties:

to drown the miller to put too much water into tea (the supply of water is so great that even the miller, who uses a water wheel, is drowned with it)

stranger (Sussex) a single tea-leaf floating in a cup of tea

laptea (US slang) a crowded tea party where guests sit in each other's laps

to smash the teapot (late 19C) to abandon one's pledge of abstinence from alcohol (the symbolic rejection of tea as one's sole liquid stimulant)

DOWN AT THE OLD BULL AND BUSH

In Britain the drinking of alcohol has always been, for better or worse, at the heart of the community. The Romans had *tabernae* (the origin of our word tavern), which turned into the Anglo-Saxon alehouses, where a brewer would put a green bush up on a pole when the ale was ready to drink:

kiddleywink (1830) an unlicensed public house

build a sconce (18C) to run up a large bill at a tavern especially when one has no intention of paying

brendice (1673) a cup in which a person's health is drunk

spit chips (Australian slang 1901) to have extreme thirst (from the idea of having dry wood in your mouth)

flairing (Sydney slang) the action of bartenders of balancing, catching, flipping, spinning or throwing bottles, glasses, napkins or straws with finesse and style

MINE'S A NIPPITATUM

The traditional pint comes in many forms:

arms and legs (UK slang 19C) weak beer (i.e. a drink that has no body)

nippitatum (1576) exceptionally strong beer
barbed wire (Australian slang, Darwin) Four X beer (from the xxxx
   symbol)
parson's collar (1940s) the froth on top of a glass of beer
neckum, sinkum and **swankum** (Berkshire) the three draughts into
   which a jug of beer is divided

ON THE NAIL

Though for refined types more Continental beverages may be preferred, whatever their quality:

supernaculum (1592) the finest wine, which is so good it is drunk to the last drop, referring to the custom of turning over a drained glass and letting the last drop of wine fall onto the thumbnail (from the Latin 'upon the nail')
butler's perks (UK euphemism) opened but unfinished bottles of wine
beeswing (1860) the scum found on the surface of aged wine
balderdash (1611) adulterated wine

PEARLY GATES

The names of British pubs are not all that they seem – certainly if you're looking at the picture on the sign hanging outside them. **The Cat and Fiddle** didn't derive from a music-loving publican who kept cats, but is a corruption of Catherine le Fidèle, which refers to the faithfulness of Catherine of Aragon, Henry VIII's first wife. The **Hope and Anchor** comes from the Biblical text 'We have this as a sure and steadfast anchor of the soul, a hope'; **The Cross Keys** is the symbol of St Peter, the gatekeeper of heaven; and **The Royal Oak** commemorates the tree that hid Charles II from Oliver Cromwell's forces after his defeat at Worcester.

LAST GASPER

In Tudor times **drink** actually meant to smoke tobacco, something you could once do inside the bar. Now the **misocapnists** (1839), those who hate the smell of smoke, are in charge, so that's a pleasure restricted to the pavements outside:

smirting (US slang New York) flirting between people who are smoking cigarettes outside a pub, office etc.

vogueress (Polari slang) a female smoker

casablanca (Tommies' slang 1914–18) the last one, especially of cigarettes

doofer (workmen's slang b.1935) half a cigarette

toss the squares (US black slang) to pass a packet of cigarettes

whiffler (1617) a smoker of tobacco

JUST THE ONE

Take it or leave it, boozing is a serious business:

cagg (UK military slang b.1811) a solemn vow or resolution used by private soldiers not to get drunk for a certain time

parson palmer (late 18C) a term of reproach, to one who stops the decanter circulating by preaching over his liquor (as was done by a parson of that name whose cellar was under his pulpit)

duffifie (Aberdeenshire) to lay a bottle on its side for some time, after its contents have been poured out, so that it may be completely drained of the remaining few drops

SPEAKEASY

Just make sure your companions understand the importance of paying their way:

to raddle someone's toe (Australian late 19C) to request someone to buy a round of drinks

twizzling (Sussex) spinning a pointer on a pub ceiling to decide who should buy the next round

decorate the mahogany (Hobo slang) to buy the drinks; to line the bar with thirsty throats and brimming glasses

shot-clog (1599) an unwelcome drinking companion tolerated because he pays for the drinks

DRINK AND BE MERRY?

Soon, if you're not exactly **zig-zag** – Tommies' slang from the First World War for the state where it's impossible to walk in a straight line – the booze will certainly be making itself felt:

hozzy nozzy (Rutland) not quite drunk

bleezed (Scotland 19C) the state of one on whom intoxicating liquor begins to operate: especially describing the change produced in one's facial expression

cherubimical (Benjamin Franklin 1737) benevolently drunk

tenant in tail (mid 17C) one whose drunkenness promotes indiscriminate displays of affection

whiffled (P. G. Wodehouse: *Meet Mr Mulliner* 1927) drunk

FROM SHEEP TO SOW

In Lincolnshire they marked out four distinct phases of intoxication. A man was **sheep drunk** when he was merry and easily handled; then **lion drunk** when he was brave and boastful; **ape drunk** when he got up to silly, irresponsible tricks; and finally **sow drunk** when he fell to the ground in an alcoholic stupor.

TWO TOO MANY

Sailors are legendary for their drinking prowess but watch out for these two:

admiral of the narrow seas (early 17C) a drunkard who vomits over his neighbour

vice admiral of the narrow seas (1811) a drunken man that pisses under the table into his companions' shoes

THE MOURNING AFTER

Being drunk means never having to say you're sorry, until the next morning of course when you forswear alcohol for tea again:

take a sheep-bed (Wiltshire) to lie down like a sheep to sleep in a grass-field, till one is sober

woofits (1918) a hangover; a vague unwell feeling; a headache; a moody depression

gunfire (Service slang) early morning tea (because it often has to be of considerable strength to counteract a bad head)

to feel as if a cat had kitten'd in one's mouth (16C) to feel the nauseous after-effects of drinking

crambazzled (Yorkshire) prematurely aged through drink and a dissolute life

---

WORD JOURNEYS

bonkers (early 20C) slightly tipsy

tobacconist (16C) a tobacco smoker

grape (11C from Old French) a hook for gathering fruit; then a cluster of fruit growing together

stale (13C) old and strong (applied to wine and ale having stood long enough to clear of sediment)

FOOTER-FOOTER
Taking off

A traveller must have the backe of an asse
to beare all, a tung like the taile of a dog to
flatter all, the mouth of a hogge to eate what
is set before him, the eare of a merchant
to heare all and say nothing

(1594)

Going for a walk is the quintessential English form of relaxation; but there are many varieties within the basic idea of putting one foot in front of another ...

mantle (Lincolnshire) to walk aimlessly up and down with short steps
starp (North East) to walk with long strides
footer-footer (Scotland 1894) to walk in an affected mincing manner
nuddle (Suffolk) to walk alone with the head held low
slochet (Bedfordshire 1809) to walk with shoes nearly falling off the feet
festination (1878) walking faster and faster involuntarily

... and sometimes it can all seem a bit too much:

pouff (Banffshire) the act of walking with a heavy step, especially
  through weariness
plout (North East) to struggle to walk
surbater (1633) someone who tires another person out by walking
hox (Gloucestershire) to knock the feet together while walking
dot and go one (b.1811) to waddle: of people with one leg shorter than
  the other
darby-roll (19C) a style of walking that betrays an individual's
  experience of fetters and thus time spent in prison

BONE-BREAKER

So why not take up that efficient, ecological and highly fashionable way of getting around – just be sure not to flirt with its dangers:

croggie (UK school slang) a ride on the crossbar or handlebars of another rider's bicycle

blackadder (West Scotland playground slang) the action of allowing a bike to continue its journey without a rider (usually performed at the top of hills on either old, borrowed or stolen bikes)

endo (US slang San Francisco 1987) a bicycling accident in which the rider is thrown over the handlebars

SMIDSY (cyclists' acronym) Sorry Mate, I Didn't See You

acrobrat (UK playground slang 1970s) a kid who attaches poles to the front axle of his bike so he can bounce up and down on the front wheel

GO CART

Once upon a time more substantial vehicles moved slowly and with difficulty:

unicorn (1785) a coach drawn by three horses, two abreast and one in the lead

timwhisky (1764) a light carriage for one or two people, pulled by one or two horses

quarter (Shropshire) to drive a cart in a lane with deep ruts, in such a way as to keep each wheel clear of them

to hunt the squirrel (18C) for two coachmen to attempt to upset each other's vehicles as they race along a public road (veering from side to side like a frightened squirrel)

Now the opposite is too often the case:

garyboy (East Anglia slang 1995) a male who drives a car usually noticeable by its sporty appearance and souped up engine

swoop and squat (US slang 2005) to pull in front of another vehicle and slam on the brakes, deliberately causing an accident to collect the insurance money

chawbuckswar (Anglo-Indian) a rough rider

TICKET TO RIDE

Not that you need to have your own transport to get around:

fly canaries (underworld slang 1945) to pass off used tram tickets as new ones

monkey board (mid 19C) the step on the bus on which the conductor stands

hong! and **midor!** (UK transport workers' jargon) 'hurry along' and 'mind the doors'

Cinderella fare (US cabdrivers' slang) people left behind on the platform when the last train leaves late at night

---

I SPY

Travelling piquet (1785–1840) was one way bored travellers amused themselves when riding together in a carriage. Scores were given for people and objects passing by on their side of the carriage, as follows:

a man or woman walking = 1
a horseman = 2
a post chaise = 5
a flock of geese = 10
a flock of sheep = 20
a man with a woman behind him = 30
a man, woman and child, in a buggy = 40
a cat looking out of a window = 60
an old woman under a hedge = game won
a parson riding a grey horse with blue tack = game won

GRICER'S DAUGHTER

Let's not forget those who are happy just to watch. Trainspotters may be mocked by the outside world, but they don't take criticism lying down: the language of **gricing** is notable for its acidic descriptions of outsiders.

bert the majority of people on trains, only interested in getting from A to B

insects occasional railway enthusiasts who swarm at certain times of year

kettle basher someone obsessed with steam engines (looked on as an effete sentimentalist)

baglet a woman, generally looked upon with unfriendliness. Gricers are invariably male. Worst of all women is **The Baglet** – Lady Thatcher, whose reluctance to travel by train was legendary and who set the privatization of British Rail in progress

ELSEWHERE

Hopefully you will arrive safely at your destination. Though some places, traditionally, have been more euphemistic than real. You could **go to** ...

Jericho (late 18C) to become drunk
Bath (mid 17C) to take up life as a beggar
Chicago (US late 19C) to run away, especially to avoid one's debts
Copenhagen (1950s) to have a sex operation
the Bahamas (US slang) to be sent to solitary confinement
Peckham (early 19C) to sit down to eat

WORD JOURNEYS

muddle (17C) to wallow in mud

walk (from German) to press cloth, knead or roll paste; then (Old
English) to roll, toss, move about

insult (16C from Latin) to leap upon; then (16C) to glory or triumph
over

random (15C) great speed, violence; then (17C) of a shot: haphazard,
without purpose, fired at any range other than point blank

MUTTONERS AND GOLDEN FERRETS

Sport

Sport is sweetest when
there be no lookers on

(1616)

Sport has always been a part of British national life. In the beginning were
the informal games that anyone could play anywhere:

way-zaltin (Somerset) a game in which two persons standing back to
back interlace each other's arms and by bending forward alternately
raise each other from the ground

hot cockles (1580) a rustic game in which one player lay face downwards, or knelt down with his eyes covered, and being struck by the
others in turn, guessed who struck him

hinch-pinch (1603) a game where one person hits another softly, then
the other player hits back with a little more force, and each subsequent
blow in turn is harder, until it becomes a real fight

IN TOUCH

Many of our best-known sports started life in similar fashion. The earliest games of football involved one village taking on another, in violent, day-long combats where broken legs and bruised heads were common. Current slang reveals that underneath, perhaps, little has changed:

blaggudy (Wales) rough, dirty (especially of a football or rugby team)

clogger (UK slang 1970) a soccer player who regularly injures other players

sprig-stomping (New Zealand 1993) the deliberate stamping with studded boots on a recumbent rugby opponent

falling leaf a long-range shot in football which sees the ball change direction radically in the course of its flight

spaghetti-legs routine a goalkeeper's trick employed to distract a penalty taker

SECONDS AWAY

Another of our oldest sports had similar rough-and-tumble beginnings:

clow (Winchester 19C) a box on the ear

glass jaw (US slang 1940) of a boxer with an inability to withstand a
   punch to the chin

haymaker (1912) an unrestrained punch usually leading to a knockout,
   whereby the fist is swung wide in an arc

claret christening (b.1923) the first blood that flows in a boxing match

waterboy (US police slang 1930s) a boxer who can be bribed or coerced
   into losing for gambling purposes

FROM LAND'S END TO BROADWAY

Wrestling, too, has become less violent and more theatrical over the years,
with a terminology that dates back to its origins, supplemented by more
recent slang from around the world . . .

falx (Tudor–Stuart) a grip round the small of the back

Cornish hug a hug that causes one to be thrown over (Cornish men
   were famous wrestlers)

sugarbagging the tossing of an opponent onto the canvas as if he were
   a bag of sugar

whizzer an arm lock trapping one's arm against the opponent's body
   from a position behind him

potato (US slang 1990) a real hit that injures, as opposed to an orchestrated, harmless one

jobber a wrestler whose primary function is losing to better-known wrestlers

broadway a drawn result (so-called because, ideally, the result makes both men bigger stars)

OVER AND OUT

Another quintessentially English game has a host of extraordinary terms, from the **yorker** (a ball pitched directly at the batsman's feet) to **silly mid-off** (a fielding position close to and in front of the batsman). Other words have fallen out of fashion:

muttoner (Winchester College 1831) a blow from a cricket ball on the knuckles, the bat being at the time clasped by them

slobber (1851) to fail to grasp the cricket ball cleanly in fielding

bowl a gallon (Eton College c.1860) to get a hat-trick (the bowler then earned a gallon of beer)

TO THE 19TH

For the more senior sportsman, another gentler but equally demanding game with British (well Scottish, strictly) roots has been successfully exported around the world. First comes the teeing off, with all the problems that that entails:

waggle pre-stroke trial movements
sclaffing skidding the club over the grass before it hits the ball
skull to hit the ball too far above its centre
shank to hit the ball with the neck of the club
whiff a stroke that misses the ball

then the slow or fast progression down the fairway:

chilli-dip a weak, lofted shot that follows a mis-hit that has managed to hit more ground than ball (from the image of taking a taco and scooping up a helping of chilli)
fried egg a ball lying embedded in sand
golden ferret a golf stroke where the ball is holed from a bunker
mulligan a free extra shot sometimes taken as a second chance in a social match to a player who has made a bad one, not counted on his score-card

before the triumphant arrival at the green:

frog hair the well-cut grass that divides the fairway from the green itself
and is of a length and smoothness somewhere between the two
steamy a short shot or a putt that passes over or through the green
stiff a shot that stops so close to the hole that it must be impossible to
miss the putt

TOUCHÉ

Fencing, by contrast to all of the above, originated on the Continent and so
has a language with a very European feel:

mandritta (Tudor–Stuart 1595) a cut from right to left
passado (Shakespeare: *Love's Labour's Lost* 1588) a motion forwards and
a thrust
volt (1692) to leap with both feet in the air by your opponent's left
shoulder
appel a tap or stamp of the foot, serving as a warning of one's intent to
attack
derobement an evasion of the opponent's attempt to take or beat the
blade while keeping the sword arm straight and threatening the
opponent

TOUR DE FRANCE

Since their invention in France in 1860, bicycles have been eagerly embraced by our Gallic neighbours. So it's hardly surprising that cycling is a sport with French jargon:

musette a small cotton shoulder bag containing food that's handed to riders during a race

domestique a member of a professional cycling team, whose job is to ride solely for the benefit of the team and team leader, instead of their own glory

lanterne rouge the overall last-place rider in a stage race (from the red light found on the back of a train)

But as soon as things start going wrong, we're back to good old English:

bonk a cyclist's feeling of being devoid of energy

sag wagon the vehicle that carries bicyclists that have withdrawn from the event (due to injury, bicycle malfunction, tiredness etc.)

HEY DUDE!

Surfers follow the waves; and though you can find something to ride on in Newquay, they're altogether bigger, better and harder to stay on in Big Sur and Bondi . . .

shark biscuit (Australian slang *c*.1910) a novice surfer

hang five (US 1960s) to ride with the toes of one foot hooked over the front of the board

knots the bruises and cuts gained from battling the waves and his board (a surfer's status mark)

grubbing falling off your board while surfing

frube a surfer who does not catch a wave for the whole time they are in the water

hodad (1962) a show-off who hangs around surfing beaches, boasting of his exploits and trying to pick up girls, who has rarely, if ever, tried to surf

cowabunga! (Australian slang 1954) a shout of elation on surfing down a superb wave

COLORADO CLIFFHANGER

Climbing terms, likewise, come from mountainous places:

gingich (Scotland 1716) the chief climber or leader in climbing rocks

flash (Canada 1995) to climb a wall successfully on the first try

dynoing (Colorado 1992) leaping to a distant or out-of-reach hand hold

hang-dogging (Colorado 1992) a derogatory term for inexperienced climbers who hang on the rope while attempting feats beyond their ability

TROLLING AND YUMPING

Every sport, indeed, has both specialized terminology and also the kind of insiders' slang that makes seasoned practitioners feel quietly different, whether that be . . .

Rowing . . .

gully-shooting (b.1891) pointing oars upwards when rowing
gimp seat seat number 3 in an eight-person boat (often regarded as having the least responsibility)
blip-o! (late 19C) a derisive cry at a boat's coxswain colliding with anything

Tennis . . .

ketchepillar (early 16C) a tennis player
nacket (1833) a tennis ball-boy

Gymnastics . . .

coffee grinder a manoeuvre from a squatting position on the floor involving a circle of the leg while keeping both hands on the floor
fliffis a twisting double somersault performed on the trampoline
fly-away a horizontal-bar dismount method with a backward somersault

Billiards . . .

feather to run the cue backwards and forwards across the bridge between finger and thumb prior to making a shot
english the spin imparted to the ball
cocked hat a shot in which the ball hit by the white rebounds off three different cushions towards a middle pocket

or any of the other ways active people have found to pass their time, from long ago . . .

cock-squailing an old Shrove Tuesday sport involving flinging sticks at a cock tied by the leg, one penny per throw and whoever kills him takes him away

strag (Lancashire) to decoy other people's pigeons

trolling (Yorkshire) rolling hardboiled eggs down a slope (on Easter Monday)

dwile flunking (Suffolk) floorcloth throwing (a serious, competitive game)

postman's knock (Oxfordshire) a method of sliding on ice (by moving on one foot and tapping the ice with the other)

to right now . . .

to do an Ollie (skateboarding) to flip your ride in the air and stay aloft upon it

yump (rally-driving) to leave the ground in one's vehicle when going over a ridge

sandbagging (motorcycle racing) a stratagem whereby the favourite lets the rest of the field go on ahead, confident that when necessary he can regain the lead and win the race as expected

bulldogging (rodeo) to leap off a horse and then wrestle with a steer (the intention being to twist it by the horns and force it over onto the ground)

zorbing (New Zealand) harnessing oneself inside a huge inflatable PVC ball, then rolling more than 650 feet downhill

WORD JOURNEYS

upshot (16C) the final shot in archery that decided a match
racket (16C from Arabic via French) the palm of the hand
umpire (15C from Latin: *non par*, via Old French) not equal
gymnasium (16C from Ancient Greek via Latin) a school for
　　exercising in the nude

RUBBY-DUBBY

Country pursuits

He that would have good luck in
horses must kiss the parson's wife

(1678)

By long tradition in Britain, certain outdoor activities have been elevated to a higher category, that of 'field sports'. The most controversial of these is currently banned by law, though what this ban actually amounts to is anyone's guess:

own the moment in a hunt when the hounds show that they have found a scent

cut a voluntary to fall off one's horse while hunting

craner (*c.*1860) one who hesitates at a difficult jump

tantivy (1641) at full gallop

shoe-polisher a derisive term for a dog that doesn't stray far from a hunter's feet

TALLY HO!

Since 2004 deer can no longer be pursued with hounds in the UK, marking the end of a tradition dating back well before these terms from the Tudor–Stuart period:

abatures the traces left by a stag in the underwood through which he has passed
velvet-tip the down upon the first sprouting horns of a young deer
rascal a lean deer not fit to hunt
rechate the calling together of the hounds in hunting
dowcets the testicles of a deer

GAME ON

You may however still stalk and shoot these animals, as you may game birds such as pheasant or grouse. Which is perhaps ironic when you consider how much more efficient an instrument a gun is than a pack of hounds. As the Victorian dramatist W. S. Gilbert put it, 'Deer stalking would be a very fine sport if only the deer had guns'.

collimate (1837) to close an eye to aim at a target
nipshot (1568) in shooting: amiss in some way
fire into the brown (1871) shooting into the midst of a covey instead of singling out one bird
tailor (1889) to shoot at a bird, trying to miss
air washed a bird that lands and doesn't move or falls dead in the air and hits the ground (thus giving off very little scent on the ground and being difficult for dogs to find)
making game of a dog when it finds fresh scent

BIRDING

A gentler approach to our feathered friends has its own special terminology. And as any **birder** will tell you, it's simply not accurate to call them all **twitchers**:

squeaking noisily kissing the back of your hand in order to attract
  hidden birds
lifer a particular bird seen for the first time
getting a tick seeing a bird you've not seen before
gripping off seeing a bird when someone else doesn't
stringer a person suspected of lying about bird sightings
dipping out missing seeing a bird
whiffling of geese: descending rapidly from a height once the decision
  to land has been made, involving fast side-slipping first one way and
  then the other

GETTING HOOKED

Another ancient field sport remains highly unlikely to be banned (at least while Britain remains a democracy):

broggle (1653) to fish, especially for eels, by thrusting a sharp stick with
  bait on it into holes in the river bed
zulu (1898) an artificial fly
fizgig (1565) a kind of dart or harpoon with which seamen strike fish
guddle (1818) to catch trout by groping with the hands under the stones
  or banks of a stream
angletwitch (*c.*940) a worm used as bait in fishing
rubby-dubby (game fishing jargon) the minced fish (mackerel, pil-
  chards etc.) used as a bait for larger fish especially sharks
angishore (Newfoundland) a man too lazy to fish

ROYAL FLUSH

One pursuit of folk from country and town alike is known also as 'the sport of kings', a moniker that certainly remains appropriate with our current crop of royals:

persuader (Australian slang) the jockey's whip

poppism (1653) the smacking sound with which riders encourage their horses

call a cab the jockey's action in waving one arm to hold his balance when he and the horse are taking a fence

drummer a horse that throws about his fore legs irregularly

morning glory a horse '**catching pigeons**' (showing great promise on the training gallops) but unable to repeat the form on a racetrack
airedale (US slang 1960s) a worthless racehorse
post the blue (b.1909) to win the Derby

GIFT HORSES

With large sums of money involved, the temptation to tamper with the proper result is as old as racing itself:

ingler (underworld slang 1797) a crooked horse breeder
bishop to disguise the age of a horse by tinkering with its teeth
drop anchor fraudulently to cause a horse to run slowly in a race
hook (New Zealand 1910) to ride a horse with the aim of losing

ODDS ON

Down by the track, there's little that passes the bookies by:

pencil-fever (*c.*1872) the laying of odds against a horse certain to lose
springer (UK slang 1922) a horse on which the odds suddenly shorten
skinner (Australian slang 1891) a horse which wins at long odds (a betting coup for bookmakers who do not have to pay out on a heavily backed favourite)
stickout (US slang 1937) a racehorse that seems a certain winner
nap (bookies' jargon) a racing tipster's best bet of the day
scaler (New Zealand 1908) a bookmaker who decamps without paying out

They've even developed their own method of communication without words, known as **tic-tac**, where they signal with their arms to communicate complicated changes in the odds to outside bookmakers. To these professionals, there's slang for any bet you care to make:

> **macaroni** odds of 20/1
> **carpet** odds of 3/1
> **elef a vier** odds of 11/4
> **bottle** odds of 2/1
> **shoulder** odds of 7/4
> **ear'ole** odds of 6/4
> **up the arm** odds of 11/8
> **wrist** odds of 5/4

VERY GOOD GOING

In the US and Australia (amongst other places) they have their own words for particular combinations of winners:

exacta or **perfecta** a wager in which the first two finishers in a race, in exact order of finish, must be picked

quinella a wager in which first two finishers must be picked, but payoff is made no matter which of the two wins and which runs second

trifecta to pick three horses in a particular race to finish 1st, 2nd and 3rd (the payout is determined by the betting pool on the turnover of the particular bet)

superfecta a bet that forecasts in correct order the first four horses in a given race

WORD JOURNEYS

jockeys (16C) horse traders (once called Jocks: men of the people)

allure (15C from Old French) to bait: a device in falconry used by hunters to call back their hawks

relay (15C from Old French) to loose the hounds; a pack of fresh hounds held in reserve to relieve a previous pack

croupier (18C from French) a pillion rider, a rider on the croup of a horse; then someone who stood behind a gambler and gave advice

MADHOUSE

Indoor games and hobbies

Cards and dice ... the devil's books
and the devil's bones
(1676)

There's no shortage of enjoyable activities for those who would rather not brave our famously awful weather. Even the simplest-seeming have a complex terminology worth getting to know:

murgatroyd a badly manufactured tiddlywink, flat on both sides

squopped of a free tiddlywink that lands on another wink

blitz an attempt to pot all six winks of your own colour early in the game

crud a forceful shot whose purpose is to destroy a pile of winks completely

lunch to pot a squopped wink (usually belonging to an opponent)

boondock to send an opponent's tiddlywink a long way away, preferably off the table

LOW ROLLERS

The number of nicknames for marbles indicates what a popular game this is too (and still so in the age of the Game Boy® and the computer). In the dialect of the north-east of England, for example, marbles have been known as **alleys**, **boodies**, **glassies**, **liggies**, **marvels**, **muggles**, **penkers**, **parpers** and **scudders**. That's just the start of it:

flirt (Yorkshire) to flick a marble with finger and thumb
fullock (Shropshire) to shoot a marble in an irregular way by jerking the
    fist forward instead of hitting it off by the force of the thumb only
deegle (Cheshire) a stolen marble
neggy-lag (Yorkshire) the penultimate shot
hawk (Newfoundland) to win all an opponent's marbles
smuggings! (UK teen slang mid 19C) mine! (the exclamation used at
    the end of a game of marbles or spinning tops when the child who
    shouted first was allowed to keep the toy in question)

DICEMAN

When you get a little older, it becomes more interesting to throw objects with a more challenging set of possibilities:

snake eyes (North American slang 1929) getting double ones, the low-
    est score (supposedly resembling a snake's stare)
box cars (underworld slang 1937) double 6 (from their similarity to the
    wheels of freight cars)
gate to stop the dice moving before they have actually come to rest

ARRERS

Many grown-up indoor games are found in that fine old British institution, the pub. One pastime in particular speaks of generations of players with fine imaginations and plenty of time on their hands:

monger a person who deliberately scores many more points than needed to win the game

Robin Hood when a dart sticks into a previous dart

married man's side the left-hand side of a dart board (numbers 12, 9, 14, 11, 8 and 16) that would get a reasonable score (the rationale being a married man should always play safe)

right church, wrong pew hitting a double but the wrong number

slop darts that score, but not where you wanted them

masonry darts darts thrown so that they miss the board entirely and hit the wall instead

spray 'n' pray darts thrown by an irate and less talented player, rather quickly

bunting the art of throwing while on your knees

FEVVERS

And that's just a fraction of the jargon. All the scores in darts have their own names too. Remember, when playing darts you're counting down, not up, starting from a set 301 or 501 and trying to end up with exactly zero, a process which is known as **doubling out**:

madhouse double 1 (i.e. what you're left in until you finish the game by achieving it)

fevvers a score of 33 (from the 19C Cockney tongue twister: 'thirty-three feathers on a thrush's throat')

scroat a dart that is aimed for treble 20, but ends up in double 20

fish and globe a score of 45 (when competing on a fairground darts stall, 45 was a score that traditionally would win the customer a small paper bag of peanuts which later became the offer of a jar (globe) and a goldfish)

Lord Nelson a score of 111 (as he had one eye, one arm, one leg)

POKER FACE

A cool head and an expressionless face will serve you well in a game that otherwise relies on luck – unless of course you have other tricks up your sleeve:

runt a poker hand worth less than a pair

motown a poker hand consisting of 'jacks-on-fives'

vole the winning by one player of all the tricks of a deal; a grand-slam

pone the player who cuts the cards

hop a secret move made after the cut which puts the cards back in the original position and negates that cut for the cheat's benefit

crimp to bend one or more cards so that a cheat will be able to cut the deck as he wishes, or to know that an innocent player will be cutting the deck at that same desired card

there's work down the announcement by one player that someone somehow is cheating

BIDDING WAR

The king of card games requires not just luck, but skill of the highest level:

chicane (1886) the condition in a game of bridge of holding no trumps

bumble-puppy (1936) a game played at random (of people who play no conventions)

yarborough (19C) a bridge or whist hand with no card higher than a 9 (from a certain Earl of Yarborough who used to bet 1000 to 1 against the occurrence of such a hand; the actual odds are 1827 to 1)

flag-flying (1917) to make an overbid that will almost inevitably fail, just to liven up the game

huddle (US 1934) a period of thought in which a player considers his next move

FULL HOUSE

For those habitués of the pack, there's a fine range of nicknames for individual cards:

devil's bed-post (*c.*1835) the four of clubs, held to be unlucky

grace-card (Irish mid 19C) the six of hearts in cards

curse of Scotland (early 18C) the nine of diamonds (diamonds imply royalty and traditionally every ninth king of Scotland has been considered a tyrant and a curse to that country)

blankets (1915) the tens in a pack of cards (from the rolling of blankets in the military in tens for the convenience of transport)

noddy (Gloucestershire) the knave

suicide king the king of hearts (as the fifteenth-century French picture shows him about to impale himself on his sword)

the boy with the boots (Anglo-Irish late 19C) the joker in the pack of cards

HIGH STAKES

When you start to bring money into the picture, of course, both dice and cards can easily lose their innocence:

shill a decoy player, allied to the promoters of the game, who pretends to bet, and is allowed to 'win' in street games of three-card monte; his successes are intended to lure the public into laying down their money

tattogey (underworld slang 1753) one who uses loaded dice to cheat

langret (mid 16C) a die so loaded that it shows 3 or 4 more often than any other number

DESPERATE BIDS

For some unfortunates, the impulse to win can stop being a game and become more a part of their lives. As the Aussies say, there are some people who would **bet on two flies walking up the wall**:

martingale to continue doubling one's stake after losing in the hope of eventual recovery

ring in one's nose to be losing and betting heavily and impetuously in an attempt to get even (like a bull)

fishing remaining in a card game in the hope of a vital card

bird dog a small time or novice gambler who hangs around experienced professional gamblers to pick up tips

nut the living expenses and other overheads that a gambler must meet from his winnings

MONTE CARLO OR BUST

For people like this, home games are soon no longer enough; a professional arena for their habit beckons; and there, of course, under the patina of respectability, pretty much anything goes:

ladder man a casino employee who sits on a high chair and watches for any errors or cheating by players or croupiers

booster a bit player in a casino who entices genuine players to bet (and usually lose) their money

top-hatting in roulette, the surreptitious placing of more casino chips on top of existing ones after the outcome has been decided

BINGO LINGO

Better to switch to a sociable game often favoured by the older woman, which comes with its own inimitable terminology. **Two fat ladies** (88) and **legs eleven** are well-known but there are many other traditional coinages:

1 buttered scone
6 Tom Mix (more modern: **chopsticks**)
7 Gawd's in 'eaven
12 monkey's cousin (from rhyming slang for dozen)
23 a duck and a flea (from the shape of the figures)
50 half-way house (1940s) (since there are 100 numbers available to the caller)
76 was she worf it? (from 7/6d, the old price of a marriage licence)
77 two little crutches (from the shape of the figures)
80 Gandhi's breakfast (as he 'ate nothing')

ANORAKS

Or else give it up entirely and settle on a worthwhile and productive hobby:

notaphily (1970) the collecting of paper currency as a hobby
deltiologist (1959) a collector of picture postcards
cartophily (1936) the hobby of collecting cigarette cards
arctophile (1970s) a person who loves or collects teddy bears
cruciverbalist (US slang 1970s) a crossword puzzle addict
bowerbird (Australian slang) a person who collects an astonishing array of sometimes useless objects

WORD JOURNEYS

hazard (13C) a game of dice

forfeit (13C from Latin via Old French) 'done beyond the bounds of' the law, a crime

depart (13C from Latin via Old French) to divide into parts, distribute

MUSH FAKERS AND APPLESQUIRES

The world of work

He that hopes to thrive must rise at five;
he that has thriven, may lie till seven;
but he that will never thrive
may lie till eleven

(1640)

Even in these days of welfare, or **national handbag** as Polari slang (see page 157) evocatively has it, most of us have to work at something to make ends meet. However specialized or odd our occupation may be, we can take comfort from the fact that in harsher times, jobs came in all shapes and sizes:

legger (Yorkshire) a man employed to move canal boats through tunnels by walking on the roof or sides of the tunnel

fottie (Scottish) a female wool-gatherer

murenger (Cheshire 1706) an officer appointed to keep the walls of a city in repair

sewer (Tudor–Stuart) an attendant at a meal who superintended the seating of the guests and the tasting and the serving of the dishes

shore-man (Cockney) one who searches sewers for rats

pure-finder (c.1850) a street collector of dogs' dung

applesquire (late 16C) the male servant of a prostitute

gong-farmer (1596) a person who cleaned out privies at night and sold the waste as a fertilizer

screever (1851) a professional writer of begging letters

glutman (1796) a temporary customs officer (hired because of his ability to be numerate)

lodger-remover (underworld slang 1889) a seller of fine-toothed haircombs

mush faker (1821) an umbrella repairer ('mushroom-faker')

resurrection doctor (1800s) a doctor who buys corpses which are stolen from graves, or has people murdered and delivered to him

whiffler (1539) an officer armed with a weapon who clears the way for a procession

COLOUR CODED

Nowadays many jobs can be seen as either **white** or **blue collar**, where the former are those who wear a suit and work in offices, and the latter those getting their hands dirty in a boilersuit. The designation white came first, in 1921, and blue followed in 1950. Since then imaginative business writers and others have added yet more categories:

pink (1975) secretaries and other clerical staff

steel (1980) robots

grey (1981) skilled technicians; employees whose job descriptions combine some white- and some blue-collar duties

green (1984) environmentalists

gold (1985) professionals or those with in-demand skills; employees over 55

black (1998) miners (especially coal miners) and oil workers

scarlet (2000) female pornographic shop operators

ELBOW GREASE

But whatever your job, whether it be typing at a word-processor or hauling coal, there is one element in common: at some point you have to get stuck in to doing the work:

swallow the frog to tackle the hardest task possible
knife-and-fork it to deal with it bit by bit
antisocordist (1680) an opponent of laziness or idiocy
fluttergrub (Sussex) a man who takes a delight in working about in the dirt, and getting into every possible mess
work for Jesus (US industrial relations) to put in extra work without asking for extra pay

JOBSWORTH

Of course there are always those who manage to slow productivity in some way or other. As the Australians say, they're **as useless as an ashtray on a motorbike**:

chair plug (2006) someone who sits in a meeting but contributes nothing
boondoggle (1935) to carry out valueless or extremely trivial work in order to convey the impression that one is busy
to be on the shockell (Warwickshire) to neglect one's work through beer
headless nail (1950s) a worker who, once he got into a job, was impossible to get out, even if unsuitable
sunlighting (US 1980s) doing a quite different job on one day of the working week

BRAINSTORMING

Ideas, as they say, are two a penny. But a sudden brainwave can be worth a month of pointless toil:

quaesitum (1748) the answer to a problem
just-add-water (UK current office jargon) an idea that is so brilliantly
    simple yet effective that it requires little by way of preparation
limbeck (1599) to rack or fatigue the brain in an effort to have a new idea

NO-DAY

However hard we try not to, we all have those days where our hard work seems to come to nought:

blue duck (New Zealand 1890) something unprofitable
windmill-tilt (US jargon 2006) a fruitless and frustrating venture:
    attacking imaginary enemies or fighting otherwise-unwinnable battles
salmon day (1990s) the entire day spent swimming upstream only to
    get screwed in the end

PUSHING THE ENVELOPE

The jargon of contemporary corporate life may seem absurd to the outsider, rich as it is in the most colourful of metaphors. But it's certainly guaranteed to brighten up even the dullest day:

takeaway nuggets insights or information resulting from a meeting or interaction

sunset clauses stipulations that a contract or regulation will lapse unless renewed

to wash its own face to justify or pay for itself

push the peanut to progress an arduous and delicate task forward

ketchup-bottle a long period of inertia followed by a burst of exaggerated activity; the unplanned release of pent-up forces

swallow your own smoke to take responsibility for and/or suffer the consequences of your mistakes

MANAGERIE

Why are things so often discussed in animal terms? Is it because of a desperate subliminal desire to get out of the office?

shoot the puppy to dare to do the unthinkable

prairie dogging popping one's head above an office cubicle out of curiosity or to spy on colleagues

lipstick on a pig an attempt to put a favourite spin on a negative situation

a pig in a python a surge in a statistic measured over time

boiling frog syndrome a company which fails to recognize gradual market change (as a slowly boiled frog may not detect a slow temperature increase)

moose on the table an issue which everyone in a business meeting knows is a problem but which no one wants to address

seagull manager a manager who flies in, makes a lot of noise, shits all over everything, and then leaves

---

THANK GOD IT'S FRIDAY – OFFICE ACRONYMS

SWOT Strengths, Weaknesses, Opportunities, Threats (a favourite of consultants)

PICNIC Problem In Chair, Not In Computer

WOMBAT Waste Of Money, Brains And Time

POET'S day Piss Off Early Tomorrow's Saturday (refers to Friday)

BULLS AND BEARS

In good times and bad, the highly paid practitioners of both the City of London and Wall Street have couched their dubious activities in their own specialized jargon:

J-Lo (Wall Street) the rounding bottom in a stock's price chart (after the curvaceous Jennifer Lopez)

Bo Derek (Wall Street) the perfect stock (after her famous film *10*)

poop and scoop to drive down a share price by spreading malicious rumours

mattressing the term used by other traders and bank managers to hide their results

barefoot pilgrim someone who has lost everything on the stock market, but might still be persuaded to invest again

catch a falling knife to buy a stock as its price is going down, in the hope that it will go back up, only to have it continue to fall

ROOM AT THE TOP

If you have ability, however, and enough patience to continue to play the game, you will slowly but surely make your way up the corporate ladder:

royal jelly flashy projects fed to someone whom the boss is grooming for promotion

marzipan layer the group who are ranked below the very top in their profession, but ahead of the majority

tribal chiefs bosses who dominate through charisma and patronage

deceptionist a secretary whose job it is to delay or block potential visitors on behalf of their boss

FIRM HAND

Though we'd all like to believe that hard work is always rewarded, with the best jobs going to the most productive people, the sad fact is that the realities of employing people are not always so straightforward:

muppet shuffle the redeployment of problem staff

featherbedding (1949) the practice of forcing the employer (by union rule etc.) to hire more workers than needed (or to limit his workers' production)

kicked upstairs (1697) removed from the scene of action by promotion to an ostensibly higher post

other shoe syndrome when a number of executives in a firm are being made redundant, those survivors, rather than feeling relieved, find their own morale sabotaged as they wait for 'the other shoe' to come down on them

chainsaw consultants outside experts brought in to reduce the employee headcount (leaving the top brass with clean hands)

THE SACK

So unpleasant is it to ask people to clear their desks and take their skills elsewhere, that a huge number of words and phrases has grown up to euphemistically describe the simple fact of redundancy. You might have been **handed your cards** or perhaps you're **clearing your desk**, **considering your position** or maybe becoming a **consultant**. Maybe you've been **deselected** or you're taking an **early bath**. Then again, perhaps you're **excess to requirements** or you've even been **excluded**. You're leaving to **give time to your other commitments** or else you're off on **gardening leave**. If you're lucky you'll have negotiated a **golden handshake** rather than merely being given a **leave of absence** or **let go**. When you're **given notice** let's hope they don't say it's **natural wastage** or that you've been **stood down**. No, you're **spending more time with your wife and family,** as it's your right to do, even if your **contract has been terminated** and nobody could really describe this as a **voluntary relocation**.

SMALL IS BETTER

As for the ruthless companies themselves, why, they're doing nothing more unnatural than a bit of **recruitment**. They are in fact **degrowing**, **dehiring**, **delayering** and **destaffing**. In a process of **downsizing** some employees have had to take **early release**. Yes, there is a bit of **executive outplacement** and **force reduction** going on. Shall we call it **internal reorganization**? Nobody is being **put out to grass**. There's been a **personnel surplus reduction**, indeed a straightforward **rationalization of the workforce**. Some people have been **redeployed**. There's been a bit of **restructuring**, some **retrenching** and **rightsizing**, not to mention **schedule adjustment**, **selective separation** and **skill-mix adjustment**. It's all nothing more than a bit of **transitioning**, **vocational relocation** and **workforce imbalance correction**.

MY OLD MAN'S A . . .

Once upon a time, we were all quite happy to say exactly what it was we did. But as status has become ever more important, some quite straightforward occupations have developed some quite preposterous titles:

vision clearance engineer a window cleaner
stock replenishment adviser a shelf stacker
dispatch services facilitator a post room worker
head of verbal communications a receptionist/secretary
environment improvement technician a cleaner

HAWKERS AND HUCKSTERS

However you dress him (or her) up, there's no denying that a salesman is always a salesman. It's an occupation that's been around since men first started trading beads and barley:

chafferer (1382) a vendor who enjoys talking while making a sale

mangonize (Tudor–Stuart) to sell men or boys for slaves

bend-down plaza (Jamaican English) a row of roadside pedlars, specializing in items that are hard to get in shops, because of import restrictions

amster (Australian slang 1941) one who works outside a carnival, side-show, strip club etc. touting the pleasures inside and pulling in the customers

click (1748) to stand at a shop-door and invite customers in

jaw-work! (mid 18C) a cry used in fairs by the sellers of nuts

WIDOWS AND ORPHANS

These guys know the price of everything, and its value too, and they've plenty of lingo to describe what they're trying to get rid of . . .

zhing-zhong (Zimbabwean slang) merchandise made in Asia; cheaply made, inexpensive or substandard goods

halo model a super-product which enhances an entire brand

orphan (second-hand motor trade jargon) any discontinued model of a car

widow's piano inferior instruments sold as bargains (from an advertisement announcing that a widow lady is compelled to sell her piano, for which she will take half price)

. . . how they do it . . .

deaconing (US slang 1866) the practice of packing food so that the finest specimens are visible

shillaber (North American slang 1913) someone posing as an enthusiastic or successful customer to encourage other buyers

trotting (auction jargon) the tactic whereby a dealer's ring will force an outsider up to an unrealistically high bid, at which point they will drop out and leave their rival with a large bill

bovrilise (1901) to condense an advertisement to essentials

. . . and those to whom they're pitching their spiel . . .

nose picker a salesman's derogatory description of a potential client who cannot make up their mind and has no power of decision-making within the firm

twack (Newfoundland 1937) a shopper who looks at goods, inquires about prices but buys nothing

grey panthers (US slang) assertive and/or exigent elderly consumers

THE READIES

At the end of it there's one glorious commodity that makes it all worth-while:

stadge (Lancashire and Cheshire) the date of issue stamped upon coins
mule (industry jargon) a coin or note which has two mismatched sides
drink-link (Ireland slang 1990s) a cash dispenser
squiddish (Northumberland) the twentieth part of a farthing
chapmoney (Shropshire) money which the seller gives back to the
    buyer for luck
wergeld (1214) money paid by the killer's family by way of compensation
    to free the offender from further punishment
fornale (1478) to spend one's money before it has been earned

LILIES OF THE FIELD

Although for some fortunate people, such vulgar considerations really
don't figure:

oofy (1896) rich
slippage (US slang 2005) the percentage of people who get a cheque
    and forget to cash it
set the Thames on fire (UK late 18C) to make a great success in life
stalko (1802) a man who has nothing to do and no fortune to support
    him but who styles himself as a squire

WORD JOURNEYS

robot (20C from Czech) servitude, forced labour

cattle (13C) property, wealth; then (16C) moveable property; then livestock

up the spout (UK slang b1894) from the spout (lift) used in pawnbrokers' shops; when items were handed over in return for money they were sent 'up the spout' to the storeroom where they stayed until their owner could afford to redeem them

customer (14C) a customs house officer; then (16C) someone the customs officer had to deal with

BULK AND FILE
Crime and punishment

He that helpeth an evill man,
hurteth him that is good

(1597)

The line between making money by sheer hard work and from more dubious practices has always been thin:

vigerage (underworld slang 1935) a loan shark's 20 per cent weekly interest

flim-flam (underworld slang 1881) the various dodges by which a thief, in changing money, obtains more than he gives from tradesmen and bank-tellers

mocteroof (costermongers' jargon 1860) to doctor damaged fruit or vegetables

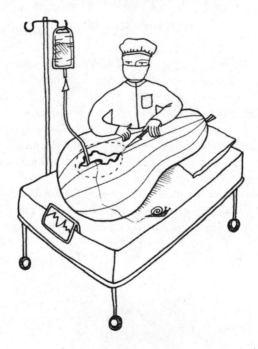

striping the lot (North American slang) the painting of the parking lot at a new shopping mall with extra-wide spacing for the positioning of cars (this gives the impression of the mall attracting more customers than it really does, and when business picks up, the spaces can be repainted somewhat narrower)

quomodocunquize (1652) to make money by any means possible

MY DEAR FELLOW!

Other ways of getting booty out of people may be more extreme:

gagging (*c.*1825) persuading a stranger that he is an old acquaintance and then borrowing money from him

bull trap (Australia 1930s) a villain who impersonates a policeman and preys on couples in lovers' lanes, extorting money from those who should not be there

queer plungers (underworld slang 1785) crooks who threw themselves into the water and pretended to be drowning, before being taken by accomplices to one of the Humane Society houses for the recovery of drowned persons, where they were rewarded with a guinea each for rescuing the bogus victim

jibber the kibber (Cornwall 1781) a wrecker's tactic of fixing a lantern round the neck of a horse which at night appeared like a ship's light. The ships bearing toward it ran aground, and were plundered by the locals

NOT QUITE MY COLOUR

Even the most upright of us may not be totally straight all the time:

wardrobing (US slang) buying an item and then returning it after wearing it

bilker (1717) a person who gives a cabman less than his fare and, when remonstrated with, gives a false name and address

manoeuvring the apostles (b.1811) robbing Peter to pay Paul (i.e. borrowing from one man to pay another)

oyster (underworld slang 1920) a society woman employed to wear stolen jewellery in the hope that she will receive an offer from a fence, and will, because of her social position, remain unsuspected by the police

PANHANDLER

Just because you've been reduced to begging, it doesn't mean that you're dishonest. Having said that, some bums have always known that cheating pays:

dommerers (1567) men who pretended to be deaf and dumb

cleymes (b.1811) artificial sores, made by beggars to excite charity

scaldrum dodge (mid 19C) the practice of deliberately burning the body with a mixture of acids and gunpowder to simulate scars and wounds to soften the hearts of those from whom one begs

whip-jacks (1562) vagabonds who pretended to be shipwrecked sailors

aurium (16C) a wandering beggar posing as some kind of priest

CUTPURSE

Others, fitter and more fleet of foot, make better boodle by being proactive:

maltooling (b.1861) the picking of pockets in omnibuses
bulk and file (1698) two pickpockets operating together (the **bulk** jostles the party that is to be robbed and the **file** steals the treasure)
reef (*c*.1860) to draw up a dress-pocket until a purse is within reach of the fingers
pappy (underworld slang 1910) an elderly man whose clothes and pockets are baggy (the ideal victim for a pickpocket)

SLEIGHT OF HAND

As in many another career paths, the professional pilferer, too, likes to develop his expert knowledge:

feeder-prigger (late 18C) a thief specializing in silver spoons
badger (US mid 19C) a rogue who specializes in robbing clients who are visiting a brothel
efter (underworld slang 1846) a thief who robs theatre patrons during a show
tinny-hunter (late 18C) a thief who robs people whose homes are burning down, while pretending to give assistance
vamper (mid 19C) a thief who deliberately starts fights between others in order to rob them in the confusion
tosher (b.1859) one who steals copper from the bottom of ships moored in the Thames

ARTFUL DODGERS

Other tricks of the trade definitely make a crook's life easier and more productive:

trigging the jigger (early 19C) placing a small piece of paper (**trig**) in the front door keyhole of a house that is presumed to be uninhabited; if the paper is still there a day later, the robber can believe that the house is empty and can be broken into safely

treacle-man (late 19C) a good-looking man who works as a decoy for burglars by charming the housemaid while the gang slip in unnoticed

snudge (underworld slang 1665) a thief who hides himself under a bed in order to rob the house

little snakesman (1781) a little boy who gets into a house through the sink-hole, and then opens the door for his accomplices

DOLPHINS AND TURTLES

Underworld slang, old and new, covers a whole range of dodgy activity, from the relatively harmless to the downright evil:

shoulder surf (UK current slang) to use a pair of binoculars to read the PIN of people using cash dispensers

slaughter (1950s) an immediate dumping ground for recently stolen property, before it is shared out or hidden more permanently and securely

turn turtle (early 19C) to flip a carriage upside-down

airmail (US prison jargon 1950s) concrete, bricks and so on hurled down from rooftops onto patrol cars responding to a call

rifling (underworld slang 1885) plundering dead bodies in the river (especially the Thames) and turning them adrift again

make one's bones (New York slang 1969) to kill a person as a requirement for membership in a criminal gang

OLD BILL

One gang who know more about all this than most are society's upholders of the law, who have a few tricks of their own up their sleeves:

flash roll (police jargon) a wad of money which is never actually used, but is flashed ostentatiously around to convince a criminal, e.g. a drug dealer, that one wishes to make a purchase, at which point an arrest will be made

Kojak with a Kodak (US 1970s) a policeman manning a radar speed trap

mule kick (US slang 2005) the act of standing with one's back to the front door and kicking the door in

attitude-adjuster (US black slang) a club; a police officer's stick

to get a fanner (Hobo slang) to be hit on the soles while sleeping on a park bench and moved on by the police

ghetto bird (US slang) a police helicopter

wiggle seat (US police jargon) a special lie detector that can be fitted to a chair and which will measure the bodily reactions of a suspect to various crucial questions

BAD APPLES

Upstanding members of society can only hope that their local rozzers are worthy of the power entrusted in them:

mumping (UK slang 1970) the acceptance by the police of small gifts or bribes from tradespeople

swim in golden grease (UK slang 17C) to receive many bribes

banana (UK street slang 1990s) a corrupt police officer (initially of the Special Patrol Group because they were, allegedly, yellow, bent and hanging around in bunches)

shoo-fly (US slang 1877) a policeman, usually in plain clothes, whose job is to watch and report on other police officers

accommodation collar (US police jargon) an arrest only made to raise the officer's arrest record and thus improve his standing in the hierarchy

JUST DESERTS

There are some who would prefer that criminals were treated with the summary justice of yesteryear; without faffing around with all that tedious business of innocent until proved guilty:

alfet (*c.*1000) a vat of boiling water into which the accused plunged his arm in lieu of a trial

keelhaul (1626) to punish in the seamen's way, by dragging the criminal under water on one side of the ship and up again on the other

ride the stang (UK b.1828) to be carried on a pole through the town on men's shoulders and pelted with refuse for the amusement of a hooting crowd (a derisive punishment for a breach of decorum or morality, especially on the part of a married man)

corsned (Anglo-Saxon law *c.*1000) a trial by ordeal that required a suspect to eat a piece of barley bread and cheese to test his innocence (if guilty, it was believed the bread would cause convulsions and choking)

whiffler (underworld slang 1859) a fellow who cries out in pain

PETTIFOGGERS

Undoubtedly the intervention of the legal profession does complicate matters, and sometimes completely unnecessarily:

kilburn (police jargon) the official police notebook that is produced in court (rhyming slang: Kilburn Priory for diary)

gunner (US slang) a law student who always needs to volunteer an answer to show off how smart he are

ambulance-chaser (underworld slang 1897) a lawyer who attends scenes of accidents and hospitals to get business from the injured or bereaved, who are not in a position to resist

dock asthma (police and prison jargon 1950s) gasps of (usually feigned) surprise and disbelief by prisoners in the dock

boot-eater (1880) a juror who would rather 'eat his boots' than find a person guilty

PORRIDGE

A spell inside should be enough to make anyone think twice about reoffending:

oubliette (Scott: *Ivanhoe* 1819) a dungeon whose only entrance is in the ceiling

dry bath (1933) a search of a prisoner who has been stripped naked

broken arse (New Zealand) a prisoner who has sided with the authorities and thus ranked the lowest in the inmate hierarchy

carpy (1940s) locked away in one's cell at night (from Latin tag *carpe diem* for 'seize the day')

to polish the King's iron with one's eyebrows (underworld slang 1785) to look longingly out of prison windows

Although not necessarily so:

gate fever (UK slang 2007) terror at the prospect of release from prison

phoenix (underworld slang 1925) one who enters the world after long imprisonment

boomerang (US slang) to return to prison almost immediately on finishing the last sentence

CLEAN SHIRT

Career criminals have always had to make calculations about the possible punishment they may have to endure, leading to a wide range of names for different prison sentences. Here's a selection:

thirteen clean shirts (late 19C) three months' imprisonment (at the rate of one shirt a week)

magazine (US 1920s) a six month jail sentence (the time it would take to read one if one could barely read)

the clock (Australian slang 1950) twelve months' imprisonment (from the hours on a clock face)

pontoon (UK prison jargon 1950) a twenty-one month jail sentence (from the card-game in which a score of twenty-one is the optimum hand)

rouf (UK back slang* 1851) a four year sentence

taxi (US slang 1930) between five and fifteen years' imprisonment (from the fares in cents displayed in New York taxis)

neves (UK back slang* 1901) a seven year sentence

work under the armpits (early 19C) to confine one's criminality to such activities that would be classed as petty larceny (bringing a maximum sentence of seven years' transportation rather than hanging)

working above the armpits (early 19C) to commit crimes that could lead to one's execution

* Slang that works when read or written backwards

WORD JOURNEYS

to pay on the nail (1596) from a practice in medieval markets where
instant justice was dealt to those who reneged on agreements or
cheated their customers. Eventually it was decided that accounts be
settled at counters (short pillars known as nails) in the open market
place and in front of witnesses. Payments were placed on these
counters for everyone to see that all was correct

not enough room to swing a cat (1771) refers to the whip used on
board ships for dealing out punishment (the whip started as a cat-
of-three-tails but became a cat-of-nine-tails by the end of the sev-
enteenth century; this method of punishment continued until 1875)

nipper (16C) a thief, person who nipped or pinched; then (19C) a
costermonger's boy attendant

villain (14C from Latin via Old French) a worker on a country estate
(in feudal terms the lord was the great landowner, and under him
were a host of tenants called villains; the notion of wickedness and
worthlessness is simply the effect of aristocratic pride and
exclusivity)

BUNTING TIME

Matters of love

After your fling,
watch for the sting

(1917)

The beginning of love is often physical. In hiphop male attractiveness is described as **pimp-juice** and its female counterpart as **milkshake**, contemporary versions of a long tradition:

bobbant (Wiltshire) of a girl: forward, romping
featous (mid 14C) of a man: handsome, good looking
clipsome (1816) eminently embraceable

DISCO JUDGES

Women have long known just how critical others can be of their looks, whether they be English country folk or American teenagers:

sinful-ordinary (Wiltshire) plain to the last degree in looks
bridlegged (Cheshire) a farmer's contemptuous description of a woman as having legs not strong enough to work on the farm
sphinx (US black teen slang) a woman who is beautiful from the neck up
Medusa (US black teen slang) a woman who is beautiful from the neck down
strobe-light honey (US black teen slang) a woman who seems attractive in flickering light but not otherwise

ZEPPELINS

One aspect in particular often receives close attention:

bathycolpian (1825) having a deep cleavage

headlamps (UK slang early 20C) female breasts: this was when large, raised car headlights were the norm (a century earlier the common expression was **barges**)

dead heat in a Zeppelin race (UK slang) an admiring description of large breasts

fore-buttocks (Pope: *The Dunciad* 1727) breasts

Cupid's kettledrums (18C) breasts

SUPERSIZE ME

So how do you get your feelings across? **Do fries go with that shake**? was a phrase called out by black men in 1970s America to a passing woman they fancied; while the object of admiration might mutter to her friend: **He can put his shoes under my bed anytime** ...

boombaloomba (Australian slang) an expression of a man's attraction to a woman

look that needs suspenders (1940s) a very interested glance at a woman (the suspenders were needed to keep the man's eyeballs attached to their sockets)

HUNTER DITHERERS

Not that everyone finds it easy to be so forward:

stick-up (Wiltshire) to make the first tentative advances towards
   courting
dangle (late 18C) to follow a woman without actually addressing her
quirkyalone (US slang 1999) someone who just wants the right person
   to come along at the right time even if that means waiting

FAINT HEART

Sometimes one just has to take the risk and get a bit proactive:

tapper (1950s) a boy who repeatedly pestered a girl for a date
wingwoman (US slang from the film *Top Gun* 1986) a professional female matchmaker who escorts a man to a bar or club, engages in light
   conversation to draw in other females, and then withdraws
strike breaker (1920s) a young woman who was ready to date her
   friend's beau when a couple's romance was coming to an end
rabbit's-kiss (Anglo-Manx) a penalty in the game of 'forfeits' in which
   a man and woman have each to nibble the same piece of straw until
   their lips meet

DELIGHTFUL

Until 1958 debutantes and their mothers exchanged information about the respectable young men to whom they were introduced by using a special code:

FU Financially Unsound
MTF Must Touch Flesh
MSC Makes Skin Crawl
NSIT Not Safe In Taxis
VVSITPQ Very, Very Safe In Taxis, Probably Queer

THE WILDER SHORES OF LOVE

As homosexuality was illegal in the UK until 1967, the secret language of Polari was used to disguise gay subculture from the disapproving gaze of the law. It was originally used by circus and fairground performers who were equally keen to communicate with each other without their audience understanding. Drawn from Italian, Yiddish, Cockney rhyming slang and full of backwards words (such as **ecaf** for face) Polari provided various terms that we all use today, such as **drag**, **camp** and **bimbo**, as well as some less well-known but equally colourful expressions:

omi-polone a gay man (literally man-woman; a lesbian was **polone-omi**, a woman-man)
alamo hot for him
basket the bulge of male genitals through trousers
naff awful, dull, bad (said to stand for Not Available For F***ing)

CHEAP DATE

Whatever your proclivities, there are numerous reasons why one should beware of giving too much too soon:

couch cootie (US 1920s) a poor or miserly man who prefers to court a woman in her own house than take her out on the town

flat-wheeler (US college slang 1920s) a young man whose idea of entertaining a girl is to take her for a walk

cream-pot love (b.1811) professed by insincere young men to dairy-maids, to get cream and other goods from them

GETTING DOWN TO IT

In the less permissive 1950s, a **Nottingham goodnight** was the phrase used of a courting couple who had got back from their date, and then slammed the door and said 'goodnight' loudly before retiring quietly to the sofa, hoping they would not be disturbed for some time ...

suaviation (1656) a love kiss

cow-kissing (US slang mid 19C) kissing with much movement of the tongues and lips

lallygagger (1920s) a courting male who liked to kiss his sweetheart in hallways

bundling (b.1811) a man and a woman sleeping in the same bed, he with his clothes on, and she with her petticoat on

COUNTRY LOVING

But if the weather's good, why bother to go home at all?

sproag (Scotland late 16C) to run among the haystacks after the girls at night

to give a girl a green gown (late 16C) to tumble her onto the grass

bunting time (1699) when the grass is high enough to hide young men and maids courting

boondock (Tennessee campus slang b.1950) to neck, pet or make love in an automobile

gulch (Newfoundland 1895) to frequent a sheltered hollow to engage in sexual intimacy

---

SEALED WITH A LOVING KISS – LOVE LETTER ACRONYMS

During the Second World War all mail was opened and read by the official Censor. So acronyms of places written on the backs of envelopes were used to convey secret messages of love (and lust) between servicemen and their wives or girlfriends:

HOLLAND Hope Our Love Lasts And Never Dies

MEXICO CITY May Every Kiss I Can Offer Carry Itself To You

MALAYA My Ardent Lips Await Your Arrival

CHINA Come Home I Need Affection

NORWICH (K)nickers Off Ready When I Come Home

BURMA Be Undressed Ready My Angel

EGYPT Eager to Grab Your Pretty Tits

SIAM Sexual Intercourse At Midnight

ALL LOVED UP

Limerence (US Connecticut 1977) is the word for that initial exhilarating rush of falling in love, the state of 'being in love'. During that time the besotted of either sex should be careful not to **deff out**, the American slang for women who immediately lose contact with their female friends after acquiring a steady boyfriend. And this is just one of the pitfalls of sudden love:

fribbler (1712) one who professes rapture for a woman, but dreads her consent

batmobiling (US slang) putting up protective emotional shields just as a relationship enters an intimate, vulnerable stage (with reference to the car's retracting armour)

THEY FLEE FROM ME

Once things start to go wrong, the slide can be all too rapid . . .

to wear the willow (late 16C) to have been abandoned by one's lover

. . . so do try and avoid being cynical . . .

sorbet sex (US slang popularized by *Sex and the City*) a casual sexual relationship undertaken in the period between two more serious relationships

pull a train (US slang 1965) sexual intercourse with a succession of partners (like a string of boxcars, they have to be coupled and uncoupled)

... or sentimental ...

desiderium (Swift: letter to Pope 1715) a yearning for a thing one once
   had but has lost

anacampserote (1611) a herb that can bring back departed love

DROIT DE SEIGNEUR

Take heart from the fact that anything goes; and the history of love tells of some decidedly odd arrangements:

gugusse (early 1880s) an effeminate youth who frequents the private company of priests

panmixis (1889) a population in which random mating takes place

Shunamitism (b.1901) the practice of an old man sleeping with, but not necessarily having sex with, a young woman to preserve his youth (the rationale was that the heat of the young woman would transfer to the old man and revitalize him, based on the Biblical story of King David and Abishag)

HE DOESN'T UNDERSTAND ME

Just beware the types for whom lovemaking has become habitual (or even professional):

mud-honey (Tennyson: *Maud* 1855) the dirty pleasures of men about town

cougar (Canadian slang 2005) an older woman on the prowl, preferably for a younger man

lovertine (1603) someone addicted to sex

play checkers (US gay jargon 1960s) to move from seat to seat in a cinema in search of a receptive sex partner

twopenny upright (UK slang 1958) the charge made by a prostitute for an act of sexual intercourse standing up out of doors

WORD JOURNEYS

boudoir (French 18C) a place to sulk or pout in
friend (Old English) a lover; then (12C) a relative or kinsman
buxom (12C) obedient, compliant; then (16C) plump and comely
harem (17C from Turkish via Arabic) forbidden to others; then
   sacred to the women and their apartments

WITTOLS AND BEER BABIES
Marriage and family life

Marriage halves our griefs,
doubles our joys,
and quadruples our expenses

(1902–4)

However giddy and capricious at first, it's certainly true that Love moves, inexorably, towards the recognized and the formalized:

wooer-bab (Burns: *Halloween* 1785) a garter tied below the knee of a young man as a sign that he was about to make an offer of marriage
subarrhation (Swinburne: *Spousals* 1686) a betrothal accomplished by the man's showering presents on his incipient bride
acquaintance (Shropshire) a fiancé/e
maiden-rent (17C) a fee paid by every tenant in the Welsh manor of Builth at their marriage (given to the lord for his omitting the ancient custom of **marcheta**, whereby he spent the first night with his tenant's new wife)
gluepot (b.1811) a parson (from joining men and women together in matrimony)

IN THE PAPERS

In the UK, people of a certain class have traditionally advertised marriage, just as they do births and deaths, with an announcement in their newspaper of choice. This trio defining a person's life is colloquially known as **hatched, matched and dispatched** (with some believing that these really are the only times your name should appear in the papers). In Australia, similar announcements are known as **yells, bells and knells**. But though established through long custom, marriage has come in many varied and interesting forms . . .

paranymph (1660) the best man or bridesmaid at a wedding

levirate (1725) the custom requiring a man to marry his brother's widow

punalua (1889) a group marriage in which wives' sisters and husbands' brothers were considered spouses

adelphogamy (1926) a form of marriage in which brothers share a wife or wives

jockum-gagger (1797) a man living on the prostitution of his wife

bitch's blind (US slang) a wife who acts as a cover for a homosexual male

opsigamy (1824) marrying late in life

VIRAGO

Maritality (1812) is a charming word, meaning 'the excessive affection a wife feels for her husband', while **levament** (1623) describes one of the best aspects of a good marriage, 'the comfort a man has from his wife'. But in general the words and phrases our language has thrown up speak of more demanding realities, with wives all too often in the frame:

loudspeaker (underworld slang 1933) a wife

alarm clock (US slang 1920s) a nagging woman

tenant at will (late 18C) one whose wife arrives at the alehouse to make him come home

ten commandments (mid 15C) the ten fingers and thumbs especially of a wife

curtain-lecture (b.1811) a reproof given by a wife to her husband in bed

cainsham smoke (1694) the tears of a man who is beaten by his wife (deriving from a lost story relating to Keynsham, near Bristol)

AFTERPLAY

Love and marriage, the song goes, go together 'like horse and carriage'. So why doesn't fidelity always fit so easily into the equation?

wittol (15C) a man who is aware of his wife's unfaithfulness but doesn't mind or acquiesces

court of assistants (late 18C) the young men with whom young wives, unhappy in their marriages to older men, are likely to seek solace

to pick a needle without an eye (West Indian) of a young woman, to give oneself in marriage to a man whom one knows will be of no use as a sexual partner

gandermooner (1617) a husband who strays each month, during the time of the month when his wife is 'unavailable'

stumble at the truckle-bed (mid 17C) to 'mistake' the maid's bed for one's wife's

UP THE DUFF

The desire to expand the family is all too natural; though the actual circumstances of conception may vary considerably:

beer babies (Sussex) babies sired when the man was drunk

Band-Aid baby (UK slang) a child conceived to strengthen a faltering relationship

basting (UK slang 2007) being with a gay male friend who offers to give the baby a woman longs for

sooterkin (1658) an imaginary kind of birth attributed to Dutch women from sitting over their stoves

THE STORK DESCENDS

In parts of America they say you have **swallowed a watermelon seed** when you become pregnant. In Britain, children were once told that the new baby boy in the family had been found **under the gooseberry bush**, while the girl was found **in the parsley bed**:

omphalomancy (1652) divination by counting the knots in the umbilical cord of her first born to predict the number of children a mother will have

nom de womb (US slang 2005) a name used by an expectant parent to refer to their unborn child

infanticipate (US 1934) to be expecting a child

quob (b.1828) to move as the embryo does in the womb; as the heart does when throbbing

pigeon pair (Wiltshire dialect) a boy and a girl (when a mother has only two children)

PRIVATE VIEWS

As soon as Baby appears, of course, there is much excitement. Relatives and friends crowd round to check out the new arrival, and any gossip about the timing of the pregnancy melts away:

barley-child (Shropshire) a child born in wedlock, but which makes its advent within six months of marriage (alluding to the time which elapses between barley sowing and barley harvest)

jonkin (Yorkshire) a tea-party given to celebrate a birth of a child

crying-cheese (Scotland) a ritual where cheese was given to neighbours and visitors when a child was born

FIRST STEPS

Then there is the long, slow process of bringing up the little darling; beset with many dangers, but not, fortunately, as many as in the past ...

vagitus (Latin 17C) a new-born child's cry
marriage music (late 17C) the crying of children
blow-blow (Jamaican English 1955) babbling baby-talk
chrisom (*c.*1200) a child that dies within a month of its birth (so called from the chrisom-cloth, anointed with holy unguent, which the children wore until they were christened)
quiddle (Midlands) to suck a thumb
gangrel (1768) a child just beginning to walk
dade (Shropshire) to lead children when learning to walk

CHIPS OFF THE OLD BLOCK

It's an exhausting time, but hopefully rewarding, whatever the extra commitments:

antipelargy (1656) the love of children for their parents
philostorgy (1623) natural affection, such as that between parents and children
butter-print (Tudor–Stuart) a child bearing the stamp of its parents' likeness
stand pad (Cockney) to beg in crowded streets with a written statement round one's neck, such as 'wife and five kids to support'
sandwich generation (Canadian slang) those caring for young children and elderly parents at the same time (usually 'baby boomers' in their 40s or 50s)

POPPING OFF

*S*adly, not all men seem able to stay the course:

zoo daddy (US slang) a divorced father who rarely sees his child or children (he takes his kids to the zoo when exercising his visiting rights)

baby fathers (Jamaican English 1932) males who abandon their partner and offspring

goose father (US slang 2005) a father who lives alone having sent his spouse and children to a foreign country to learn English or do some other form of advanced study

jacket (Jamaican English 2007) a man tested and proven not to be the father of the children said to be his

EARLY PROMISE

*A*nd what a course it can prove to be ...

glaikut (Aberdeenshire) of a child too fond of its mother and refusing to be parted from her at any time

chippie-burdie (Scotland) a promise made to a child to pacify them

killcrop (1652) a child who is perpetually hungry

vuddle (Hampshire and Wiltshire) to spoil a child by injudicious petting

ankle-sucker (Worcestershire) a child or person dependent on others

COLTISH

ot necessarily made any easier as the offspring grow older ...

dandiprat (1583) an urchin
daddle (Suffolk) to walk like a young child trying to copy its father
liggle (East Anglian) to carry something too heavy to be carried easily
(e.g. of a child with a puppy)
airling (1611) a person who is both young and thoughtless

... though getting them outside in the fresh air is always a good plan ...

grush (Hiberno-English) of children, to scramble for coins and other
small gifts thrown at them
duck's dive (Newfoundland) a boy's pastime of throwing a stone into
the water without making a splash
poppinoddles (Cumberland 1885) a boyish term for a somersault
triltigo (Derbyshire) a word used to start boys off in a race
treer (c.1850) a boy who avoids organized sports, but plays a private game
with one or two friends (by the trees at the side of the ground)

ABC

School can take some of the heat off the parents ...

abecedary (1440) a table or book containing the alphabet, a primer
minerval (1603) a gift given in gratitude by a pupil to a teacher
brosier (Eton College c.1830) a boy with no more pocket money
nix! (1860) a warning especially among schoolboys and workmen of
somebody's approach

MANNERS MAKYTH MAN

At Winchester College, as elsewhere in times gone by, discipline was strictly maintained by corporal punishment. If it wasn't from the authorities, you could count on the bullies for trouble:

tin gloves (*c.*1840) a criss-cross of blisters methodically made by a bully on the back of a victim's hand
bibler (*c.*1830) six cuts on the back
tund (1831) to flog a boy across the shoulders with a ground-ash
rabbiter (1831) a blow on the back of their neck with the edge of the open palm
to sport eyesight (1920) to deliver all the blows on the same spot in beating

FIGHTING YOUR BATTELS

Similar slang was adopted at many universities. At Oxford, your **battels** (Tudor–Stuart) were (and still are) your college bills; if you didn't get to an exam you **ploughed** (1853) it; and **academic nudity** (b.1909) was appearing in public without a cap or gown. At Cambridge, in Victorian times, a **brute** (19C) was one who had not matriculated and a **sophister** (1574) was an undergraduate in his second or third year. In both places a **whiffler** (*c.*1785) was one who examined candidates for degrees, while at Dublin a **sizar** (1588) was one who got a college allowance. At Aberdeen, from the eighteenth century on, you were a **bajan** in your first year, a **semi** in your second, a **tertian** in your third, and a **magistrand** (1721) if staying for a fourth year to sit an MA.

JUST MISSED A GEOFF

Much more recently, a new slang has grown up to describe the various kinds of degrees that one may hope to get. The much-prized First has been known as a **Geoff** (Hurst), a **Damien** (Hirst) or a **Patty** (Hearst), a **raging** (thirst) or a **James** (the First). A 2:1 is known as an **Attila** (the Hun) or a **Made-In** (Taiwan). A 2:2 is known as a **Desmond** (Tutu) and a Third as a **Douglas** (Hurd), a **Thora** (Hird), or even a **Gentleman's Degree,** though who would admit to having one of those these days?

RETURN TO THE COOP

Education over, for more than a few the appeal of moving back home can be strong, especially in these days of high rents and generous parental expectations:

twixters (US slang) fully grown men and women who still live with their parents

ant hill family (UK slang) the trend whereby children move back in with their parents so that all can work together towards group financial goals

LIFE IS SHORT

Life races on, and all too soon comes that point when some feel the need to start lying about their age ...

agerasia (1706) looking younger than one really is
paracme (1656) the point at which one's prime is past
menoporsche (UK slang) the phenomenon of middle-aged men attempting to recapture their lost youth by buying an expensive sports car

... a pointless activity, for your years will always catch up with you:

prosopagnosia (1950) an inability to recognize familiar faces
sew the button on (UK slang b.1898) to have to jot down at once what you wish to remember
astereognosis (1900) the loss of the ability to recognize the shapes and spatial relationships of objects

---

WORD JOURNEYS

debonair (13C from Old French: de bonne aire) of good disposition or family
puny (16C from Old French: puis né) born later, a junior; then inexperienced
husband (Old English) master of a house; then (13C) husbandman: tiller of the soil (an extension of his duties); then (15C) housekeeper or steward; then (16C) a man who managed affairs generally

OYSTER PARTS
Culture

Literature should be my staff
but not my crutch

(Scott: *Lockhart's Life* 1830)

here's little doubt that as a culture we have a passion for a good story well told:

anecdotard (1894) an old man given to telling stories

ackamarackus (US slang 1934) a specious, characteristically involved tale that seeks to convince by bluff

SHAZAM (1940) Solomon's wisdom, Hercules' strength, Atlas's stamina, Zeus's power, Achilles' courage and Mercury's speed (an acronymic magic word like 'abracadabra' used to introduce an extraordinary story)

shark-jump (US media jargon 1997) instances that signal the imminent decline of a TV series by introducing plot twists inconsistent with the previous plot

bridges, bridges! (*c.*1880) a cry to arrest a long-winded story

THE BEST WORDS IN THE BEST ORDER

Poetry too seems to be in the blood, and judging by the activity in pubs around the nation, in no danger of declining:

genethliacon (1589) a poem written for someone's birthday

amphigory (1809) a poem that seems profound but is nonsense

randle (b.1811) a set of nonsensical verses, repeated in Ireland by school-boys and young people, who have been guilty of breaking wind backwards before their companions

rhapsodomancy (1727) fortunetelling by picking a passage of poetry at random

musophobist (Swinburne 1880) a person who regards poetry with suspicious dislike

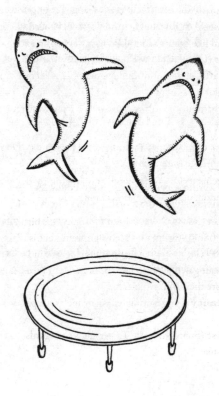

PENMEN

Scribblers still throng a land where people have long been under the illusion that there is something glamorous about the business of writing:

purlicue (1808) a dash or flourish at the end of a written word
wegotism (1797) the excessive use of 'we' in writing (particularly in newspaper editorials)
parisology (1846) the use of ambiguous language or evasive writing
macaronic (1638) mixing words from different languages
Patavinity (1607) the use of local slang or expressions when writing
cloak-father (*c*.1639) a pretended author whose name is put forth to conceal the real author

CRITICAL MASS

The best advice for authors is Somerset Maugham's: 'Don't read your reviews, dear boy. Measure them'...

Zoilist (1594) a critic, especially one who is unduly severe or who takes joy in faultfinding (after the fourth-century Greek critic)
histriomastix (Tudor–Stuart) a severe critic of playwrights
squabash (1818) to crush with criticism
praise sandwich (US slang Houston 1987) criticism prefaced by and followed by compliments

BOOKS DO FURNISH A ROOM

here remains one important group that no one in the business can afford to take for granted – the dear old readers:

enchiridion (Late Latin 1541) a book carried in the hand for reference

thumbscall (Shropshire) a piece of paper or card inserted in a book to mark a page

bibliotaph (1824) a person keeping his or her books secret or locked up

grille-peerer (1940s) one of a group of clergymen who used to haunt the stacks of the London Library to look up the skirts of women browsing above

to have a face-ticket (British Museum Reading Room 1909) to be so well known to the janitors that one is not asked to present one's ticket

ARE YOU WORKING?

Sitting in a corner with a mere book has never been enough for another creative group who flourish in our supposedly inhibited culture:

oyster part an actor who appears and speaks or acts only once (like an oyster he opens but once)

nap-nix (c.1860) an amateur playing minor parts for experience

crawk (1930s) a performer acting as an animal imitator

cabotinage (1894) behaviour typical of a second-rate actor or strolling player, implying a tendency to play to the gallery or overact

come back Tuesday pseudo-friendly advice from theatrical directors and management to hopefuls really meaning 'go away!'

flag-fallen (16C) unemployed (used first of actors: the playhouse flag was lowered where there was no performance)

AGAIN FROM THE TOP

Many are the tricks of the trade to be learnt in this most demanding of callings; and theatre has developed a fine jargon to describe it:

swallow the cackle to learn a part

ping to speak one's lines softly, with no special emphasis

pong to speak in blank verse after forgetting one's lines

stagger the first rehearsal without a script in one's hands

wing to fasten one's script to one of the wing flats or some part of the scenery when one has failed to learn it properly and thus needs an occasional reference during the performance

Mummerset (J. B. Priestley: *Festival at Farbridge* 1951) fake peasant accents adopted by actors to denote a supposed rural origin (from a mix of Somerset and mummer)

SMOKE AND MIRRORS

Normal costume apart, a range of cunning accessories assist the thespian's art:

heart the padding out of their tights by acrobats, actors etc. to prevent an otherwise painful fall

wafters (Geordie) swords made with blunt edges for performers

bronteon (Ancient Greek 1849) a device used in theatre or movies to create thunder

scruto (1853) a spring trap-door, flush with the floor of a stage, for a ghost to rise through, for sudden falls and other effects

pepper's ghost a trick used to create a 'ghost' on stage by using an inclined sheet of plate glass onto which an actor can be projected as if 'walking through air'

bird's nest crepe wool used to construct false beards

LIGHTS UP

But once you're out there, darling, all you can do is stick to the script and hope for the best:

ventilator a play so appallingly bad that the audience leaves well before the final curtain, and their seats are filled only with fresh air
exsibilation (1640) the collective hisses of a disapproving audience
handcuffed an actor's description of an audience who will not applaud
stiff (1930s) a terrible joke, rewarded only by silence
soso (1930s) a joke rewarded by a smile, but not a laugh
gravy easy laughs from a friendly audience
crack the monica (music hall jargon *c.*1860) to ring the bell to summon a performer to reappear

BUMS ON SEATS

Though you may be deep into your role, you'll still have one eye on the view beyond the footlights:

plush family empty seats in the auditorium (i.e. the plush-covered seats that can be seen from the stage)
paper the house to give away free theatre tickets in order to fill up an undersubscribed performance
whiskey seats seats on the aisle (popular both with critics, who need to get out before the rush and phone in their reviews, and those who like to escape to the bar when the action palls)
baskets are in a full house (from the one-time practice of leaving the prop baskets as security against the income of a touring company: if the house didn't guarantee the payment of the theatre's rent, the props were theoretically forfeit)

MAGIC CIRCLE

But let's please never forget that the stage is not simply a venue for actors. Other fine artists offer equally enjoyable entertainment:

burn (conjuring jargon) staring at the magician's hands without averting your gaze, no matter what misdirection is thrown

riffle (conjuring jargon) to let cards come out of the hand, creating a noise

grimoire (French 1849) a magician's manual of black magic for invoking demons

cultrivorous (1846) actual or illusory knife-swallowing

drollic (1743) pertaining to a puppet show

swazzle (1942) a mouthpiece used by a puppeteer to make the squeaking voice of Mr Punch

MORE WHIFFLE

Other performers don't even need a stage. From break to Morris dance, a pavement or floor is more than enough:

gaff a dancer's belt, the protection under his tights for his genitals

garlic (17C) a lively jig

applejack (1980s) a basic move to challenge another breakdancer to a competition, squatting down, falling back onto your hands, and kicking one leg high in the air, then springing back onto both legs

whiffler the man with the whip in Morris dancing

CROONERS

Singers, too, can operate anywhere:

griddle (b.1851) to sing in the streets

woodshedding (1976) spontaneous barbershop singing (originally meaning a place to rehearse music privately)

barcarole (French 1779) a gondolier's song

rumbelow (1315) a meaningless song or refrain sung by sailors while rowing a boat (e.g. Heave Ho or Hey-Ho)

aubade (Franco-Provençal 1678) a song at sunrise

scolion (Ancient Greek 1603) a song sung in turn by the guests at a banquet

ROCK FOLLIES

Though why be a busker when you could be a star? Or at least get as near to one as possible ...

guerrilla gig a performance by a band in an unlikely venue, where they play until they are evicted

mosh to engage in uninhibited, frenzied activities with others near the stage at a rock concert (**mosh pit** the place near the stage at a rock concert where moshing occurs)

wollyhumper a bouncer employed by a rock band to make sure no fans manage to climb on stage while they play or, if they have climbed up, to throw them down again

résumé on a rope a backstage pass

woodpecker people who nod their heads to the music being played while paying no attention

GOGGLE BOX

There is one contemporary venue where almost all performers are happy to be seen; and behind the scenes in TV land, too, a whole rich lingo has grown up:

toss in television news, an onscreen handover from one host to another

golden rolodex the small handful of experts who are always quoted in news stories and asked to be guests on discussion shows

bambi someone who freezes in front of the camera (like a deer caught in headlights)

clambake the possibility of two or three commentators all talking over each other and thus confusing listeners

goldfishing one politician talking inaudibly in an interview (you can see his lips move but only hear the reporter's words)

>O

WORD JOURNEYS

explode (16C from Latin) to reject; then (17C) to drive out by clapping, to hiss off the stage

tragedy (16C from Ancient Greek) a goat song

anecdote (from Ancient Greek) unpublished things; then (17C) secret history

charm (from Latin carmen) a song; then (13C) an incantation, the singing or reciting of a verse that was held to have magic power

enthusiasm (from Ancient Greek) divinely inspired; then (17C) possession by a god, poetic frenzy; misguided religious emotion

DIMBOX AND QUOCKERWODGER

Military and political concerns

Soldiers in peace are like
chimneys in summer

(1598)

We all claim to love a peaceful time, but somehow squabbles keep breaking out:

breed-bate (1593) someone looking for an argument
conspue (1890) to spit on someone or something with contempt
cobble-nobble (Shropshire) to rap on the head with the knuckles
donnybrook (1852) a street brawl (named after the famously violent annual Fair in Dublin)
recumbentibus (b.1546) a knock-down blow either verbal or physical
sockdolager (1830) a decisive blow or answer that settles a dispute

SHADOW DANCING

Fights come in all shapes and sizes:

batrachomyomachy (b.1828) a silly and trifling altercation (literally, a battle between frogs and mice)

sciamachy (1623) fighting with a shadow or with an imaginary enemy

holmgang (1847) a duel to the death fought on an island

ro-sham-bo (US slang 1998) a competition employed to determine the ownership of an object when in dispute (the two parties kick each other in the groin until one falls to the ground: the person left standing wins)

hieromachy (1574) a conflict of ecclesiastics, a fight between persons of the cloth

... and brave the person who tries to come between the opposing parties:

dimbox (Scotland) the 'smoother-over' of disputes, an expert at getting others to make up

redder's lick (Scott: *The Abbot* 1820) the blow one receives in trying to part combatants

autoclaps (Jamaican English 1970s) trouble that leads to more trouble

GOING REGIMENTAL

When it comes to the bigger disagreements between nations, we still, it seems, need armies to protect us – the perfect breeding ground for specialized lingo and tradition:

boots (b.1811) the youngest officer in a regimental mess, whose duty it is to **skink** (b.1811) to stir the fire, snuff any candles and ring the bell

militaster (1640) a soldier without military skill or knowledge

egg (early 20C) an inexperienced airman, not yet 'hatched'

knapsack descent (late 19C) a soldier or soldiers in every generation of a family

alvarado (Tudor–Stuart) the rousing of soldiers at dawn by beating the drum or the firing of a gun

yomp (1982) to march with heavy equipment over difficult terrain; a forced military march in full kit

YELLOW-BELLY

Not that everyone is equally eager to join the battle:

murcous (1684) of one who cuts off his thumb to escape military service

troppo (Australian slang) nervously affected by the privations of war service in the Tropics

ear-flip (Service slang) a very cursory salute

chamade (French 1684) the drum beat or trumpet blast which announces a surrender

poodle-faker (Service slang 1902) an officer always ready to take part in the social side of military life

WEIGHING ANCHOR

The navy, too, has developed some colourful jargon over the years:

anchor-faced someone, usually an officer, who lives and breathes the
Royal Navy even when retired

mushroom troop a complaining description used by those who feel
that they are not being told enough about what is happening (i.e. fed
on dirt and kept in the dark)

Dockyard Olympics the old process of refitting a warship whereby
all the tradesmen lined up at the start of the day and then raced off to
various places within the ship

upstairs (submariner's jargon) the surface of the sea

swallow the anchor to leave the navy

MAGNIFICENT MEN

Our newest military service was at first rather looked down on by the other two. But it didn't take long to prove its usefulness:

spike-bozzle (1915) to destroy (an enemy plane)
bombflet (New Zealand 1940) a propaganda leaflet dropped from an aeroplane
brolly-hop (b.1932) a parachute jump
vrille (French 1918) an aerobatic spinning manoeuvre (twisting, like the tendril of a vine)

Whatever the difficulties . . .

socked in (aerospace jargon) an airfield shut for flying because of poor visibility
penguin (Air Force jargon 1915) an aeroplane unable to leave the ground
dangle the Dunlops (Royal Navy jargon) to lower an aircraft's under-carriage prior to landing

or the dangers . . .

cigarette roll (US slang 1962) a parachute jump in which the parachute fails to open
angry palm tree (Royal Navy jargon) a burning and turning helicopter
buy the farm (US Service slang 1955) to crash an aircraft, usually fatally (referring to government compensation paid to a farmer when an aircraft crashes on his farm)

at least it had its compensations:

modoc(k) (US slang 1936) a man who becomes a pilot for the sake of the glamorous image it conveys

SHOCK AND AWE

As the airforce role becomes ever more important, and the machines more powerful and hi-tech, the lingo just keeps on coming:

green air (US slang) flying with night-vision goggles

play pussy (RAF jargon) to fly into cloud cover in order to avoid being discovered by hostile aircraft

glass ball environment (US intelligence jargon 2004) of the weather in Iraq being often conducive to collecting images from above

---

PANCAKE! – SERVICES' WATCHWORDS

popeye! (air intercept code) I am in cloud; I have reduced visibility

state tiger! (air intercept code) 'I have sufficient fuel to complete my mission as assigned'

Geronimo! (1940s) the favoured shout of paratroopers as they leapt from airplanes

Pancake! (Service slang) the order given in the air to land

lumpy chicken! (US military use) loud and clear

SPOOKS

Our fourth service lurks in the shadows, complete with its own covert terms of communication:

cut-out someone acting as a middle-man in espionage

starburst losing a tail by having several similar cars suddenly drive off in different directions, making it hard to know which to follow

swallow a woman employed by the Soviet intelligence service to seduce men for the purposes of espionage

lion tamer in a blackmail operation, a strong-arm man who makes sure that the target, once told that he is being blackmailed, does not make an embarrassing and potentially destructive fuss which could thus ruin the operation

ill arrested on suspicion for questioning

demote maximally to kill one of your associates (the victim's career as a spy certainly can fall no lower)

POLITICOS

We can only hope that all these fine operatives are given wise and honourable direction by that class of men and women we choose to run things for us:

tyrekicker (New Zealand 1986) a politician who discusses and debates but takes no action (from car sales where a person examines a car at length but does not buy it)

snollygoster (1846) a burgeoning politician (especially a shrewd or calculating one) with no platform, principles or party preference

dog-whistle politics (Australian slang 2005) to present your message so that only your supporters hear it properly

quockerwodger (mid 19C) a pseudo-politician; a politician acting in accordance with the instructions of an influential third party, rather than properly representing their constituents (a quockerwodger was a wooden toy figure which, when pulled by a string, jerked its limbs about)

moss-back (late 19C) a right-winger (as they move so slowly that moss could grow on their back)

doughnutting (UK slang 2005) a carefully created seating plan which places an ideal group of members of Parliament (women, photogenic, ethnic minority etc.) around a leader for the ideal television shot

mugwump (New York 1884) one who holds more or less aloof from party politics, professing disinterested and superior views

girouettism (1825) frequently altering one's opinions or principles to follow trends

TWO CHEERS FOR DEMOCRACY

We live, after all, in the finest political system yet devised by man:

pot-waller (Somerset) one whose right to vote for a member of Parliament is based on his having a fireplace on which to boil his own pot

flusher (US slang 2008) a volunteer who rounds up non-voters on Election Day

astroturfing (US slang) a PR tactic in which hired acolytes are used to offer ostensibly enthusiastic and spontaneous grassroots support for a politician or business

barbecue stopper (Australian slang 2002) an issue of major public importance, which will excite the interest of voters

WORD JOURNEYS

opportune (15C from Latin via Old French) (of wind) driving towards the harbour; seasonable

bounce (13C) to beat, thump; then (16C) a loud, exploding noise

borough (Old English) a fortress

the devil to pay (1783) from the time of old sailing ships when the devil was a long seam beside the keel of a ship which was sealed with tar (if there was no hot pitch ready the tide would turn before the work could be done and the ship would be out of commission longer)

SCURRYFUNGE
Domestic life

A lyttle house well fylled,
a lytle ground well tylled and
a little wife well wylled
is best

(1545)

ᴾundits talk of the global village, but the world is still a huge and deeply varied place, offering any number of environments for people to settle in:

Periscii (1625) the inhabitants of the polar circles, so called because in summer their shadows form an oval

Ascians (1635) inhabitants of the Tropics, who twice a year have the sun directly overhead at noon (hence 'without shadows')

antiscian (1842) a person who lives on the opposite side of the Equator

epirot (1660) a person who lives inland

paralian (1664) a person who lives near the sea

owd standards (Lincolnshire) old folk who have lived in a village all their lives

carrot cruncher (UK slang) a person from the country, a rural dweller

BRIGHT LIGHTS

Countryside, town or something in between, take your pick:

agroville (1960) a community, a village stronghold (relating to South Vietnam)

tenderloin district (1887) the area of a city devoted to pleasure and entertainment, typically containing restaurants, theatres, gambling houses and brothels

huburb (US slang) its own little city within another city

HIGHLY SOUGHT AFTER

Local features may add to or subtract from the desirability of one's residence:

hippo's tooth (US slang) a cement bollard

witches' knickers (Irish slang) shopping bags caught in trees, flapping in the wind

urbeach (US slang) an urban beach generally built along a riverbank

generica (US slang) features of the American landscape (strip malls, motel chains, prefab housing) that are exactly the same no matter where one is

packman's puzzle (Wales) a street or housing estate where the house numbers are allocated in a complicated fashion which causes problems to visitors, tradesmen etc.

SOILED BY ASSOCIATION

If you stay too long in one place you might saddle your children with a nickname they never asked for:

beanbelly (17C) a native of Leicestershire (a major producer of beans)
malt-horse (17C) a native of Bedford (from the high-quality malt extracted from Bedfordshire barley)
yellow belly (18C) a native of Lincolnshire (especially of the southern or fenland part where the yellow-stomached frog abounds)

LOVE THY NEIGHBOUR

It's generally wisest to try and meet the neighbours before you actually move in; though the horrid truth is that the people next door can change at any time:

baching (New Zealand 1936) living usually apart from a family and without domestic help, 'doing for oneself' (especially of a male)
scurryfunge (coastal American 1975) a hasty tidying of the house between the time you see a neighbour and the time she knocks on the door
exhibition meal (Hobo slang) a handout eaten on the doorstep: the madam wants the neighbours to witness her generosity
flying pasty (c.1790) excrement wrapped in paper that is thrown over a neighbour's wall
to have the key of the street (b.1881) of a person who has no house to go to at night, or is shut out from his own

HOUSEPROUD

Once you've settled in, though, you're free to make what you like of the rooms . . .

piggery (UK college slang early 20C) a room in which one does just as one wishes and which is rarely cleaned
chambradeese (Scotland) the best bedroom
ruelle (Tudor–Stuart) the space in a bedroom between the bed and the wall
but and ben (Geordie) outside and inside (refers to a two-roomed house with an outer and inner room)

though you're all too likely to become swamped in the details of domesticity:

flisk (Gloucestershire) a brush to remove cobwebs
izels (Lincolnshire) particles of soot floating about in a room, indicating that the chimney needs to be swept
beggar's velvet (1847) downy particles which accumulate under furniture from the negligence of housemaids
winter-hedge (Yorkshire 18C) a clothes-horse (from the way a full clothes-horse 'hedged off' a portion of a room: summer washing was dried out of doors)
wemble (Lincolnshire) to invert a basin or saucepan on a shelf so that dust does not settle on the inside
poss (Shropshire) to splash up and down in the water, as washerwomen do when rinsing their clothes

just make sure you don't take it so far that that you upset your cohabitants . . .

spannel (Sussex) to make dirty foot marks on a clean floor
heel (Gloucestershire) to upset a bucket
spang (Lincolnshire) to shut a door by flicking the handle sharply so that it slams without being held

HOUSEWARMING

With the place spick and span, perhaps it's time to throw that party:

tin-kettling (New Zealand 1874) a house-warming custom whereby a newly wed couple were welcomed by friends and neighbours circling the marriage home banging on kerosene tins until provided with refreshments

cuddle puddle (New York slang 2002) a heap of exhausted ravers

buff-ball (1880) a party where everyone dances naked

THE THREE NIGHT RULE

A well-known proverb says that fish and guests go off after three nights, so if you ask people to stay for longer, make sure you have some way of getting rid of them if need be:

thwertnick (Old English law) entertaining a sheriff for three nights
agenhina (Saxon law) a guest at an inn who, after having stayed for three nights, was considered one of the family
sit eggs (US black slang 1970s) to overstay one's welcome (from the image of a hen awaiting her chicks)

BATHTIME

Because, in the end, what could be nicer than closing the front door to all outsiders and taking the relaxing ablution of your choice:

offald (Yorkshire) tired and dirty, in need of a bath
muck-rawk (Yorkshire) a dirty line (e.g. on neck) showing the limit of where it has been washed
cowboy (US slang) a quick bath using little water (since cowboys bathed sparingly)
psychrolutist (1872) one who bathes in the open air daily throughout the winter

BEDDY-BYES

Before sinking into a well-deserved rest, wherever in the house the fancy takes you:

nid-nod (1787) to nod off

counting rivets (Royal Navy jargon) going to sleep: it refers to lying
   down and looking at the rivets above the bunk

hypnopompic (1901) the fuzzy state between being awake and asleep

to sleep in puppy's parlour (Newfoundland 1771) to sleep on the
   floor in one's clothes

bodkin (1638) a person wedged in between two others when there is
   proper room for two only (a bodkin was a small sharp dagger)

admiral's watch (underworld slang 1905) a good night's sleep

to drive one's pigs to market (US 19C) to snore

WORD JOURNEYS

detect (15C from Latin) to unroof

climax (from Ancient Greek) a ladder; then (16C) in rhetoric, an
   ascending series of expressions

curfew (13C from Old French: couvre feu) to cover the fire

AW WHOOP

Animals

You may beat a horse till he be sad,
and a cow till she be mad

(1678)

In a world where dogs are unclean in some cultures and on the menu in others, the British Isles is one place where the life of the average mutt might not be so bad:

snuzzle (1861) to poke around with one's nose, as dogs do
flew (1575) the pendulous corner of the upper lip of certain dogs, such as the bloodhound
lill (Gloucestershire) used of the tongue of a dog dropping his saliva
slink (Shropshire) to draw back, as a dog does when about to bite
pudding (underworld slang 1877) liver drugged for the silencing of house-dogs
ar dawg's a sooner (Ulster) my dog prefers to pee on the carpet rather than go outside

GRIMALKIN

Our other favourite domestic animal is supposed to have nine lives and knows how to enjoy all of them:

ess-rook (Shropshire) a cat that likes to lie in the ashes on the hearth
tawl-down (Somerset) to smooth down a cat's back
brebit (Shropshire) a cat that continually hunts for food
furs bush (Sussex) the cat's tune when purring

PRANCERS AND DOBBINS

The Queen is said to prefer horses to people, and there's little doubt they get to mix in the best of company:

fossple (Cumberland 1783) the impression of a horse's hoof upon soft ground

trizzling (Devon) the slow, lazy trot of horses

brills (1688) a horse's eyelashes

skewboglish (Lincolnshire) a horse that is apt to shy

reeaster (Yorkshire) a horse making less effort than the others in a team

feague (UK slang b.1811) to put ginger or a live eel into a horse's anus to make him lively and carry his tail well

jipping (horsetraders' slang mid 19C) staining part of a horse with Indian ink to conceal a blemish

LIVESTOCK

It's all very well going to the races, but where would we be without the milk and cheese from our herds of Jerseys and Guernseys (to say nothing of the beef from Herefords, Galloways and Lincolns)?

ganners (Shetland Isles) the inside of a cow's lips

noit (Yorkshire) the period during which a cow gives milk

tulchan (1789) calf's skin set beside a cow to make her give milk freely

shick (Caithness) to set the head as a bull does when intending to toss

giddhom (Ireland) the frantic galloping of cows plagued with flies

LAND OF THE LONG WHITE FLEECE

Sheep are the animal most mentioned in the bible (lions and lambs came in second and third). In New Zealand, where there have long been more sheep than people, a whole separate language grew up for talking about them:

break back (1864) to run or dash in the reverse direction to the drive
pink (1897) to shear a sheep carefully and so closely that the skin shows
raddle (1910) to mark an unsatisfactorily shorn sheep
huntaway (1912) a noisy sheepdog trained to bark on command and drive sheep forward from behind
drummer (1897) the worst or slowest sheep-shearer in a team
cobbler (late 19C) the last and least willing sheep to be sheared

PORKER

In strong competition with the Danes, our hogs and sows do their level best to bring home the bacon:

hodge (Shropshire) the large paunch in a pig
wurtle (Cumberland) to work underneath or in the ground like a pig
treseltrype (Somerset 1883) the youngest in a litter of pigs

FOWL PLAY

Some birds we keep as hunters or pets, some we breed to mow down with guns, a few we eat . . .

turdoid (1823) akin to a thrush
ostreger (1400) a keeper of goshawks
hack (1575) eagles before they become acclimatized and can hunt on their own
ossiger (Orkney Isles) the condition of a fowl when moulting
jollop (1688) to gobble like a turkey
zoo-zoo (Gloucestershire) a wood pigeon (from the sound it makes)

. . . but they're always worth listening to:

quit-quit (Wiltshire 1900) the note of the swallow
quee-beck (Scotland 1901) the cry of grouse when startled
hoolie-gool-oo-oo (Banffshire 1876) the cry, hooting of an owl
valentine (1851) to greet with song at mating-time (said of birds)
chavish (1674) the sound of many birds chirping together, or many people chatting at once

QUEENS AND WORKERS

In other parts of the world they eat fried grasshopper and chocolate-coated ants; but with one glorious exception, insects are not much help in our national diet:

warp (Tudor–Stuart) bees in flight working themselves forward
cut (Gloucestershire) the second swarm of bees in the same season (**hob**
  or **kive**: the third swarm of bees)
spear (Sussex) the sting of a bee
narrow-wriggle (East Anglian) an earwig (the Yorkshire version is
  forkin robins)
dulosis (Modern Latin 1904) the enslavement of ants by ants

GREAT AND SMALL

The ordinary garden mole was known in Middle English (1100–1500) as a **mowdiwarp.** Later he became known as the **little gentleman in black velvet** (early 18C), the subject of a famous Jacobite toast to the mole that raised the hill that caused their oppressor King William to fall from his horse and die. Other animals have avoided such glorification . . .

fuz-pig (Somerset) a hedgehog
bubbly jock (Scottish) a turkey
pilser (b.1828) the moth or fly that runs into a candle flame

. . . but nonetheless their most obscure parts have been carefully noted . . .

junk (New Zealand 1837) the soft part of a sperm-whale's head
dewlap (1398) the pendulous skin under the throat of cattle, dogs etc.
cnidocil (1884) a stinging bristle of the tentacle of a jellyfish
katmoget (Shetland Isles 1897) having the colour of its belly different
  from the rest of the body

acnestis (1807) that part of an animal (between its shoulders and lower back) that it cannot reach to scratch

fleck (Essex) the soft hair of a rabbit

... not to mention their intriguing behaviours ...

mather (Gloucestershire) to turn round before lying down, as an animal often does

squeem (Ayrshire) the motion of a fish as observed by its effect on the surface of the water

pronk (1896) to leap through the air, as an antelope does

traffic (Gloucestershire) the tracks worn by rabbits or rats near their holes

... to say nothing of their mating habits ...

epigamic (1890) attracting the opposite sex at breeding time

clicket (b.1811) the copulation of foxes

amplexus (1930s) the mating embrace of a frog and a toad

caterwaul (Middle English) the cry of cats at mating time

YELLS BELLS

At rutting time a badger **shrieks** or **yells**; a boar **freams**; a buck **groans** or **troats**; a ferret or stoat **chatters**; a fox **barks**; a goat **rattles**; a hare or rabbit **beats** or **taps**; a hart **bells**; an otter **whiles**; a roe **bellows** and a wolf **howls**.

SAFETY IN NUMBERS

Most of us know that geese on the ground come in **gaggles.** But were you aware that when they take to the air they become a **skein**? The collective nouns for other animals are often bizarre in the extreme:

a **murder** of crows
a **watch** of nightingales
an **unkindness** of ravens
a **crash** of rhinoceroses
a **deceit** of lapwings
a **convocation** of eagles
a **business** of ferrets
a **wedge** of swans

JUG JUG IN BERKELEY SQUARE

When it comes to the sounds of animals, some of our attempts at mimicry may leave something to be desired:

curkle (1693) to cry as a quail
winx (15C) to bray like a donkey
desticate (1623) to squeak like a rat
chirr (1639) to make a trilling sound like a grasshopper
cigling (1693) chirping like the cicada
jug (1523) the sound of the nightingale
skirr (1870) a whirring or grating sound, as of the wings of birds in flight
gi'-me-trousers (Jamaican English 1958) the sound a cock makes
    when it crows

PEN AND INK

In Lincolnshire, the sounds of horses' hoofs were onomatopoeically described as **butter and eggs, butter and eggs** for a horse at a canter. If the animal happened to be a **clicker**, that is, it caught its front hoofs on its rear ones when it was running, there were extra beats in the rhythm and it went **hammer and pinchers, hammer and pinchers**. A horse at a gallop went **pen and ink, pen and ink**.

RUTH RUTH

And who knows how this strange variety of human calls to animals developed over the years?

muther-wut (Sussex) a carter's command to a horse to turn right

woor-ree (East Anglian 1893) a waggoner or ploughman's call to his horse to come to the right

harley-harther (Norfolk 1879) a call to horses to go to the left

aw whoop (Gloucestershire) an order for a horse to go on

fwyee (Northern) a peculiar noise made in speaking to a horse

rynt ye (Cheshire) what milkmaids say to their cows when they have milked them (similar to **aroint thee** – get ye gone)

ruth ruth (Ireland) an encouragement to a bull to service a cow

habbocraws (Scotland 1824) a shout used to frighten the crows from the cornfields

way leggo (New Zealand 1945) a musterer's cry to recall a dog

midda-whoy (Lincolnshire) an instruction to a horse to turn left

bumbeleery-bizz (Lanarkshire) a cry used by children when they see cows startling, in order to excite them to run about with greater violence

soho (1307) a call used by huntsmen to direct the attentions of a dog to a hare which has been discovered

whoo-up (Lancashire and Yorkshire 1806) a shout of huntsmen at the death of the quarry

poot, poot, poot (Orkney Isles) a call to young pigs at feeding time

cheddy-yow (Yorkshire) a call to sheep being brought down from the fell, to come closer

poa poa (Northamptonshire) a call to turkeys

tubby (Cornwall) a call used to pigeons

pleck-pleck (Scotland 1876) the cry of the oyster catcher

RSPCA

However good we are as a nation to our furry and feathered friends, there's certainly no room for complacency:

shangle (Cumbria) to fasten a tin or kettle to a dog's tail

hamble (1050) to make a dog useless for hunting by cutting the balls of its feet

brail (1828) the leather strap to bind a hawk's wing

gablock (1688) a spur attached to the heel of a fighting cock

bdellatomy (1868) the act of cutting a sucking leech to increase its suction

spanghew (1781) blowing up a frog through a straw inserted into its anus; the inflated frog was then jerked into the middle of the pond by being put on a cross stick, the other end being struck, so that it jumped high into the air

EXCREMENTAL

American slang has the phrase **alley** or **road apple** for a lump of horse manure. Back home in the Middle Ages the language of hunting meant that you didn't need slang to describe the specific faeces of an animal: there were the **crotels** of a hare, the **friants** of a boar, the **spraints** of an otter, the **werderobe** of a badger, the **waggying** of a fox and the **fumets** of a deer.

➤○ WORD JOURNEYS

mawkish (17C) from a maggot; nauseated

tabby (1630s) from Attabiyah, a quarter of Baghdad, renowned for its production of striped cloth

rostrum (16C from Latin) a bird's beak; then from the orator's platform in the Roman forum which was adorned with the prows of captured ships

white elephant (1851) from successive kings of Thailand who gave a white elephant to any courtier who irritated them; although the animals were considered sacred, their maintenance was so expensive that anyone who was given one was inevitably ruined

SWALLOCKY

Rural life and weather

Spring is here when you can
tread on nine daisies at once
on the village green

(1910)

Out in the sticks are things not dreamt of by those who remain in town:

goodman's croft (Scotland 19C) a corner of a field left untilled, in the belief that unless some such place were left, evil would befall the crop

loggers (Wiltshire) lumps of dirt on a ploughboy's feet

dudman (1674) a scarecrow made of old garments

icker (1513) a single ear of corn

squeaker (Newfoundland 1878) a blade of grass held upright between the thumbs and producing a shrill vibration when blown upon

cowpat roulette (Somerset 2004) a game in which villagers bet on which plot of land will be the first to receive a cow's calling card

FIGHTING FOR THE CLAICK

Dialects and local language identify particular aspects important to rural folk . . .

plud (Somerset) the swampy surface of a wet ploughed field
fleet (Somerset) the windward side of a hedge
wamflet (Aberdeenshire) the water of a mill stream, after passing the mill
chimp (Wiltshire) the grown-out shoot of a stored potato
griggles (Wiltshire) small worthless apples remaining on the tree after the crop has been gathered in

. . . as well as gadgets and techniques that have been developed over long years of experiment:

atchett (Devon and Cornwall) a pole slung across a stream to stop cattle passing
averruncator (1842) a long stick with shears for cutting high branches
stercoration (1605) the process of spreading manure
baggin-bill (Shropshire) an implement for reaping peas
reesome (Lincolnshire) to place peas in small heaps
claick (Scotland) the last armful of grain cut at harvest (also called the **kirn-cut, mulden,** or **kirn-baby**: it was often kept and hung by a ribbon above the fireplace; in Suffolk harvesters threw their sickles to compete to reap it)

GREEN FINGERS

On a smaller scale, gardeners always have plenty to talk about ...

platiecrub (Shetland Isles) a patch of enclosed ground for growing cabbages

olitory (1658) belonging to the kitchen garden

chessom (1626) of soil; without stones or grit

pissabed (Jamaican English 1801) a dandelion (as it is a diuretic)

... and things can get pretty technical on occasion:

suckshin (Yorkshire) liquid manure

sarcle (1543) to dig up weeds with a hoe

graff (Shropshire) a spade's depth in digging (**delve** is two spades' depth)

cochel (Sussex) too much for a wheelbarrow but not enough for a cart

BOSKY

0ut on the slopes beyond the hedge the trees too need careful categorizing:

maerapeldre (Anglo-Saxon) an apple-tree on a boundary
pollard (Newfoundland *c.*1900) a dead tree still standing
rampick (1593) a tree bare of leaves or twigs
stub-shot (Somerset) the portion of the trunk of a tree which remains
   when the tree is not sawn through

... and beyond that, Nature may be wilder and more magnificent still:

borstal (South English 1790) a pathway up to a steep hill
brucktummuck (Jamaican English 1943) a hill so steep that it seems to
   break the stomach of one who tries to climb it

UP ON THE DOWNS

Critics from abroad often claim that English weather is dreadful. But this
is only one point of view; for others relish the huge variety of effects to be
found in such a changeable climate. These are just those found in Sussex:

port-boys small low clouds in a clear sky
windogs white clouds blown by the wind
eddenbite a mass of cloud in the form of a loop
slatch a brief respite or interval in the weather
swallocky sultry weather
shucky unsettled weather
truggy dirty weather
egger-nogger sleet
smither diddles bright spots on either side of the sun

THE RAIN IT RAINETH EVERYDAY . . .

It may rain often but that's not to say that there aren't some happy aspects to the experience:

petrichor (1964) the pleasant smell that accompanies the first rain after a dry spell
eske (Orkney Isles) small spots of rain that precede a heavy storm
fog dog (mid 19C) the lower part of a rainbow
water-gall (Tudor–Stuart) a second rainbow seen above the first
monkey's wedding (South African 1968) simultaneous rain and sunshine

although its less enjoyable side is also well documented . . .

trashlifter (Californian slang) a heavy rain (**loglifter**: a really heavy
   rain)
duck's frost (Sussex dialect) cold rain rather than freezing
New York rain (Hong Kong slang) the local term for water that drips
   annoyingly from air-conditioners onto passers-by

BLOWN AWAY

or those who live on coasts and hills, the wind has always been a constant
presence:

pipple (Tudor–Stuart) to blow with a gentle sound (of the wind)
wyvel (Wiltshire) to blow as wind does round a corner or through a hole
whiffle (1662) to blow, displace or scatter with gusts of air; to flicker or
   flutter as if blown by the wind

not to be trifled with if you're out on the water . . .

williwaw (1842) a sudden and powerful downdraught of wind (originally
   in the Straits of Magellan)
the dog before its master (nautical late 19C) a heavy swell preceding
   a gale

or a storm is imminent ...

brattle (Newcastle 1815) the noise of a thunderclap
rounce robble hobble (b.1582) a representation of the tumult of thunder
heofonwoma (Anglo-Saxon) thunder and lightning, literally a terrible noise from heaven
levin (13C) a bolt of lightning

THE LIVING IS EASY

Every now and then the sun appears, and everyone goes crazy with delight:

apricate (1691) to bask in the sun
crizzles (1876) rough, sunburnt places on the face and hands in scorching weather
jack-a-dandy (Shropshire) the dancing light sometimes seen on a wall or ceiling, reflected from the sunshine on water, glass or other bright surface
king's-weather (Scotland 18C) the exhalations seen rising from the earth during a warm day (while **queen's weather** (19C) is a fine day for a fête as Queen Victoria was famous for having fine weather when she appeared in public)

SNOW ON THE LINE

While at the other end of the year the country grinds to a halt for another reason:

devil's blanket (Newfoundland) a snowfall which hinders work or going to school
pitchen (Bristol) snow that is settling
cloggins (Cumberland) balls of snow on the feet
tewtle (Yorkshire) to snow just a few flakes
sluppra (Shetland Isles) half-melted snow

although the novelty does often rather pass after the building of the second snowman:

two thieves beating a rogue (b.1811) a man beating his hands against his sides to warm himself in cold weather (also known as **beating the booby** and **cuffing Jonas**)
to beat the goose (c.1880) to strike the hands across the chest and under the armpits to warm one's chilled fingers (the movement supposedly resembles a goose in flight)
shrammed (Bristol) feeling really cold

WORD JOURNEYS

aftermath (16C) after mowing (i.e. the second crop of grass in autumn)

derive (14C from Latin via Old French) to draw away from the river bank

damp (14C) noxious vapour, gas; then (16C) fog, mist, depression, stupor

sky (13C from Old Norse) a cloud

aloof (nautical 16C) windward

FEELIMAGEERIES
Paraphernalia

None are so great enemies to knowledge
as they that know nothing at all

(1586)

The English language has a name for pretty much everything, even things you've never imagined needing to describe:

feazings (1825) the frayed and unravelled ends of a rope
ouch (Tudor–Stuart) the socket of a precious stone
swarf (1566) the metallic dust that accumulates after sharpening or grinding metal
ferrule (Dickens: *Nicholas Nickleby* 1838) the metal tip on an umbrella
nittiness (1664) the condition of being full of small air bubbles

DRIBS AND DRABS

If that wasn't enough, dialect supplies a few more:

charmings (Lincolnshire) paper or rag chewed into small pieces by mice
swailing (Rutland) wax drips from a candle
smut (Dublin) the remains of a nearly burnt-out candle
catamaran (Devon 1836) anything very rickety and unsafe
swiggle (East Anglia) to shake liquid in an enclosed vessel
noraleg (Shetland Isles 1899) a needle with a broken eye

ROUGHLY SPEAKING

When it comes to describing other aspects of objects, there are some surprisingly useful words out there:

scrawmax (Lincolnshire) anything badly formed or out of shape

ullage (1297) the amount of liquid by which a container falls short of being full

wee-wow (Shropshire) more on one side than on the other, ill-balanced, shaky

cattywampus (US Middle and Southern slang) diagonally across from something else

by scowl of brow (Gloucestershire) judging by the eye instead of by measurement

ostrobogulous (1951) unusual, bizarre, interesting

... as there are for directions too:

widdershins (1513) in the opposite direction, the wrong way

deasil (1771) clockwise, or 'in the direction of the sun's course' (considered by some to bring bad luck)

antisyzgy (1863) a union of opposites

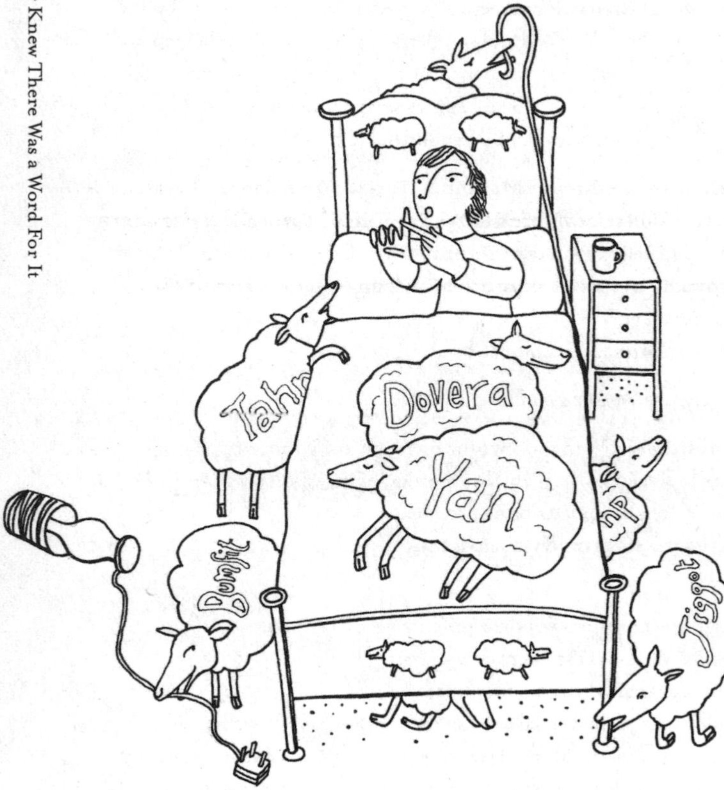
Dovera
Tahn
Yan
Bumfit
Jiggot

COUNTING SHEEP

Being able to count was a matter of survival long before education for all. **Yan Tan Tethera** is a numerical sequence once used widely by shepherds in northern England and southern Scotland to count their sheep. It was also used in knitting to count stitches. The words differ according to accent and locale (in the Lake District versions alter according to which valley you find yourself in). In Westmorland it goes like this:

Yan · Tahn · Teddera · Meddera · Pimp (5) · Settera · Lettera · Hovera · Dovera · Dick (10) · Yan Dick · Tahn Dick · Teddera Dick · Meddera Dick · Bumfit (15) · Yan-a-Bumfit · Tahn-a Bumfit · Teddera-Bumfit · Meddera-Bumfit · Jiggot (20)

The monotonous nature of the rhyme, which would have been repeated many times during the day, also supposedly gave rise to the idea of 'counting sheep' in order to get off to sleep.

WHO WANTS TO BE A VIGINTILLIONAIRE?

When numbers give way to mathematics, things start to get a bit more daunting:

zenzizenzizenzic (1557) the eighth power of a number
lemniscate (1781) the ∞ or 'infinity' symbol
preantepenult (1791) the fourth last
shake a unit of time equal to a hundred-millionth of a second (from top secret operations during the Second World War based on the expression 'two shakes of a lamb's tail', indicating a very short time interval)
vigintillion (1857) the number expressed as a one followed by sixty-three zeros

EVEN STEVENS

Colloquial English takes delight in rhyming expressions, officially known as Reduplicative Rhyming Compounds:

nibby-gibby (Cornwall 1854) touch and go
winky-pinky (Yorkshire) a nursery word for sleepy
hockerty-cockerty (Scotland 1742) with one leg on each shoulder
inchy-pinchy (Warwickshire) the boy's game of progressive leapfrog
fidge-fadge (Yorkshire) a motion between walking and trotting
boris-noris (Dorset) careless, reckless, happy-go-lucky
wiffle-waffle (Northamptonshire) to whet one's scythes together

Shropshire, in particular, has some fine examples:

aunty-praunty (Ellesmere) high-spirited, proud
bang-swang (Clee Hills) without thought, headlong
holus-bolus impulsively, without deliberation
opple-scopple (Clun) to scramble for sweets as children do

This is not just a local phenomenon, as these transatlantic modern versions demonstrate:

stitch 'n' bitch sewing or knitting while exchanging malicious gossip
denture venturer a long trip away from work pre-retirement
chop shop a stolen car disassembly place
zero-hero the designated driver: someone who doesn't drink alcohol
   at a social gathering etc. to drive those who do drink home safely

YOUR NUMBER'S UP

In the drugstores of 1930s America, staff often found it easier to talk in numerical code about certain sensitive matters:

13   a boss is roaming
14   a special order
86   we're out of what was just ordered; to refuse to serve a customer
87½ a pretty woman just walked in
95   a customer is walking out without paying
98   the manager is here

MMMMM . . .

We all know there are twenty-six letters in the alphabet. But don't think that's the end of it:

izzard (Swift 1738) an archaic name for Z

lambdoidal (1653) shaped like the letter L

tittle (1538) the little dot above the letter i (it's also the name for a pip on dice)

hyoid (1811) having a U shape

octothorpe (US 1960s) the official name of the '#' (aka the hash mark)

annodated (b.1913) anything bent somewhat like the letter S (from heraldry)

mytacism (b.1913) the incorrect or excessive use of the letter M

NEVER ODD OR EVEN: PALINDROMES

The English word palindrome was coined by the playwright Ben Jonson in around 1629 to describe words that read the same forwards as backwards; an ongoing source of fun with phrases too:

no, it is opposition

Niagara, o roar again!

rats live on no evil star

nurse, I spy gypsies, run!

murder for a jar of red rum

harass sensuousness, Sarah

a man, a plan, a canal, Panama

sums are not set as a test on Erasmus

sir, I demand - I am a maid named Iris

a new order began, a more Roman age bred Rowena

SOUND EFFECTS

Noises sometimes seem to defy description. But not in this language:

fremescence (Thomas Carlyle 1837) an incipient roaring

rimbombo (1873) a booming roar

cloop (1848) drawing a cork from a bottle

amphoric (1839) the hollow sound produced by blowing across the mouth of a bottle

wheep (Kipling: *Life's Hand* 1891) a steel weapon when drawn from a sheath

callithumpian (1836) a big parade, usually accompanied by a band of discordant instruments

rip-rap (1894) fireworks detonating

swabble (1848) water being sloshed around

crepitation (1656) the crackling and popping sound of a wood fire

jarg (1513) the creaking of a door or gate

juck-cum-peng (Jamaican English 1943) a wooden-legged person walking

whiffle (1972) a soft sound as of gently moving air or water

TINCTURE

We can all name the primary colours: red, yellow and blue; not to mention the secondaries: purple, green and orange; after that, it's anyone's guess:

gamboge (1634) bright yellow (from gum-resin)
fulvous (1664) tawny, yellow tinged with red
ianthine (1609) violet coloured
glaucous (1671) a pale green passing into greyish blue
nacreous (1841) a pearly lustre
lyard (Chaucer *c*.1386) silvery grey almost white

VERY FLAT, NORFOLK

Dialects have their own words for colour, often reflecting the landscapes they come from:

blake (Cumberland) a yellowish golden colour
bazzom (Newfoundland) purplish tint, heather-coloured; of flesh, blue or discoloured
watchet (Midlands 1891) light blue
dunduckytimur (Norfolk and Suffolk) a dull, indescribable colour

UP BETIMES

Time waits for no man. So we might as well be certain precisely what we mean:

ughten (971) the dusk just before dawn
blue o'clock in the morning (1886) pre-dawn, when black sky gives
    way to purple
beetle-belch (RAF jargon) an ungodly hour
sparrow-fart (b.1910) daybreak, very early morning
beever (Sussex) eleven o'clock luncheon
upright and downstraight (Sussex) bedtime when the clock says six
blind-man's-holiday (Shropshire) twilight
cockshut (1594) evening time

PROVIDENTIAL

If you want something to come off well, choose your date with care:

Egyptian day (Yorkshire) an unlucky day, a Friday, which was a day of abstinence

pully-lug day (Cumberland 1886) a day on which traditionally ears might be pulled with impunity

cucumber time (b.1810) the quiet season in the tailoring trade (hence the expression **tailors are vegetarians** as they live on cucumber when without work)

Saint Tibb's Eve (Cornwall) a day that never comes
when hens make holy water (1631) never

THINGUMMY

When all is said and done, however, there are just some things that remain very hard to put your finger on:

oojiboo (1918) an unnamed thing, a whatsit
feelimageeries (Scotland 1894) knick-knacks, odds and ends
hab nab (1580) at random, at the mercy of chance, hit or miss
gazodjule (Australian slang) a name for an object of which one cannot remember the name
floccinaucinihilipilification (1741) the categorizing of something that is useless or trivial

---

→O
WORD JOURNEYS

point-blank (16C from French) a white spot (as in a target)
punctual (14C from Latin) pertinent to a point or dot
normal (17C from Latin via French) rectangular, perpendicular
paraphernalia (17C from Ancient Greek) articles of personal property which the law allows a married woman to regard as her own
algebra (14C from Arabic via Medieval Latin) the reunion of broken parts

ANNE FADIMAN

EX LIBRIS
ANNE FADIMAN

'Witty, enchanting and supremely well written' Robert McCrum, *Observer*

This witty collection of essays recounts a lifelong love affair with books and language. For Fadiman, as for many passionate readers, the books she loves have become chapters in her own life story.

Writing with remarkable grace, she revives the tradition of the well-crafted personal essay, moving easily from anecdotes about Coleridge and Orwell to tales of her own pathologically literary family. As someone who played at blocks with her father's 22-volume set of Trollope ('My Ancestral Castles') and who only really considered herself married when she and her husband had merged collections ('Marrying Libraries'), she is exquisitely well equipped to expand upon the art of inscriptions, the perverse pleasures of compulsive proof-reading, the allure of long words, and the satisfactions of reading out loud. There is even a foray into pure literary gluttony – Charles Lamb liked buttered muffin crumbs between the leaves, and Fadiman knows of more than one reader who literally consumes page corners.

Perfectly balanced between humour and erudition, *Ex Libris* establishes Fadiman as one of the world's finest contemporary essayists.

'*Ex Libris* will provide enjoyable moments of recognition for all book obsessives' Alain de Botton

Penguin Language

THE STORIES OF ENGLISH
DAVID CRYSTAL

How did a language originally spoken by a few thousand Anglo-Saxons become one used by more than 1,500 million people? How have all the different versions of English evolved and changed? In this compelling global tour, David Crystal turns the traditional view of the history of the language on its head and tells the *real* stories of English that have never before been fully told.

'A spirited celebration . . . Crystal gives the story of English a new plot' *Guardian*

'Rejoices in dialects, argots and cants . . . enlightening – in a word, excellent' *Sunday Times*

'An exhilarating read . . . Crystal is a sort of latter-day Johnson' *The Times Higher Education Supplement*

'*The Stories of English* reads like an adventure story. Which, of course, it is' Roger McGough

'A marvellous book . . . for anyone who loves the English language(s) it will be a treasure-house' Philip Pullman

He just wanted a decent book to read ...

Not too much to ask, is it? It was in 1935 when Allen Lane, Managing Director of Bodley Head Publishers, stood on a platform at Exeter railway station looking for something good to read on his journey back to London. His choice was limited to popular magazines and poor-quality paperbacks – the same choice faced every day by the vast majority of readers, few of whom could afford hardbacks. Lane's disappointment and subsequent anger at the range of books generally available led him to found a company – and change the world.

'We believed in the existence in this country of a vast reading public for intelligent books at a low price, and staked everything on it'
Sir Allen Lane, 1902–1970, founder of Penguin Books

The quality paperback had arrived – and not just in bookshops. Lane was adamant that his Penguins should appear in chain stores and tobacconists, and should cost no more than a packet of cigarettes.

Reading habits (and cigarette prices) have changed since 1935, but Penguin still believes in publishing the best books for everybody to enjoy. We still believe that good design costs no more than bad design, and we still believe that quality books published passionately and responsibly make the world a better place.

So wherever you see the little bird – whether it's on a piece of prize-winning literary fiction or a celebrity autobiography, political tour de force or historical masterpiece, a serial-killer thriller, reference book, world classic or a piece of pure escapism – you can bet that it represents the very best that the genre has to offer.

Whatever you like to read – trust Penguin.